The Art of Living

American University Studies

Series VIII
Psychology

Vol. 13

PETER LANG
New York • Bern • Frankfurt am Main • Paris

Gerhard P. Knapp

The Art of Living

Erich Fromm's Life and Works

PETER LANG
New York • Bern • Frankfurt am Main • Paris

Library of Congress Cataloging-in-Publication Data

Knapp, Gerhard Peter
    The art of living : Erich Fromm's life and work /
Gerhard P. Knapp.
        p. cm. — (American university studies. Series VIII,
Psychology ; vol. 13)
            Bibliography: p.
            Includes index.
            1. Fromm, Erich, 1900-   . 2. Psychoanalysts —
United States — Biography. I. Title. II. Series: American
university studies. Series VIII, Psychology ; v. 13.
BF109.F76K59   1989   150.19'57'0924 — dc19   88-38026
ISBN 0-8204-1034-9   CIP
ISSN 0740-0454

CIP-Titelaufnahme der Deutschen Bibliothek

Knapp, Gerhard P.:
The art of living : Erich Fromm's life and works /
Gerhard P. Knapp. — New York; Bern; Frankfurt
am Main; Paris: Lang, 1989.
    (American University Studies: Ser. 8,
    Psychology; Vol. 13)
    ISBN 0-8204-1034-9

NE: American University Studies / 08

© Peter Lang Publishing, Inc., New York 1989

Printed by Weihert-Druck GmbH, Darmstadt, West Germany

Preface

The Art of Living addresses both the uninitiated reader and the specialist. As the first large-scale critical appraisal of Erich Fromm's biography, his work as an academic teacher and psychoanalyst, as well as the whole of his printed oeuvre in English, this book not only aspires to inform, but it seeks to engage its reader in a debate on the heritage of one of this century's most influential thinkers. For the non-specialist, exposure to Fromm's thought may well stimulate an ongoing dialectic process with the ultimate potential to change his or her perspectives on life and society. Hardly any other psychologist/sociologist managed, especially during the years after the Second World War, to touch so many minds and to bring a brighter awareness of the human condition for so wide a readership. The informed specialist, on the other hand, is bound to find new and challenging arguments in these pages--controversial arguments that will, as I hope, engender constructive dissent.

Dissent was the driving force in Erich Fromm's life. Humanist socialism was his credo. At the time of this writing, both humanism as such and socialist theory are among the most frequently misunderstood and even bedevilled concepts in the English-speaking world. Even for the "informed" public, clichés and misconceptions spread by the mass media have attained the status of truths. To enter a dialogue with Erich Fromm means to abandon such prefabricated truisms and prejudices: to start at the very beginning. It means the re-definition of terms like "socialist" and "humanist." And it means to accept their challenge for a better understanding of today's ideologies and their societal manifestations. For Fromm --and for all of us--humanist socialism may indeed be the last resource for the survival of the Western *and* the Eastern worlds, provided its true potential can be realized. Admittedly, Fromm's theories often border on the utopian. There is, however, a point of convergence for reality and utopia, as world history has proved innumerable times. It is the purpose of this study to pinpoint the real substance Erich Fromm so often presented in a utopian shell. Humanity's ability to change *from within* and instrument societal progress on a larger scale is Fromm's "categorical imperative." Its strengths and its limitations are discussed in the following chapters.

The writing of this book necessitated work in archives and libraries on two continents. To all those who contributed to its completion I am greatly indebted. Numerous colleagues in a variety of fields offered assistance and generous help. I would like to express my thanks to all. A posthumous homage is due to my academic teachers Max Horkheimer and Theodor W. Adorno with whom I studied during the formative years of my own life. Both kindled my love for Critical Theory, and their intellectual legacy has accompanied me throughout the years. To my parents, both accomplished psychiatrists, I owe my interest in psychology and much help in the exploration of this discipline. I also want to thank Zoltan Tár, the preeminent expert on the Frankfurt School, for making available to me some of Fromm's unpublished correspondence, and for his unflagging encouragement. And my heartfelt thanks go to Mona Knapp, without whose support and criticism this book would not have been written.

I dedicate it to all who share my hope for a better and more dignified life for *all* of humanity: to those unwilling to accept the status quo.

Salt Lake City, January 1988

Contents

Greed and peace preclude each other.
   -Erich Fromm, *The Sane Society*, 1955

There is a tragic alliance between society as a whole and its economic conditions. With a grim relentlessness those conditions tend to bring up the man of to-day as a being without freedom, without self-collectedness, without independence, in short as a human being so full of deficiencies that he lacks the qualities of humanity.
   -Albert Schweitzer, *The Philosophy of Civilization*, 1949

For the first time in history the physical survival of the human race depends on a radical change of the human heart. However, a change of the human heart is possible only to the extent that drastic economic and social changes occur that give the human heart the chance for change and the courage and the vision to achieve it.
   -Erich Fromm, *To Have or to Be?*, 1976

There is no right life in the Wrong.
   -Theodor W. Adorno, *Minima Moralia*, 1951

1

In the Name of Life: A Controversial Legacy

A collection of essays dedicated to Erich Fromm by friends, colleagues and disciples on the occasion of his seventieth birthday is pertinently entitled: *In the Name of Life.*[1] And indeed, if one attempts to summarize Fromm's written oeuvre, as well as his various other activities as one of the most influential humanists of this century, it is evident that he consistently devoted himself and his work to one single goal: the propagation of a great visionary hope for a better and more dignified life for all of humanity.

Beyond this safe generalization--which, as is the nature of most generalizations, will probably be equally acceptable to his admirers and his critics--there is as yet little or no consensus on Fromm's stature and impact. Apart from a multitude of articles, reviews, and lectures, Fromm wrote and edited some twenty book-length studies within the fifty years of his career. These books have been read by a greater number of non-specialist lay readers than those of any other psychologist/sociologist since Freud. Both in the United States, where they have been widely received and discussed since the 1950s, and in Europe, where they became popular somewhat belatedly during the mid-1960s, they have generated both fervent acclaim and harsh criticism. This ongoing and often heated debate is fueled both by prejudice and by reason. Fromm's adversaries like to ridicule him as a "kind of Dr. Spock for adults" (Kenneth Minogue). Herbert Marcuse, himself one of the most influential thinkers of this century, denounced Fromm as a neo-Freudian revisionist. Numerous scholars have belittled his grasp on scientific method. Yet he is one of the most popular authors to emerge from the entire American do-it-yourself-psychology trend of the 1960s, and within the small immediate circle of his disciples he is celebrated as a visionary and even a "prophet" (Rainer Funk). On the whole, his work in the fields of psychoanalysis and sociology has thus far eluded sober, non-partisan evaluation. It is this study's primary aim to provide a solid basis for such an assessment.

The controversies among Fromm's admirers and critics result, no doubt, from the contradictions inherent in his work itself. Throughout his life, he sternly refused to be labeled. His closer associations with professional and political groups were scarce and usually brief. Asked by an interviewer during the last decade of his life for a self-definition, he described himself as "an atheistic mystic, a Socialist who is in opposition to most Socialist and Communist parties, a psychoanalyst who is a very unorthodox Freudian."[2] A facetious reply, perhaps, but one whose validity is in fact borne out by Fromm's life and development as a thinker. It captures three essential paradoxes that shaped his life and can well serve to summarize it: he was a rationalist with strong faith; he held fervent socialist convictions despite his allegiance to Western capitalism, and combined orthodox psychoanalysis with highly unorthodox large-scale theorizing on human social behavior.

Fromm undoubtedly owed these cornerstones of his thinking and his entire *Weltbild* to his family background and formative childhood years. He came from an orthodox Jewish family and began intensive Talmud studies at age thirteen. This not only brought him into contact with the leading members of the Jewish community in Frankfurt, but also laid the moral foundations for his later life and writings. Officially, Fromm abandoned the orthodox Jewish faith in 1926, but he was to remain under the general influence of its tenets throughout his life. His thinking never lost the mystical center formed by a Jewish upbringing and extensive studies of the Old Testament and the Talmud. Clearly, the ever-present moral framework of his argumentation must be seen as a product of Talmud exegesis.

In his later writings, this moralist viewpoint frequently leads him to abandon the stringencies of an academic approach and *condemn* societal ills in addition to objectively analyzing them. Through this moral appeal his books, which have often been criticized as a potpourri of science and entertainment, reach out to a far greater audience than would ordinarily be addressed by theoretical texts on psychology and sociology. Fromm's writings are most effective and persuasive *not* by virtue of their logical argument, but through their conveyance of a supra-rational faith in humanity's potential to redeem itself from misery and establish a Golden Age on earth. Fromm's unflagging belief in this eventual progression toward a better world runs like a red thread through his books' central passages.

In the last interview given before his death, Fromm touches on the Judaism of his childhood and its inherent messianic content. He summarizes its importance for his own development as follows:

> And the thing that freed me from isolation and loneliness was, from an early age, the idea of the prophets and especially concepts like: Hope for the messianic era, hope that the saviour ultimately would construct a better world . . . This messianic motif contains two crucial messages: firstly a religious one in form of the perfection of humanity . . . the concentration of life on intellectual, religious and moral norms. And secondly a political one, namely actual change in the real world, a new constitution for society, which would enforce these religious principles.[3]

Indeed, it is this utopian component in Fromm's thinking that underlies his untiring insistence on inner human renewal and "quiet" revolution, despite the advanced exploitation of human beings in the 20th century. His relationship to politics (and specifically to the ideologies of capitalism and socialism), however, is not as simple as the above quote might indicate. Again we must examine the roots of his childhood for clues. Born exactly at the turn of the century, he later frequently referred to the pre-World War I city of Frankfurt, and particularly to his own familial environment, as a "medieval world." This implies, in his own terminology, a world yet uncorrupted by the alienation and aggression typical of modern

capitalist society. In his first book, *Escape from Freedom*, he describes in great detail humanity's exodus from a once-intact society
of trades and crafts, away from the conglomerate of guilds typical
for the medieval polis, into the age of monopolistic capitalism. Historically, of course, this transition already took place roughly during the time of the Reformation. But personally, Fromm saw his
own Frankfurt childhood as a last bastion of pre-capitalism, in
which, as in the medieval world, the closed Jewish community was
characterized by a solid hierarchy, strict rules, and a virtually intact
morality. In this close-knit community, nearly everyone had a secure place and a firm identity. Fromm's own hope for a new epoch
through "actual change in the real world," beyond the competitive
commercialism which was to surround him in the later decades of
his life, is therefore inextricably bound to his personal quest for a
lost childhood.

Fromm's first observations of practical politics took place during
his teenage years, when he was witness to the eruption of the First
World War, which he called a "hysteria of hatred." His early leanings toward socialism were further strengthened during the unsuccessful German revolution of 1918/19. In practice, however, the
eighteen-year-old Frankfurt student had little sympathy for the
Bolsheviks, for Spartakus and the Munich commissariat. Now the
paradoxical makeup of Fromm's character becomes visible: his re-
fusal to become involved in organized political action on the one
hand, and his theoretical espousal of progressive thought on the
other. As the facts of his biography have it, forty more years will
pass before Fromm, despite his constant commitment to social
change, is ready to appear publicly in connection with a political
cause. Even then, his official association with the American Socialist Party and his infatuation with the peace movement are
short-lived. Both end in disillusionment. Erich Fromm was never
comfortable in parties or organizations of any sort. His above-
quoted self-assessment as a socialist who is against socialist and
communist parties could not be more accurate.

It is, however, only one side of the coin. Fromm's popular and
scholarly works written after 1940 are based almost without excep-

tion on his prima facie observation and analysis of the social structure of the United States. Reading between the lines of his diagnosis of all aspects of society, it becomes evident that Fromm's critique of capitalist society is shaped by a strong love-hate relationship to modern capitalism as witnessed in North America. Fromm indeed recognized the destructive tendencies in this society. Beyond that, however, he could neither truly support any of the existing socialist systems in the contemporary world, nor could he formulate his own concrete political alternative. His critique of capitalist society, therefore, often dissolves into the realm of myth, when he appeals to the oppressed to cast off the chains of authority and break out of a de-humanized world. In this appeal, he glosses over the fact that for many victims of modern, alienated society, such an escape is simply not possible. Fromm's attempts to provide *practical* suggestions for speeding up the evolution of a more human socio-economic environment--such as the book *The Revolution of Hope* (1968)--are in fact invariably his weakest works.

The third paradox intrinsic to the man and thinker Erich Fromm has to do with his peculiar relationship to psychoanalytic theory. He was appointed a psychological consultant by the Frankfurt Institute of Social Research in 1930--the details of his training are explained in Chapter 2 below.[4] In the same year, he opened his own psychoanalytical practice, an aspect of his profession he was to maintain for more than forty years with only rare interruptions. One of these came relatively early, when in 1931 he contracted tuberculosis and spent more than a year in a Davos sanatorium. The following year he emigrated first to Chicago and finally to New York, where he immediately resumed his private practice. After the first decade, during which he was still unilaterally under the influence of Sigmund Freud, he gradually rejected traditional Freudianism and established his own method, which entailed a much more dynamic relationship between patient and therapist. Heated controversies arose from Fromm's vocal dissention against traditional psychiatry and against his colleagues in this field--they were to go on until the end of his life, and are described in detail in the following chapters. Suffice it to say here that the method he worked out for himself is unique and could never be claimed by any orthodox branch of the psychiatric profession.

Erich Fromm's life ended during the night of March 17/18, 1980, in the Swiss village of Muralto, near Locarno. He was a researcher who worked untiringly in the name of human dignity and freedom, and whose work was always inspired by hope. The goal of this book is to scrutinize open-mindedly the questions raised by his life's work, while recognizing the contradictions therein for what they are. And in fact, they are often no less than mirrors of the major ideological and political contradictions of our times: chasms only thinly covered over by the seemingly smooth veneer of existence in a highly technological environment. Today, more than ever, as technology reaches out into untold spheres, as the conflict between East and West burgeons and the world political scene is dominated by relentless escalations of hostility, the "necrophilous" element of human nature, diagnosed by Fromm more eloquently than anywhere else in sociological literature, is clearly on the increase. But its declared counter-force, the "biophilous" element, is growing as well. This is evidenced by the expanding peace movement and the various "green" parties, especially in Europe--the old world, Erich Fromm's lost homeland. In view of the present world situation, Fromm's work and the critical debate resulting from it have gained a new dimension of relevance.

2

The Beginnings: Frankfurt, Heidelberg, and Berlin

The city of Frankfurt, as it was during the first two decades of this century, must be seen as an element of singular importance for Erich Fromm's early intellectual development. At the turn of the century, this city, a major center for trade and business since the Middle Ages, already had a population of 290,000, which grew by 1905 to 320,000. The Jewish community within that population comprised a solid eight percent and included, in addition to the large number of small merchants, many financiers, doctors, and scholars of all disciplines. The pillars of orthodox Judaism in Frankfurt were primarily members of the merchant class. Fromm's family descended from a long line of rabbis and Talmud scholars. Erich Fromm's father, Naphtali Fromm, was born on 30 November 1869 in Homburg vor der Höhe, and was buried after his death on 29 December 1933 in the old Jewish cemetery located in the Eckenheimer Landstrasse. He was the son of a well-known rabbi, Dr. Seligmann Pinchas Fromm (1821-1898), and the grandson of two rabbis. Seligmann Fromm, Erich's paternal grandfather, spent the years from 1852 to 1875 in the service of the Count of Homburg, where he held a position as Talmud scholar. In 1875, he entered the employment of Baron Willi Carl von Rothschild in Frankfurt, and accepted a well-paid post as his personal rabbi. This move provided him with material security and guaranteed the future for his ten children. In the eyes of Naphtali and later of Erich (who never met his grandfather), however, he had sold his freedom for financial reasons, and he was criticized sharply by his family for having done so. The Fromms' relationship to their rabbinical heritage was, therefore, not unblemished by occasional friction.

Naphtali's wife, Rosa Fromm (née Krause), was born on 29 January 1877 in Posen (today: Poznan), the same city in which Erich Fromm's parents were married on 16 June 1899. Rosa Fromm's father was a cigar manufacturer, and his brother Ludwig Krause was known as one of the most influential Talmud scholars of his time. Originally, the Krause family came from Russia, but had emigrated at the time of the Revolution to Finland, were they converted to the Jewish faith. Six years after the death of her husband, Rosa Fromm, upon the urgent entreaties from her son, emigrated to England. In 1941, Erich Fromm secured her passage to the United States. She lived in New York until her death on 26 February 1959. Thus Rosa Fromm was spared the fate met by millions of European Jews under National Socialism.

Erich Seligmann Fromm, whose middle name was given in deference to his grandfather,[1] was born on 23 March 1900 in Frankfurt. He was to be his parents' only child. In the same year, Leo Löwenthal was born, and three years later, Theodor Wiesengrund-Adorno, both in the same city and to prominent Frankfurt Jewish families. Their paths are later to cross with Fromm's. At the time of Erich's birth, his parents lived at Königsteiner Strasse 49, close to the Altkönig-Platz and to the Palmengarten. In 1903, they moved to a larger flat in a parallel street, at the address Liebigstrasse 27, where Erich grew up.

Naphtali Fromm owned a modest but flourishing fruit-wine business. Contemporary photographs show him as a vulnerable and definitely introverted personality. In his political and religious convictions, Naphtali Fromm was decidedly conservative. Obviously, he would have preferred the life of a rabbi to his own profession as a merchant. In this respect, he personified to the adolescent Erich the "medieval" concept of life, firmly ensconced in religious orthodoxy and righteousness. Erich's father was one of the co-founders of the Jewish Hermann-Cohen-Loge, and he served as its president in 1924/25.

Fromm's mother Rosa, née Krause, appears to have been the more energetic partner in this marriage. Later in life, Fromm described his parents as "neurotic" and "overly fearful." Both appear to have been almost hysterically concerned for the well-being of their only child. As much as Erich's father supported his early inclinations to become a Talmud scholar, he would not permit him to go to Riga and pursue his studies there. Rosa Fromm was not overly attached to her husband. She disapproved of his political and religious conservatism and had quite different plans for her son's future: he was to become a famous pianist. In 1918, when Fromm graduated from the renowned Wöhler High School, he gave up his piano practice, and his mother grudgingly relinquished her dream.

During the formative years of his adolescence, Erich Fromm saw his father live out the conflict between the "medieval" and the "modern" worlds, i.e. between a rabbi's calling which Naphtali would rather have followed, and the world of business which supported his family. This was apparently the only major dissonance in an otherwise essentially happy childhood. In the last interview before his death, Fromm succinctly summarizes this conflict again: "My father was a merchant, and he was ashamed of it, because he would really rather have become a rabbi. As a small boy, I always felt shame when someone said 'I'm a businessman,' because I thought: how shameful it must be for him to admit that he spends his whole life earning money. That, then, was the medieval standpoint, as opposed to the modern one."[2]

This discrepancy between a supposedly intact, pre-capitalist world, and the modern consumer society not only characterized Fromm's early home life, but is also to run through his later works like a red thread. It is this distinction which lays the foundation for Fromm's theory of humanity's evolution as presented in *Escape from Freedom* (1941).[3] In the years following, it crystallizes into the very cornerstone of Fromm's critique of monopolistic capitalism. The idea takes on its sharpest contours in the polarity of Having and Being as two diametrically opposed concepts of existence in the book *To Have or To Be?*, written in 1976. When, as a child and as an adolescent, Erich Fromm both participated actively in his father's business life and at the same time progressively rejected it as shameful, he prefigured to some degree his own later career, as well as his compelling love-hate relationship to American capitalism.

As a pupil, Fromm was noted for both diligence and talent. During his high school years, he excelled particularly in Latin, French, and English, and passed the graduation examination in 1918 with honors. At age thirteen, he had begun to study the Talmud, both at home and at the Synagogue under the direction of the rabbi Dr. Jakob Horowitz. He also received instruction from his 70-year-old great-uncle Ludwig Krause. Later, his teachers included the renowned mystic Dr. Nehemiah Anton Nobel at the new synagogue at Börneplatz, as well as the socialist Dr. Salman Baruch Rabinkov in Heidelberg. Fromm pursued intensive Talmud studies on a daily basis until 1926. Thereafter, however, he gradually turned away from orthodox Judaism. But the insights gained from these studies were to be integrated directly as the strong moralistic focus of his entire later works. In his later study on the teachings of the Old Testament, *You Shall be as Gods* (1966), the author himself strongly emphasizes this lasting indebtedness to Judaism.[4] There is also a humorous footnote to be attached to Fromm's renunciation of orthodoxy. An anecdote has it that in this fateful year of 1926, Fromm--who at that time had completed his psychoanalytical training in Munich--stood in silent contemplation in front of a street vendor's grill filled with sizzling pork sausages. Like Eve in front of the biblical apple tree, he could not resist temptation: he bought and of course consumed one of the sausages. With that, Fromm had passed the point of no return and expelled himself from the paradise of his childhood.[5] In the same year, he also had his first brief encounters with Buddhism. This religion was to play a major role in his life more than thirty years later. Also, at a much later stage of his career, he will turn to the teachings of Master Eckhart, the medieval German mystic, theologian, and theist. These heterogeneous leanings ultimately blend to provide the mainstream of Fromm's eclectic mystical thinking.

Fromm's early personality development was greatly influenced by the people with whom he came into contact in Frankfurt Jewish circles. At his parents' home, he met Ernst Bloch, who was 15 years his senior, and whose *Spirit of Utopia* (1918) he read while in high school. The circle of scholars surrounding the Rabbi Nobel included the religious philosopher Franz Rosenzweig, Ernst Simon, Siegfried Kracauer (author of the influential study *From Caligari to Hitler*) and Martin Buber, who impressed Fromm considerably. It was in this context that Fromm first came into contact with the idea of messianic socialism. This made such an impact on his thinking that, in reminiscences years later, Gershom Sholem caustically described him as a "psychoanalytical bolshevist."[6] The fact is, however, that it was not until the mid-1920s that Fromm actually began to study Marx's writings. Prior to that, he read Siegfried Kracauer's *Sociology as Science* (1922), a work which probably influenced him more deeply and permanently than any other sociological theory encountered in the entire course of his studies.

Early impressions made on the adolescent Fromm included experiences of individual and collective suffering. It is known that, at the age of twelve, he was extremely shaken by the suicide of a young and talented friend of the family--a painter who chose to follow her elderly father in death. Her choice of death and burial together with her father remained incomprehensible to the high school student. In his eyes, she was youthful, beautiful, and gifted, and surely *must* have chosen the joys of life over willful self-destruction.[7] Undoubtedly, this occurrence proved to be a formative experience for the adolescent, as it allowed him a first--and yet unreflected--glance at those conflicting forces at work in every human personality: the death-wish and the will to live. Fromm will incorporate them much later in his psychoanalytical theory as the "biophilous" and the "necrophilous" factors.

Much more devastating were his observations of the events of the first World War, which began two years thereafter with the assassination of the Austro-Hungarian crown prince Franz Ferdinand and his wife on 28 June 1914 in Sarajewo, and the consecutive opening of hostilities on various European fronts. After a brief outburst of enthusiasm for this war in most European nations, the death of friends and relatives quickly doused the flames of mass patriotic fervor. The sobering, indeed shattering experience of large-scale destruction, the war in the trenches, and the senseless waste of human life left a deep impression on all those at the front and at home. Even at that point in his youth, Fromm must already have divined the dimensions of the phenomenon he was later to describe as "necrophilia." In his "intellectual autobiography" written in 1962, he expounds on his impressions of the First World War:

> When the war ended in 1918, I was a deeply troubled young man who was obsessed by the question of how war was possible, by the wish to understand the irrationality of human mass behavior, by a passionate desire for peace and international understanding. More, I have become deeply suspicious of all official ideologies and declarations, and filled with the conviction "of all one must doubt."[8]

Fromm was eighteen when he began his study of law at the University of Frankfurt. At that time, Germany was in a state of political upheaval. For all practical purposes, the second Reich and its allies had, even before the armistice of 11 November 1918, lost the war. While Kaiser Wilhelm II fled into exile in the Netherlands, the social democrat Philipp Scheidemann had declared Germany a republic. Various political factions, including the Spartakus group and other militant proponents of a commissariat government, fought for control in the following months of revolutionary chaos. A temporary unification was then reached in the Weimar Republic, a fragile and short-lived attempt at democracy which served ultimately as a stepping-stone for National Socialism on its way to dictatorial power. Fromm, characteristically enough, agreed in principle with the need for social reform as propagated by the leftist groups during the revolution. He had, however, as mentioned before, little or no sympathy for their practical goals, as much as he abhorred the brutality of the political struggle of the day. Sholem's above-quoted quip about the self-declared "bolshevist" thus must certainly be taken with more than a grain of salt. When Rosa Luxemburg and Karl Liebknecht, the leaders of the Communist Party, were brutally murdered by members of the ultra-right volunteer corps and the reactionary army, many liberals were deeply shocked and dismayed. As opposed to his fellow socialists, Fromm made no comment on these events or on the two political leaders, who rapidly became symbolic martyrs for the lost cause of the social revolution in Germany. Only much later, in some of his political writings and in his *opus magnum*, *The Anatomy of Human Destructiveness* (1973), does he mention the name of Luxemburg in passing.

After two semesters, Fromm realized that the practice of law would never be his vocation. He changed both universities and fields of study. On 21 October 1919, he matriculated at the University of Heidelberg, concentrating on courses in psychology, sociology, and philosophy. One of his teachers at this time was the philosopher Karl Jaspers, whose existentialist thinking made a lasting impression on him. Another influential professor was the neo-Kantian philosopher Heinrich Rickert, who also became a mentor of Walter Benjamin. At this time, Fromm developed a personal friendship with the sociologist Alfred Weber, who was later to become his dissertation supervisor. Alfred Weber was the brother of Max Weber, the eminent sociologist who died in Munich in 1920. Although Fromm doubtlessly became acquainted with Max Weber's writings during his Heidelberg years and even quoted Weber frequently in his own later works, a direct impact on his own development appears to be unlikely.

As a student, Fromm regularly spent his vacation time between semesters with his family in Frankfurt. There he was intensely involved in the Jewish Community. Together with the prominent rabbi Georg Salzberger, he helped found the *Gesellschaft für jüdische Volksbildung* (Society for the education of Jewish people) in February, 1920. Under the auspices of this Society, lectures on religious and ethnic issues were provided on a regular basis. Nehemiah Nobel gave the inauguration speech. Fromm also lectured frequently on a variety of topics. On 17 October 1920, the *Freies Jüdisches Lehrhaus* (Free Jewish Academy) was founded in collaboration with the Society. Franz Rosenzweig, a renowned philosopher of Judaism and also--strangely enough--a Hegelian scholar, was appointed its director. His so-called "common sense" interpretation of religious dogma and, concomitantly, his "experiential" and humanistic approach to Talmud exegesis deeply impressed Fromm from the very outset. It is safe to say that his own life-long unorthodox relationship to Judaism is owed to a certain extent to Rosenzweig. The Free Jewish Academy soon became a focal point for meetings of the foremost personalities in the Frankfurt Jewish Community. Fromm frequently took part in lectures and other activities, and it was there that he met Leo Löwenthal, who was later to introduce him into the circles of the Frankfurt Institute of Social Research. Of the later members of that Institute, only Fromm's and Löwenthal's works will consistently reflect their early allegiance to Judaism.

In the setting of the Academy, Martin Buber's influence on Fromm blossomed. Buber's synthesis of Judaism and existentialism prefigures in certain ways Fromm's own amalgamation of religion and sociology. Through Buber, who published his important essay *I and Thou* in 1923, Fromm became increasingly aware of the importance of inter-personal relationships in any given societal context. Fromm's initial research focus, the interaction of human beings within a specific community, in fact can largely be traced to his studies of Buber's writings around this time. (It was not until many years later that Fromm extended his theoretical focus to the whole spectrum of human nature.) The importance of Buber's influence on the fledgling scholar is by no means diminished by the fact that personal relations between the self-declared prophet and his young disciple were never really warm. His intellectual debt to Buber remains unacknowledged in his writings.

In the Academy, as well, Fromm met Gershom Sholem and Walter Benjamin. Fromm's circle of friends also included Ernst Simon and Nachum Glatzer, both lecturers at the Academy. Gershom Sholem relates the anecdote that Fromm's reputation for extreme orthodoxy led his friends to compose a facetious prayer-verse: "Let me be like Erich Fromm / That I may to heaven come."[9]

Erich Fromm concluded his formal studies in the field of sociology with the dissertation entitled *Jewish Law. A Contribution on the Sociology of Diaspora Judaism.*[10] The lengthy study was written under the direction of Alfred Weber and is dated 4 September 1925 (thus contradicting the widespread misinformation that Fromm received his Ph.D. in 1922). It is an investigation of the socio-psychological structures within three Jewish sects: the Karaites, the Hassidim and the Reformed Jews. It is quite possible that Salman Rabinkov, with whom Fromm remained in constant contact after his move to Heidelberg, instilled in him the initial interest in this topic. Rabinkov's own origins derive from the Hassidim, and much advice regarding this particular group certainly came from him. In general, Fromm's dissertation stresses strongly the humanistic basis of Jewish life and community interaction--an aspect central to Rabinkov's own philosophy. The dissertation also emphasizes the historical importance of the Jewish Diaspora as a self-governing unit which remains independent of the given greater national and cultural context: "The Jewish Diaspora has--although it was always integrated into the greater civilizational processes of its host nations--preserved an individuality and autonomy in its own societal and cultural microcosm, which, in return, guaranteed its subsistence as a homogeneous historic force."[11] Although Fromm's primary method in his dissertation is sociological (already augmented freely with psychological argumentation), his later interest in and definition of the "social character" is not yet foreshadowed here. All in all, the dissertation does not attain great heights, either in terms of structural clarity or of dazzling insights. It makes for rather dull reading. Most certainly, it must be regarded as a yet very tentative, inconclusive step in the direction of Fromm's later research.

From 1926 to 1929, Fromm studied psychology and psychiatry in Munich under the direction of Wilhelm Wittenberg and in Frankfurt under Karl Landauer. Both had been trained by Sigmund Freud. Wittenberg had also studied with Emil Kraepelin, who for the first time described the syndrome of clinical schizophrenia. Wittenberg was the most orthodox Freudian of all of Fromm's teachers--and at the same time the least influential. Fromm's training was then completed at the Psychoanalytical Institute of Berlin, where he studied theoretical and practical psychoanalysis from 1929 to 1930. All of his academic teachers there were more or less strict adherents of Freudian theory: Karl Abraham, Franz Alexander, Sándor Radó, Theodor Reik and Hanns Sachs. Fromm never personally met Sigmund Freud. In the Berlin Institute circles, Fromm came into contact with Karen Horney. This resulted in a long friendship between the two psychoanalysts and also in an invitation to lecture at the University of Chicago in the fall of 1933. In addition to the sociologist Siegfried Bernfeld, the Institute's staff also included Carl Müller-Braunschweig, Harald Schultz-Hencke and René Spitz. Wilhelm Reich joined the Institute in 1930. He and Fromm established a close but short-lived association. Reich frequently lectured on Marx and on the application on his theories to sociology. It was at this time that Fromm began his passionate immersion in Marxist thought. Although he had read Marx since 1926, it was only through Reich, Henrik de Man and, of course, Max Horkheimer that Fromm became a Marxist in the true-- though somewhat controversial--sense of the word. His indebtedness to Reich, with whom he broke off contact relatively soon, has never been fully clarified in pertinent studies.

On 16 June 1926, Fromm, who was originally engaged to Golde Ginsburg (the later wife of Leo Löwenthal), married Frieda Reichmann (1889-1957), a fellow-psychoanalyst. More than ten years his senior, she was born and had studied in Königsberg (East Prussia). After she completed her doctorate in 1914, she went to Dresden and later she received her training as a psychoanalyst at the Berlin Institute. Like Fromm himself, she studied with Hanns Sachs and Emil Kraepelin. He had met Reichmann in Heidelberg where she had opened a psychoanalytic clinic in 1924. This clinic was strictly Freudian in orientation and, moreover, ruled by the rituals of orthodox Judaism. The German name of this establishment, *Therapeutikum*, was thus mockingly changed to "Torapeutikum" ("Torah-peutikum") by the initiated. Frieda Reichmann insisted that all her friends, including Ernst Simon, Löwenthal and, of course, Erich Fromm, undergo an analysis with her. Yet paradoxically, many key figures of the "Torapeutikum" were soon to drift away from orthodoxy, including Fromm and even Reichmann herself. Before this happened, however, a deeper relationship had already developed between the analyst and her patient, which resulted in their marriage. Frieda Fromm-Reichmann was clearly a mother-figure for the young psychoanalyst. (She even resembled his mother physiognomically to a certain extent.) Fromm gained considerable experience in practical and clinical analysis through his association with his first wife. Nevertheless, their marriage was not a happy one. It lasted only four years. They separated in 1930, but were divorced only much later when both had emigrated to the USA. There, Frieda Reichmann continued her work in Rockville, Maryland, and was counted for more than two decades among the foremost clinical analysts in this country.

Since the fall of 1926, Fromm had kept close ties to Frankfurt psychoanalytic circles. One of his academic teachers, Karl Landauer, was instrumental in founding a workshop there which attracted emerging analysts through its discussions of new methods and related literature. Together with his wife, as well as Clara Happel, Heinrich Meng, and Franz Stein, Fromm attended most of these workshops. The atmosphere of the group was relaxed and congenial, but their argumentation remained strictly Freudian. In 1929, on the instigation of Max Horkheimer, Landauer was then entrusted to establish a psychoanalytical "guest" institute, which remained for its lifetime under the auspices of the Frankfurt University, although it was in fact much more closely attached to the Institute of Social Research. It was officially opened on 16 February 1929, and its staff included, besides Landauer, who was appointed director of the guest institute, Heinrich Meng, Erich Fromm, and Frieda Fromm-Reichmann. During the following two years, Fromm commuted every two weeks between Berlin and Frankfurt. The first seminar he taught at the Frankfurt Psychoanalytical Institute was aptly entitled "The Application of Psychoanalysis in Sociology and Religion." Within the Frankfurt guest institute, he had close contacts with Siegfried Bernfeld and Paul Federn, who for some time had been working on a synthesis of the theories of Marx and Freud. He also met there Georg Groddeck, the prominent psychiatrist and physician who may be called the founding father of the theory of psychosomatic illness. Groddeck was also a close acquaintance of Sándor Ferenczi and Karen Horney. If Fromm experienced at that time the first doubts in the validity of orthodox Freudianism, Groddeck must be given credit for providing him with the example of a new, holistic, and thoroughly revolutionary approach to psychoanalysis.

Through Bernfeld and Federn, Fromm also met at the Psychoanalytical Institute the Belgian Socialist Henrik de Man, who had been appointed professor of social psychology by the Frankfurt University in 1929. His book *The Psychology of Marxism* (1928) had, at that time, considerable impact on European scholarly circles. Here, de Man propagated a modification or even a reversal of Marx's theory of economic determinism by means of a more irrational, spontaneous activism. He insisted on the predominance of subjective motivation for all social and political action, thus trying to displace the more objective, often mechanical psychology used by Marx. De Man's study failed to convince Max Horkheimer and his circle, who at that time represented the orthodox Marxist position at the Frankfurt University. It had, however, considerable impact on Fromm, whose own efforts to amalgamate Freud and Marx had not yet come to fruition. Together with Buber's existentialist concepts, the subjectivism propounded by de Man was definitely absorbed into his own later theories of the individual and the social character of humanity.

An overall glance at the biographical data documenting Erich Fromm's life from 1926 to 1930 reveals that these were years of self-exploration, of probing, and of quest for a distinct intellectual identity. Though his ultimate goal was not yet clear to him during these years, his various ventures served the purpose of making it more and more tangible. As at least one result of this "trial and error" method of clarifying his real direction in life, Fromm came to see many influences on his earlier thinking as relative, or even to repudiate them altogether. It was mentioned above that he eventually turned away from orthodox Judaism. This happened as a consequence of the psychoanalysis Fromm underwent in Munich in 1926. Concurrently, as if seeking a new source for mystical inspiration, he briefly embraced Buddhism, a field to which he was to return in the 1950s. While under the influence of his academic teachers at the Berlin Psychoanalytical Institute, all of whom were Freudian disciples, and of course in collaboration with the ideas of Frieda Fromm-Reichmann as an analyst, he had remained true to Freud's theories, though somewhat reluctantly, until the 1930s.

But this, too, he would later decisively reject: first challenging Freud's theory of sexuality and his evaluation of women, and later Freud's whole assessment of psychoanalysis and society insofar as it hinges on the libido theory, the life and death instinct theory and particularly the Oedipus complex. On the other hand, he adhered in his own analytical approach throughout his life to Freud's concept of the unconscious and his dynamic definition of character, as well as to the importance of dreams, neuroses, etc. Fromm was supported in his revision of Freudianism first by Groddeck, then by de Man, a compelling personality (whose role in Frankfurt's intellectual life of the late 1920s, incidentally, is still largely unresearched), and ultimately by the works of Johann Jacob Bachofen, the anthropologist and defender of matriarchy. Fromm also quickly assimilated the ideas of Bertrand Russell and Wilhelm Reich. With his initiation into the Frankfurt Institute of Social Research in the year 1930, Fromm had tentatively arrived at a first, and yet flexible, definition of his own scholarly position. Though it was enormously augmented and extended throughout the course of his career, its basic contours had been established at this time.

Fromm's early publications illustrate this process of self-definition. His dissertation relies still largely on positivistic methods and is of only limited scholarly relevance. His first major article, a spin-off from the dissertation, was published in 1927. It is entitled "Der Sabbath" and appeared in the periodical established by Freud himself, *Imago*.[12] Though still immature in style and execution, it already points vaguely in the direction of Fromm's later endeavors. Still under the spell of Judaism, this article attempts to illuminate certain aspects of Jewish custom by means of psychoanalytical arguments. It does not, however, really arrive at any programmatic insights. Fromm's next article, in contrast, is more successful. Titled "Psychoanalysis and Sociology," it appeared in 1929 in the periodical *Zeitschrift für Psychoanalytische Pädagogik*, edited by A. J. Storfer, and in fact takes first decisive steps toward a synthesis of both disciplines.[13] It defines the goal of such a synthesis as the investigation of the "relationships between humanity's social, i.e. technological/economic development, and the development of the inner emotional structures, especially in the configuration of the ego."

This short article, which represents a distilled version of Fromm's first seminar taught at the Frankfurt Psychoanalytical Institute, bears witness to the intellectual maturation undergone by its author since 1926. Already here, a slight departure from Freudian ideas is evident when Fromm describes the family as the "product" of certain societal norms which, in turn, are dependent in a greater sense upon technological evolution. Karl Marx, however, is not yet mentioned by name, although the article concludes with a brief, anonymous quote from Marx, whom Fromm calls "one of the greatest geniuses of sociology"[!]. His theory of historical/economic determinism will not be fully incorporated in Fromm's argumentation until after 1930--the year he joins the Frankfurt Institute of Social Research.

Fromm's further intellectual and scholarly development was decisively and lastingly molded by his contact with Max Horkheimer and the circle of young intellectuals who were later to become synonymous with the terms "Frankfurt School" and "Critical Theory." Though entire books have been written on the background and achievements of this Institute--*the* Institute, as it is called by insiders--a few remarks will have to suffice here. The Institute of Social Research was located at the address Viktoria-Allee 17, not far from the corner of Bockenheimer Landstrasse. It was originally founded by the Marxist political economist Carl Grünberg on 22 June 1924. In student circles, it was known at that time as "Café Marx." Grünberg resigned as the Institute's director in 1929, for reasons of health. In July, 1930, the director's position was assumed by the 35-year-old Max Horkheimer, who had only recently been appointed professor of Social Philosophy. Horkheimer's colleagues included his life-long friend Friedrich Pollock, the economist Henryk Grossmann, Julian Gumperz, the sinologist Karl August Wittfogel, Franz Borkenau, Reinhard Sorge (who was executed in 1944 in Japan as a Soviet spy), the Germanist Leo Löwenthal and, after 1932, Herbert Marcuse. The eminent philosopher, sociologist, and musicologist Theodor W. Adorno, who was to become the best-known representative of Critical Theory after World War Two, kept regular contact with the Institute members during the 1930s, especially with Horkheimer, with whom he was close friends. But he did not officially join the Institute until 1938, at which time it was already functioning in exile in New York. Fromm's first introduction into the Institute took place though Löwenthal, who had worked there since 1926. Both men had met much earlier in the circle around Rabbi Nehemia Anton Nobel and had become friends. Further contact between Fromm and the Institute occurred automatically, since he was teaching regularly at the neighboring psychoanalytical guest institute. In 1930, then, the same year in which Fromm became an associate member of the German Psychoanalytic Society and opened his own office in the city center of Berlin at Bayrischer Platz 1, he was also appointed a consultant for psychoanalysis by the Institute of Social Research. Simultaneously, he became the director of the Institute's department of psycho-sociological research, a position which included lifetime tenure.

3

Erich Fromm at the Institute of Social Research. The Foundations of his Thought

Fromm's association with the Institute of Social Research lasted only eight years: from his appointment in 1930 to his resignation in January, 1939. These years in this small but superb group of young Marxist scholars, and especially in collaboration with Horkheimer, whom Fromm greatly admired, allowed him to solidify and at the same time expand his own methods to a great extent. During this time, the foundations of his own unique combination of psychoanalytical and sociological methodology were firmly and lastingly laid. Fromm now had truly found himself. It is safe to say that the works he produced during these eight years--which included only articles and no books--already contain *every* essential thought to be found in his later, more popular writings. There exists a widespread myth, which is obediently supported in almost all related research, that Fromm's career as a writer began practically overnight, with the publication of *Escape From Freedom* in 1941. This is certainly not true. Fromm did not emerge with one stroke of genius as an accomplished writer. The purpose of the following analyses of his early work is, therefore, to show the gradual development of his thought--which will immediately dispel the above-mentioned myth--, and to introduce the reader to Fromm's early and yet widely unknown scholarly accomplishments.

In terms of style and methodological finesse, his publications of the 1930s indicate that he had now reached the peak of his scholarly development. Most of these texts have yet to be translated into English and are accessible only to readers fluent in German. It is interesting to note that the often unstructured, even rambling quality of his later books (almost all of which originally appeared in English) is practically absent from his German publications. Whether this is due to their strictly scholarly structure or to the fact that Horkheimer--a first-rate writer and stylist himself--kept an extremely tight rein on his house periodical, remains open to debate. (The *Zeitschrift für Sozialforschung* [*Journal for Social Research*] appeared throughout the nine years of its existence [1932 to 1941] under Horkheimer's editorship.)

Poor health interrupted Fromm's work at the Institute from 1931 to 1932, when he was forced to spend more than a year in a Davos sanatorium fighting tuberculosis. He fell ill a second time in 1938, and again went to Davos for several months of recuperation. It has been suggested by Rainer Funk, a most perceptive biographer of Fromm, that Georg Groddeck correctly diagnosed this illness as psychosomatic.[1] Presumably, its cause was the disintegration of Fromm's marriage to Frieda Fromm-Reichmann, since their separation coincided with the outbreak of his illness. Even so, it is difficult or impossible to verify such biographical connections. During his rest in Davos, he did not remain idle. The two major articles which appeared in the inaugural issue of the Institute's periodical (which will be discussed below[2]) must have been written, at least in part, in Switzerland.

Before engaging in a closer examination of Fromm's scholarly production during these crucial years and of the role he played within the Institute's context, a note of caution to the contemporary reader seems appropriate. As stated above, the Institute, from its inception under Carl Grünberg, continuing throughout the Horkheimer years and even into a much later phase after its return from American exile, was predominantly dedicated to the study and application of Marxist theory to practically all areas of social life and interaction. After the mid-1950s, its orientation may have changed somewhat, but the later history of the Institute is not the issue of this study. For today's American reader, who may or may not have been subjected to the years of McCarthy brainwashing and the slogans of Cold War propaganda, this dedication to Marxist thought might appear to have been subversive or at least suspicious. One has to keep in mind, though, that during the 1930s the present polarization of the superpowers and their satellites did not yet exist. Moreover, Marxism was (and still is today) regarded in many American and European intellectual circles as a socio-philosophical theory which presented a viable alternative to both capitalism and, particularly, rampant fascism. Marxism as such was certainly not considered synonymous with the party line of the Soviet Union, the only declared "Marxist" state at that time. In fact, many members of the Institute were denounced in later years by their more orthodox communist fellow-scholars in Eastern Europe as "revisionists." Only in the years after World War II, and especially in the United States, was the *philosophical* term "Marxism" used *politically* and indiscriminately to identify the "enemy" camp, i.e. the non-capitalist world. Conservative politicians in more recent years, after the demise of détente, have even further muddied the waters by branding those peoples and their governments who presumably ascribe to Marxist doctrines as the anti-Christ and as beings who do not "accept our kind of morality." All this reflects, at best, uncoordinated thinking or deliberate distortion. At worst, it may lead to another world war. It has been amply demonstrated--last but not least by Erich Fromm himself--that a person may be a Marxist and, at the same time, a deeply religious and ethical being. For the purpose of the following discussion of Marxist thought and the role it plays in Fromm's theories, it is vital to separate the *theoretical* aspects of Marxism from both their denunciation by political propaganda and from the more *practical* side of latter-day Marxism-Leninism as it may be encountered in today's socialist and/or communist countries.

Max Horkheimer was the originator of what was later to be called "Critical Theory." He first used the term in the year 1937. In approximately one dozen highly perceptive articles, all published between 1932 and 1940 in the *Zeitschrift für Sozialforschung*,[3] he defined the goals and methods of this concept. Roughly speaking,

Critical Theory is an amalgamation of certain central elements of Hegel's philosophy with particular aspects of Marx's thoughts. As opposed to Marx, however, Horkheimer does not delegate a special role to the proletariat--not to any one class in particular. Critical Theory attempts to analyze theoretically and to contribute practically to the better understanding of three focal aspects: 1) the economic basis of society; 2) the psychological development and formation of the individual; and 3) the cultural sphere. By means of this declared close interrelationship between theory and practice, Critical Theory further aspires to overcome the mental and economic impoverishment typical of the individual within capitalist society--a system which presumably is bound to self-destruct in due time. Through the creation of a new, humane social structure, Horkheimer ultimately hoped to accomplish the reconciliation of the modern human being with its natural destiny: a life in joy and dignity. As can be seen from this account (which is, admittedly, extremely simplified) of the basic tenets of Critical Theory, Horkheimer replaced the *revolutionary* impetus of Marx (even if he does not exclude the possibility of occasional revolutionary changes) with a more *evolution-oriented* concept of societal betterment. It is obvious that the goals of this change from "within" carry strong ethical overtones.

When Fromm joined the ranks of the Institute's faculty in 1930, Horkheimer had long since realized the importance of socio-historically oriented psychoanalysis within the greater framework of Critical Theory. In a programmatical lecture entitled "History and Psychology," held before the Kant Society in Frankfurt (and later published as an article in the first volume of the *Zeitschrift für Sozialforschung*), Horkheimer defines the goal of "specialized group psychology" as the intensive research of the psychological structure of individual social strata: "The key to analysing any given historical epoch lies in the recognition of the psychological powers and dispositions, the character and mutability of members of the various social classes."[4] Horkheimer himself, by the way, had undergone lengthy psychoanalysis with Karl Landauer, as he found himself incapable of extemporizing or lecturing without written notes--a serious but not altogether unusual impediment in the academic profession. Needless to say, the analysis was successful. (The author of this study, as a Frankfurt student, had the opportunity of hearing some of Horkheimer's lectures many years later. Horkheimer, at that time already a professor emeritus, was able to lecture freely, although his delivery never dazzled his audience, nor even approached the inimitable eloquence of his colleague Theodor W. Adorno. It was the *substance* of his lectures which cast a strong spell over his students.) In the above-quoted article, though he does not yet define it, Horkheimer makes a direct reference to the phenomenon of "social character" to which so much of Fromm's later work will be devoted.

In the same initial volume of the *Zeitschrift für Sozialforschung*, Fromm's article "On the Methods and Goals of Analytical Social Psychology" was published.[5] It can be considered a culmination and summation of his foregoing articles "On the Psychology of Criminals and Society" (1931) and "On the Development of The Dogma of Christ" (1930).[6] This latter work also appeared as a *separatum* in 1931 and was described by Frank Borkenau as a successful "linking of Marxism with Freudian psychoanalysis."[7] But the 1932 article in Horkheimer's periodical not only caps off Fromm's earlier work. It contains virtually all the methodological premises for his work in the decades to come. Though it is concise and in places even compressed, this article--and *not Escape From Freedom*, which was written nine years later and is generally considered to be the first foundational work--contains the author's most decisive breakthrough in his own scholarly approach. It deserves to be discussed in some detail.

Fromm proceeds from both Freud's definition of human drives and from Marx's analysis of socio-economic conditions, and arrives at his own definition of a new Social Psychology. This discipline should aim primarily at generating insight into ". . . the instinct structure, the libidinous and largely subconscious behavior of a group [=class] in the context of its socio-economic structure."[8] Psychoanalysis can "add to the conception of Historical Materialism a whole new dimension, namely the deeper understanding of one of society's most essential components, human nature itself."[9]

The theories of Dialectical Materialism, Fromm continues, fail to come to grips with the effect of material conditions on the *consciousness* of human beings. This is where psychoanalysis become important. Only psychoanalysis

> can show that ideologies are the products of certain desires, drives, interests, and needs which, though they themselves are to a great extent not realized consciously, find external expression through ideology. These instincts are themselves the result of biological drives, on one hand, but they are further formed in both quantity and content by the socio-economic situation of the individual or its class.[10]

Through the methods of psychoanalysis, Fromm concludes, it will be possible to analyze ideologies and ideas in terms of their libidinous properties. From there, conclusions may be drawn regarding the given influences of socio-economic conditions on the mental and emotional development of both the society as a whole and its individual member. Proceeding thus, it will also be possible for researchers of the "dynamic components within the social process" to make retroactive statements regarding past history, as well as to make prognoses for the future.[11] Fromm also mentions the libidinous relationship between a ruling or privileged minority and the dominated/underprivileged majority: a phenomenon which makes it possible for exploitative capitalism to maintain the status quo with little or no difficulty.

This remarkable article, which could only be briefly paraphrased here, delineates Fromm's methodology step by step and clearly stakes out the paths his later work will take. In addition, it provides striking evidence for the fact that in the Institute's environment, and especially with Horkheimer's guidance, Fromm had found both the inspiration and the necessary resonance for the further growth of his thinking. This fact, remarkably enough, was never officially acknowledged by Fromm himself after his departure from the Institute. Neither was the impact of his own thought on other members of the Institute given due credit in the years to come.

For a better understanding of his later, more popular works, a glimpse at the ensuing seminal essays of the 1930s is indispensable. These appeared in rapid succession in the *Zeitschrift für Sozialforschung*. Characteristically, these articles, like his later books, fall into three distinct, though closely interrelated categories. The first group attempts to define *the interdependence of the individual and the social character*. Coupled with "On the Methods and Goals of Analytical Social Psychology," Fromm published "The Psychoanalytical Characterology and its Relevance to Social Psychology" in the same inaugural issue of the *Zeitschrift* in 1932. Here, he demonstrates through a slight but noticeable modification of Freud's libido theory that not only the development of the individual is governed by libidinous drives, but in fact *every* societal structure is equally dominated by something which may be called a "collective libido." Fromm's theory of the "social character" emerges already from this article--it is tentative, but clearly discernible. According to Freud's character definition, the "social character" of a given organization, state, or conglomerate of societies bound by common ideological structure, must be seen as dynamic and open to change. The "social character" of capitalist societies, according to Fromm,

> must be considered the sum of the character traits typical of all human beings who live in that society. The essential aspect, however, lies in the libidinous stimuli which are responsible for these character traits, i.e. the dynamic function of the character as a whole.[12]

From there, Fromm engages in a brief but convincing description of the "libidinous structure" typical of capitalist systems. The later discussion of his popular writings, in particular of *To Have or To Be?*, will be devoted to the analysis of what is later called "social character."

Following this twosome, Fromm devotes a second, no less innovative pair of essays to the topic of *matriarchy*. In 1934, he turns to the "socio-psychological importance of the theory of matriarchy" ("Die sozialpsychologische Bedeutung der Mutterrechtstheorie"[13]) as derived from Johann Jakob Bachofen's epoch-making book *Mutterrecht* (1861). This study stresses the importance of myths for the modern human being. After a brief discourse on the historical aspects of the issue, it turns to Friedrich Engels, who used Bachofen's theories to support his own critique of the patriarchal hierarchy of nineteenth century class society. The "patricentric" society typical of modern industrialized nations is clearly described in this essay. Later, Fromm will incorporate this aspect into his large-scale social criticism. Of similar, if not equal importance is also his earlier review article, printed in volume two of the *Zeitschrift für Sozialforschung* (1933), on Robert Briffault's three-volume study of matriarchy, which was published in England in 1928.[14] Briffault, who was strongly influenced by Darwin and Freud, follows a more anthropological and ethnological line of thought than Fromm finds appropriate or convincing. His criticism is highly illustrative with regard to his own socio-psychological position.

The third and final group of studies written by Erich Fromm during these strikingly productive years is, characteristically, directed toward the more *practical* aspects of present-day society in the 1930s. In his investigation of the societal influences exerted on the practice of analytical therapy ("Die gesellschaftliche Bedingtheit der psychoanalytischen Theorie" [1935]),[15] Fromm demonstrates for the first time a distinctly critical attitude towards Freudian psychoanalysis. Freud's assessment of sexual morality is now seen as a direct result of his own background: the restricted mores and thought of the ruling bourgeoisie at the turn of the century. As alternatives to Freud's authoritarian and class-influenced viewpoint, Fromm cites the work of Georg Groddeck and Sándor Ferenczi. Both propagated a liberal, open-minded relationship between analyst and analysand. Freud's "tolerance" toward the patient thus appears to be nothing more than indifference, and therewith the product of a pseudo-liberal, but essentially patricentric and restrictive social character. In conclusion, Fromm recommends a modified application of Freudian analysis and stresses the necessity that it be connected ". . . with an independent philosophy to accept unconditionally the patient's claim to happiness and eliminating from all valuations the taboos and abstract traits."[16] This modified--or "revisionist"--stance toward Freudianism was to become the invariable basis for Fromm's own future work as a psychoanalyst. After his emigration to the United States, it brought him into sharp conflict with more orthodox Freudian professional circles--a development to be related below. His critique on Freud is further expounded in *Sigmund Freud's Mission* (1959) and in *Greatness and Limitations of Freud's Thought (1979)*.

The other three studies belonging in this group are devoted to the investigation of the social character of bourgeois (=capitalist) society during the Weimar years. Fromm wrote a remarkable contribution to the anthology *Studies on Authority and Family* (*Studien über Autorität und Familie* [1936]), dealing with the socio-psychological aspects of authoritarianism in the family context as a reflex of a generally oppressive, patriarchal societal structure. His essay is one of the better sections of this joint research venture of various Institute members.[17] At the same time, he produced one more seminal article: "The Feeling of Powerlessness" ("Zum Gefühl der Ohnmacht" [1937]), which again appeared in the *Zeitschrift für Sozialforschung.*[18] This was to be Fromm's last major essay in the *Zeitschrift*. All in all, Horkheimer's house periodical, published already at that time for the fifth consecutive year in Paris by the Librairie Félix Alcan, contains a total of five (not counting the review article on Briffault) fundamental scholarly contributions by Erich Fromm: milestones on the road of his development as a social psychologist. This does not take into account his approximately thirty reviews also published in this organ. These are, at least in part, illustrative examples of his ongoing reception of various philosophical, psychological, and sociological theories during those years.

"The Feeling of Powerlessness" is of primary import for the understanding of Fromm's later works. Within the restricted scope of this brilliant twenty-three-page essay on the essential traits of the individual and the bourgeoisie, most of the cornerstones for the author's later, more influential books are laid. The bourgeois character--as explored later in considerable depth in *Escape from Free-dom* and also in the politically oriented books of the 1950s and the 1960s, such as *The Sane Society* (1955), *May Man Prevail* (1961), as well as *The Heart of Man* (1964)--is seen as manifestly ambivalent. On the one hand, it possesses an active and creative component which enables each individual (and consequently society as a whole) to align all functions of living with the prerogatives of rea-son. Thus, the bourgeois class has been instrumental in bringing about socio-economic changes beneficial to a greater number of individuals than ever before in history. Diametrically opposed to this creative and formative drive characteristic for this class and its members, on the other hand, is an equally strong tendency toward resignation, impotence and blind obedience. This latter character trait--Fromm rightly considers it to be a neurotic quality--renders the individual ultimately helpless in the face of his/her societal am-bience:

> The work of his [i.e. the bourgeois individual's] own hands, originally meant to serve him and to make him happy, turns into an alienating world, to which he pays humble and impotent obedience. He shows this very same attitude [of blind obedience] toward the whole societal and political apparatus.[19]

This neurotic feeling of powerlessness against political powers, i.e. the "state," has in the past invariably prevented the masses from taking collective action, even when they fully realized that catas-trophic wars were imminent. A general failure to avert crises and detrimental developments in the course of history is due to this same perverse inertia. The deep-seated feeling of helplessness, however, is not restricted to "greater" social interactions. The bourgeois individual, as a rule, feels equally powerless in his inter-personal relationships, as well as toward things and objects. Even the own, individual self appears to be an unchangeable entity which can not be altered by creative introspection. The most widespread "safety-valve" of this neurotic self-limitation is, according to Fromm, anger and fury. But this feeling, again, remains largely un-channeled, as its roots and causes are not understood by the individual. Consequently, anger frequently results in fear: one of the main characteristics of the authoritarian personality.

The causes of this process appear to be bi-fold. First, patriarchal/authoritarian child-rearing produces early manifestations of helplessness in the adolescent personality. Sado-masochistic character traits are frequently found in authoritarian families, and may lastingly influence the adult life of the respective adolescent. (All this will be discussed by Fromm in depth in *The Anatomy of Human Destructiveness*.) Second, this "private," familial training toward obedience and resignation is further augmented by a presumably impenetrable and enigmatic economic system, which seems to be totally impervious to individual understanding:

> The fact that the bourgeois individual is uninformed of the psychological reasons behind his *own* actions corresponds with his total lack of knowledge regarding both economic causalities and the dictates of the market imposed on those causalities. To the contrary, he regards them as incomprehensible acts of fate.[20]

Both the private and the collective self-reduction of the bourgeoisie to passivity and societal impotence contribute, in the final analysis, to a stagnant "social" character. An overpowering feeling of dependence pervades the individual as well as the whole. No wonder, Fromm remarks in conclusion, that authoritarian ideologies fall on fertile ground in this situation. All hopes, collective and individual, are centered on the vague but fervent expectations of "change"--*any* change at *all* costs!--and on the potential rise of a Führer-personality in the name of "national destiny." Quite obviously, this article not only accurately and perceptively describes the preconditions which made European fascism and National Socialism possible. In addition, it pinpoints the inherent dangers of any societal configuration dominated by stagnation and impervious to evolution. Fromm will employ the very same model approach to his various analyses of American monopolistic capitalism.

The essay on powerlessness also enumerates all essential elements of the phenomenon Fromm later called the "social character" of capitalist society, to the exploration of which not only *Escape from Freedom*, but also many of his following publications are devoted. Moreover, the "social character" (the term is not yet used in "The Feeling of Powerlessness") is already delineated as a *dynamic* interrelation of individual *and* collective (i.e. socio-economically defined) character traits. In other words: for Fromm the character of an individual is as much formed by the given societal framework as this societal framework possesses a collective, "social" character provided for by the sum of the individual character traits of its members. Both are contingent on one another. This theory, which appears reminiscent of Leibniz' dynamic system of monads--all of which are interdependent on each other and, simultaneously, allow for the universal dynamics of the whole--will be discussed later in some detail. At this point, the remark may suffice that this configurative interdependence of both types of character, individual and "social," implies an almost circular motion of socio-economic processes. A re-distribution of the means of production or the available capital (as Dialectic Materialism suggests) would not suffice to change the "social" character of capitalist societies. This change would have to originate from within, i.e. from *all* members of the greater social context, in order to be effective.

Prior to this fundamental study, Fromm carried out a field project under the auspices of the Institute which may very well have provided him with much of the statistical material tacitly underlying the conception of "The Feeling of Powerlessness." The results of this project were buried for many years in his private files, and could only recently be edited.[21] The study was published in English under the title *The Working Class in Weimar Germany. A Psychological and Sociological Study.*[22] Already in 1930, Fromm, his friend Ernst Schachtel, and a team consisting of Anna Hartoch, Herta Herzog, and Paul F. Lazarsfeld composed a questionnaire of 641 related questions, which was distributed to approximately three thousand members of the working classes. About 1,100 completed questionnaires were returned, but many were lost when the Institute moved to the United States in 1933. Only 584 were left in 1934. This project was meant to be the first practical application of Critical Theory to a given, sharply defined societal stratum. The same questionnaire was used for the Institute's later joint venture, the *Studies on Authority and Family*.[23] Although the results of the team's efforts in 1930 remain inconclusive, the experimental project and its evaluation make for interesting reading in various respects. Not only was this a pioneering research project in itself, it also allowed many insights into the socio-psychological status of the participants at this historically crucial moment. Inasmuch as the questionnaire itself is mostly Fromm's own work, its composition and the thrust of the questions even allow a glimpse at his own *practical* orientation as a psychoanalyst at the very beginning of his career.

The text, once more, proved to be seminal for further research. A much later collaborative effort of various members of the Institute, entitled *The Authoritarian Personality*,[24] although primarily theoretical in its approach, profited from this earlier venture. For Fromm himself, the field study provided a pragmatic foundation for consecutive investigations of authoritarian character traits, especially as exemplified in *Escape from Freedom*. Much later in his life, he returned to the method of statistical field study. One of the results of these endeavors is to be found in the volume *Social Character in a Mexican Village* (1970), which carries the characteristic subtitle *A Sociopsychoanalytic Study*.[25]

The Working Class in Weimar Germany was never published under the auspices of the Institute of Social Research. Martin Jay, the foremost authority on the history of the Institute, was later informed by Friedrich Pollock that the loss of almost half of the completed questionnaires thwarted its publication.[26] This may be true in part. Much more decisive was the fact, however, that at a time when the collected materials might have been prepared for print, the rift between Fromm and his colleagues at the Institute had already deepened. The final break was only a question of time and, curiously, was further accelerated by the ongoing debate over the eventual publication of the field study.

To be sure, the relations between Erich Fromm and some of the other Institute members had been strained for quite some time. Theodor W. Adorno, who was a frequent Institute guest after his own appointment as assistant professor of philosophy at the Frankfurt University in 1931, disliked Fromm intensely. This feeling was reciprocal. Adorno had insulted Löwenthal and Fromm, who were both still orthodox in their adherence to Judaism at the time, by mockingly calling them "professional Jews." His jest about Martin Buber, whom he called a "religious Tyrolean," was not taken kindly either. Differences in temperament became obvious at an early stage: Fromm's serious, unblinking outlook on life must have clashed with the whimsical and caustically self-ironic personalities of Adorno, Horkheimer, and Friedrich Pollock. One has to keep in mind as well that the continuity of his work at the Institute suffered from the hiatus of his enforced sojourn in Davos. While Fromm was in Switzerland, the prescient Horkheimer, who became acutely aware of the imminent National Socialist threat, had opened a branch of the Institute in Geneva in 1931. Through this branch, administered initially by Pollock and later led by Andries Sternheim and Juliette Favez, Fromm maintained only sporadic contact with the Institute while he recuperated from his illness.

In March, 1933, the Frankfurt Institute was shut down by the new National Socialist government. The reason: it had demonstrated tendencies "hostile toward the state." Shortly thereafter, Horkheimer, Adorno and other Jewish faculty members were expelled from their teaching positions. Horkheimer and the majority of his co-workers managed to flee to Geneva. There, the main body of the International Institute of Social Research, as it was called after the opening of the Geneva branch, continued its work until 1934. When Horkheimer visited New York in May, 1934, he was invited by Nicholas Murray Butler, the generous president of Columbia University, to relocate the Institute in New York: "And so the International Institute for Social Research, as revolutionary and marxist as it had appeared in Frankfurt in the twenties, came to settle in the center of the capitalist world, New York City."[27] During the same year, when the Institute had found its new home at 429 West 117th Street, most of its members crossed the ocean and joined Horkheimer in American exile. Erich Fromm, who had earlier followed an invitation of the Chicago Institute of Psychoanalysis to give a series of guest lectures, was at that time already in the United States. He stayed in Chicago until the fall of 1934, when he moved to New York. The Geneva branch of the Institute remained functional through the war years, but barely so. Fromm once again revisited it in 1938/39 during his second convalescent stay in Davos.

Beginning with its relocation in the New World, the Institute rapidly underwent a process of scholarly re-orientation. The various stages of Critical Theory have been described elsewhere, and are too complex to be analyzed here.[28] Horkheimer and his closer associates, whose ranks were joined in November, 1938, by Theodor W. Adorno, became increasingly oriented toward abstract sociological and philosophical research. The staff members' individual research interests remained, at least on the surface, essentially the same: Horkheimer and Marcuse were primarily responsible for philosophy; Grossmann, Gumpertz and Pollock were devoted to economics; Fromm still represented the field of social psychology; Adorno and Löwenthal dealt with the theory of culture. But the climate within the Institute changed drastically in exile. In addition to a much more sober, even pessimistic outlook on society--strengthened by the rise of fascism in Europe, the imminence of war and, notably, their first-hand observations of American capitalism--they abandoned immediate hope for *practical* application of Critical Theory as a tool of societal change. Instead, the Institute's work shifted toward the investigation of cultural and aesthetic phenomena, a directional change due mostly to Adorno's increased influence on Horkheimer.

In the meantime, Erich Fromm had resumed his work as a psychoanalyst in the United States. He opened an office in New York City, which he maintained for many years to come. Apart from his teaching obligations, he did not participate in any of the Institute's projects after 1937. His modification and critique of Freud's theories, which had initially won him acclaim within the Institute, were now openly rejected by some of its members. His working relationship with Adorno and Marcuse rapidly deteriorated. When Fromm insisted on his intention to publish the results of his now outdated

field study (*The Working Class in Weimar Germany*), Horkheimer
vetoed the publication, arguing that the whole undertaking had
been of questionable scientific validity from the very beginning. It
has never become absolutely clear what caused the irrevocable
break.[29] Among a multiplicity of personal and methodological differences, financial considerations may finally have tipped the
scales. Friedrich Pollock, the budget director of the Institute, suggested that Fromm, who had a regular income from his analytical
practice, forego his Institute salary for the benefit of his needier
colleagues. Fromm, in turn, handed in his resignation, effective in
January, 1939. He received the amount of $20,000 as compensa-
tion for the loss of his tenure.[30] At that time, this was not a paltry
sum: the blow to the coffers of the Institute dealt by Fromm's departure was a massive one. When he left the Institute, he took all
his notes with him, including the materials on *The Working Class in
Weimar Germany*.

This departure was also a symbolic act. For Erich Fromm, both
the time of apprenticeship and his tenure as an academic theoretician had come to an end. During the following thirty years in the
New World, he rapidly attained prominence in academic and psychoanalytical circles. But much more important, his career as a
"popular" writer whose works reached many millions of readers began within two years. Through his close integration in American
life, he was now able to gain the insights necessary for his accurate
and often cutting analysis of this society's foundations. Critical
Theory, for Fromm, did not lead to philosophical introspection and
to ultimate resignation, as it did for many of his colleagues at the
Institute for Social Research. On the contrary, it reshaped and re-
vitalized his own dynamic method of social diagnosis. Characteristically, this diagnosis, even at its most dismal, is never without hope.
For Fromm, there is always light at the end of the tunnel. When
Horkheimer and Adorno had long relinquished their expectations
for drastic societal changes--even Herbert Marcuse became disillu-
sioned at a later time--, Erich Fromm clung tenaciously to his unflagging faith in humanity's potential for self-regeneration. *This*
unbroken hope is the spiritual center of his life and his works.

4

The Synthesis: *Escape from Freedom*
(1941)

As opposed to many of his fellow émigrés, academicians and writers alike, Erich Fromm achieved integration into the new societal and working situation of his host country--and not least into the new language environment--with little difficulty. Obviously, his English was sufficiently fluent. He did not, as did his more philosophically-oriented fellow members of the Institute, have to rely heavily on his native tongue as a means for precisely formulated ideas. Horkheimer and Adorno in particular were deeply chagrined by the loss of their native linguistic habitat, and greatly hampered in their expression of thought. Philosophy does not translate well into another language. In a poignant attack on those German emigrants who readily and willingly abandoned their linguistic (and thus their cultural) roots, Horkheimer described the situation: "That the German intellectuals don't need long to change to a foreign language as soon as their own bars them from a sizeable readership, comes from the fact that language already serves them more in the struggle for existence than as an expression of truth."[1] For Erich Fromm, the last part of this verdict does not hold true. English rapidly and permanently became his "first" language, the one in which he wrote his well-known books and which served him sufficiently for the expression of truth as he saw it.

In 1940, Fromm was granted American citizenship. By then, he had already established himself as a successful practicing analyst. In November, 1934, he had moved from his New York apartment in 66th Street to a flat at 444 Central Park West. Nine years later, he had moved again, this time to 32 Central Park West. From 1940 to 1941, he then held a position as visiting assistant professor at the American Institute for Psychoanalysis at Columbia University. In 1941, he joined the faculty at Bennington College, Vermont, where he taught psychoanalysis until he resigned in 1950. His busy schedule called for lectures and seminars in Bennington on Mondays, many guest engagements, as well as upholding his private practice in New York during the week. On Fridays, he usually returned to Bennington for the weekend. After 1941, he also was a frequent visiting speaker at the American Institute for Psychoanalysis.

His ready acceptance in American psychoanalytic circles was facilitated by his friendship with Karen Horney (who had been instrumental in bringing Fromm to Chicago already in 1933), and Harry Stack Sullivan. Both ranked at that time among the most influential Neo-Freudian psychoanalysts in the United States. Fromm met Sullivan, as well as Ruth Benedict, Abram Kardiner, Clara M. Thompson, and William Silverberg through Horney. His relationship to Karen Horney herself, the author of the influential work *The Neurotic Personality of our Time* (1937), warrants some comment. Both had established their first contact and, subsequently, a lasting friendship in Karl Landauer's Frankfurt circle, and in Georg Groddeck's sanatorium in Baden-Baden. Karen Horney gradually assumed the role of a strong, motherly figure in Fromm's life, especially in the years after the disintegration of his first marriage.[2] Together with Fromm's friends, Ernst and Anna Schachtel, both Horney and Fromm spent many weekends either at Horney's apartment or in the company of Sullivan, who resided on 64th Street. Clara Thompson also lived in the immediate neighborhood, on 83rd Street. At this time, Fromm was strongly influenced by Horney's theories on *individual* neuroses. On the other hand, Horney was equally impressed by his analyses of *collective* behavior and his investigation of the social character, in brief: by his sociological approach. Until 1941, Fromm, Horney, and the Schachtels (Ernst Schachtel specialized in test psychology and also became a psychoanalyst) spent several vactions together. In 1938, when Fromm becam ill again and had to recuperate in Davos, Horney visited him in Switzerland.

The dissolution of this warm and mutually productive relationship began in 1941. During the yearly meeting of the New York Psychoanalytic Society on 29 April, 1941, Horney was attacked by some of her fellow-members on the grounds of her unorthodox teaching and analysis methodology. Further, she was forbidden to supervise theses and dissertations and "demoted" to undergraduate instruction. Among her antagonists were Kardiner (who had stated his own theoretical positions in his book *The Individual and His Society* [1939][3] and vastly disagreed with Horney's theory of neurosis), as well as Sándor Rádo, Carl Binger, George Daniels, David Levy and others. Horney left the Society in protest. She was followed by Harmon S. Ephron, Sarah R. Kelman, Bernard S. Robbins, and Clara Thompson. Together with William Silverberg, they founded the Association for the Advancement of Psychoanalysis. Silverberg was elected president, and Thompson vice-president. Its paractical branch, the American Institute for Psychoanalysis, was subsequently attached to the Lower-Fifth-Avenue Hospital. Erich Fromm joined the Institute practically at its inception. His status as a lecturer and practical analyst, however, was initially questioned by various members, as he did not hold a medical degree. Although he was reluctantly granted full faculty status in November, 1941, his qualification to teach technical workshops was challenged again in 1943. Presumably, this attempt to reduce his status originated from Horney's sphere of influence. Clara Thompson, the Institute's president at the time, put an investigative committee in charge of the controversy. The committee decided to deprive Fromm of his full faculty status. Thompson was dissatisfied with this verdict, and stated during an extraordinary faculty meeting that personal differences among the three protagonists of three distinctly different analytical "schools" within the Institute--Horney, Sullivan, and Fromm--had apparently led to the present power struggle. She then suggested a reconciliation. Her entreaties were, however, of no avail. Fromm finally submitted his resignation. Together with him, Thompson, Sullivan, and various other analysts left the Institute.

There is little doubt that Karen Horney felt threatened during the early 1940's both by Fromm's steadily increasing influence on her own thought, and by his ever-growing popularity in student circles. The publication of *Escape from Freedom* in 1941 had, almost overnight, provided him with the mantle of a cult figure among his students. Already in 1937, Horney had made an unsuccessful attempt to help her friend place *Escape from Freedom* (on which Fromm was still working, and which was far from completion) with her own publisher, Norton. Norton declined. The book was eventually published by Holt, Rinehart and Winston, and it turned out to be enormously successful. Horney must have felt a certain amount of professional envy toward her protegé and close associate. Her ultimate move against his overpowering presence at the Institute, therefore, appears retroactively almost as an act of self-liberation.[4] In addition, her daughter Marianne had undergone an analysis with Fromm in 1939. As a result, she had begun to rebel against her mother's domineering personality. Karen Horney put the blame for this rift in her ralations with Marianne on Fromm. The break between Fromm and Horney was inevitable and could not be mended.

After his departure from the American Institute for Psychoanalysis, Erich Fromm maintained his close ties with Harry Stack Sullivan. In fact, they remained friends until Sullivan died in 1949. Sullivan had studied psychiatry with William Alanson White in Washington and was one of the foremost American authorities on schizophrenia. He had, already in Washington, initiated an informal gathering for friends which was jokingly called the "Zodiac Club." During the days of Prohibition, the members of this circle--which at that time included Thompson, Silverberg, Edward Shipley, and Sullivan's step-son Jimmy--enlivened their professional discussions with the frivolously illegal consumption of alcoholic beverages. Later, Fromm was a frequent guest of the "Zodiac" gatherings. It was in this circle that he met John Dollard and Margaret Mead. He also renewed his previous acquaintance with Paul Tillich, the renowned philosopher and theologian, who at that time held a faculty position at the New York Union Theological Seminary. Tillich's re-vitalization of Protestantism on the basis of modern psychology and sociology appealed to Fromm. A closer relationship, however, did not develop between the two men. Prophets usually are uneasy in each other's company.

In 1936, Sullivan founded the Washington School of Psychiatry. A New York branch was initiated in 1943 by Sullivan himself, Erich Fromm, Frieda Fromm-Reichmann, David and Janet Rioch, and Clara Thompson. In 1946, this establishment was given a new name and re-organized as the William Alanson White Institute of Psychiatry, Psychoanalysis and Psychology. Fromm served as its staff director from 1946 to 1950, and remained with its faculty for many years thereafter. He was also a close personal friend of the *Institute's later director, Earl G. Wittenberg. The innovative curriculum*, which provided for cross-fertilization among various disciplines in the natural and empirical sciences as well as in the humanities, was extremely conducive to Fromm's own dual orientation toward theory and practice. Indeed, the atmosphere at the White Institute reinforced his own belief in "the superior value of blending empirical observation with speculation."[5] Even after his permanent move to Mexico in 1951, he returned regularly to the William Alanson White Institute for summer sessions and other seminars.

Erich Fromm's early reputation as a writer rests almost exclusively on the merits of his first book, *Escape from Freedom*. In this study, which will be discussed below in some detail, he achieves a first significant synthesis of both the theoretical basis of his socio-psychological training and the practical aspects gleaned by his own observation of the two societal frameworks under discussion in the book: the authoritarian, fascist state versus American democracy. The former of these systems is welded together by the domineering power of what Fromm calls "irrational" authority, whereas the latter is based on the economic principles of monopolistic capitalism. Critical Theory in Fromm's own application now merges with psychologically oriented, large-scale social criticism. Insofar as he recognized the *processional* character of history, Fromm remains indebted to Hegel, Marx, and to the teachings of Horkheimer and others at the International Institute of Social Research. In this respect, Franz Borkenau's study *The Transition from the Feudal to the Bourgeois World View* (1934)[6] may well have inspired the historical section of his own book to a certain extent. Regarding the psychological and social interrelations of the *individual* at a given time in history with the *whole* of a specific socio-economic configuration, however, Fromm relies exclusively on his own method.

In the foreword to *Escape from Freedom*, Fromm mentions that this book is only a part of a larger study "concerning the character structure of modern man and the problems of the interaction between psychological and sociological factors," the completion of which will take a considerably longer time.[7] It must be noted here that *all* of his subsequent books and articles are devoted essentially to this topic. All may thus be regarded as individual parts of the same monumental oeuvre. Even when they are perfectly able to stand on their own premises, they are still intricately related to one another and display many overlapping and even outright repetitious versions of the very same arguments. On the other hand, this multi-faceted work not only contains ample continuation and augmentation of ideas, it also demonstrates a more or less linear development of its author's thought. Within the subsequent discussions of each particular title, some attention must therefore be paid to the cross-referential scope of the *whole* work, and allowances made for its resultant repetitive nature.

In general, it should be stressed from the outset that Fromm's "popular" writing is hampered on occasion by a tendency toward imprecision. (This aspect is conspicuously absent from his early academic publications.) It is difficult to say whether his command of English--an acquired rather than native language--is primarily responsible for this. Possibly, his intention to address a large and mostly non-specialist readership plays a major role here. The fact remains that a portion of the debate surrounding his work has been sparked by his own frequent use of oblique and even contradictory terminology. In addition, he often uses a technique of recapitulation which may frustrate his more astute readers. Chapters usually open with a summary of the arguments to follow; they conclude with a brief resumé of the preceding text, which in turn is often carried over to open the following chapter. These deliberate exercises in redundacy have exasperated various critics. They are, however, part of an intricate effort to persuade the reader by constantly rephrasing the major points: a modified "Socratic" form of hermeneutic argumentation, which may well be derived from the author's earlier studies of Talmud.

Escape from Freedom, which marks its author's breakthrough to success as a writer, is structured according to the same three-step pattern typical of his subsequent books. Chapters I to III provide the *historical* framework for his investigation of character changes. Within this part of the study, a clear-cut two-step approach can be discerned (it will be discussed below). In chapters IV and V, a *diagnostic* analysis of the modern individual's psychological makeup is supplied. Again, this diagnostic approach might be called two-pronged, as it concentrates first on the greater socio-economic conditions and, second, on the individual and collective character traits of capitalist societies. The third and final step occurs in chapters VI and VII. Here, the different behavioral patterns of persons living in a fascist, authoritarian system and those living in a capitalist, democratic society are juxtaposed. The book's main body concludes with practical suggestions for the improvement of life, both for the individual and for society at large.

Attached is an appendix entitled "Character and the Social Process." For any serious student of Erich Fromm, this is undoubtedly the book's most important element. It might be suggested that the reader concentrate *first* on the appendix, as a prerequisite to reading the text itself. In this twenty-page essay, the author reformulates and reshapes his theory of characterology. Although he had explored it previously in his essays during the 1930s, especially in "On the Methods and Goals of Analytical Social Psychology," "The Psychoanalytical Characterology and its Relevance to Social Psychology," and "The Feeling of Powerlessness,"[8] Fromm argues at this point for the first time on a predominantly theoretical basis. He also uses the important term "social character" for the first time in this essay. For non-German-speaking readers, this brief article is a prerequisite for *any* deeper insights into Fromm's work as a whole. As the following discussion of *Escape from Freedom* hinges largely on the understanding of the principles of characterology, the appendix's meaning and contents should be explained beforehand.

Fromm proceeds from the assumption that all members of a given social group share common characteristics. He had successfully tackled and proven this assumption in the above-mentioned articles, and also in his field study *The Working Class in Weimar Germany*. These character traits, taken as a whole, comprise what he calls *social character*. Deviations from this predominant behavioral pattern are discounted as not relevant to the theory. Any social process, according to Fromm, must be analyzed in terms of the given social character, because the social character is not only the *product* of the existing societal framework, but also the one and only *agent* responsible for its sustenance or eventual change. Thus, social character must be seen as the major formative influence on every individual member of a group or society:

> . . . by adapting himself to social conditions man develops those traits that make him *desire* to act as he *has* to act. If the character of the majority of people in a given society--that is, the social character--is thus adapted to the objective tasks the individual has to perform in this society, the energies of people are molded in ways that make them into productive forces that are indispensable for the functioning of that society.[9]

It then follows that those individuals who adapt most flawlessly to the given social character will be rewarded by material success, by respect and recognition from their peer groups, *and* by the feeling of being in harmony with their environment. An authoritarian and hierarchic societal environment, composed of individuals who share a strong orientation toward authority (that being the basis of their social character), will necessarily produce further individuals of equally authoritarian inclination, as they strive to emulate the prevalent social character traits. Similarly, a society based on the accumulation and consumption of material goods (that being the social character shared by the majority of its members) will invariably reinforce this character trait in child-rearing and thus eventually create an even stronger consumer-orientation in new generations. Clearly, in his description of the process of individual characteristics being shaped and molded by the dictates of the ruling majority and/or class, Fromm is strongly indebted to Marx himself and, in his wake, to Wilhelm Reich. In his fundamental study, *The Mass Psychology of Fascism* (1933), Reich had already pinpointed the problem that ". . . each society generates in the masses of its members those structures [of behavior and thought] which are needed for the achievement of its goals."[10] For Fromm, social character also includes a reciprocal function: it is, on the one hand, defined by the members of a societal group and their predominant orientation. And on the other, it helps maintain the *status quo* of the socio-economic, as well as the psychological and ideological makeup of this group. Therefore, it is responsible for those psychological factors that sustain the social order. Fromm uses the effective metaphor of the "cement" which joins the blocks of the given social structure.[11]

Primary institutions which serve to propagate the social character are the *family* and the *educational system*. The following graph may be helpful for the understanding of this rather complex interrelation between individual and social character:

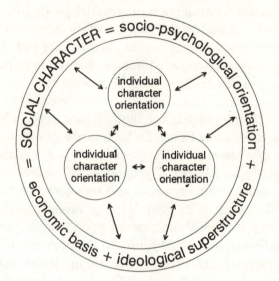

Though this delineation of social character would appear to imply that human existence is predetermined *exclusively* by societal (=external) conditions, Fromm nevertheless refutes such a conclusion as "sociological relativism." Although he concedes--in opposition to Freud, but thoroughly in line with Marx--that "man is *primarily* a social being,"[12] he nevertheless maintains a *dynamic* definition of the human character. And, far from paying mere lip service to Freud's characterology, Fromm remains adamant on this point throughout his entire work. He insists that this "dynamism" of human nature "constitutes an active factor in the evolution of the social process."[13] His assumption of a dynamic force (=human nature) within the collective and often stagnant strictures of externally imposed character traits (=social character) sets Fromm's characterology apart from both the "psychologistic" Freudian concept and Marx's "economistic" approach. As much as human nature adapts dynamically to the prevalent societal orientation, it also remains capable of altering this orientation by means of an equally dynamic intorduction of new ideas and concepts. Fromm's whole theory of evolution, in fact, hinges *exclusively* on this assumption: that human nature, through its innate and autonomous productive force, may initiate constant changes in the psychological, ideological, and economic conditions prevailing at any particular time in history.[14] This encouraging, even optimistic principle, which is to permeate practically all of Erich Fromm's subsequent books, stands in apparent contradiction to the main body of *Escape from Freedom*. The following analysis will attempt to highlight this contradiction--and its potential resolution.

The introductory chapter delineates the task of social psychology: to explore the vastly different character traits encountered in various historical settings. Freedom, like human conceptions thereof, is according to Fromm primarily a psychological "problem." As much as historical progress is propelled by human evolution, the human self in turn is shaped and molded by the changing conditions of its socio-economic environment. Of primary importance within this context is the notion of *adaptation*. Human nature adapts dynamically to the stringencies and demands imposed on it by the prevalent mode of life. This mode of life is, of course, the product of the given economic basis and ideological superstructure. The concept of "freedom," consequently, emerges as a double-edged entity: once the human being has been deprived of "the original oneness with man and nature,"[15] he or she becomes an "individual." And individual freedom rests exclusively on the decision whether to adapt more or less blindly to any given societal context (a decision which results ultimately in the *loss* of freedom), or to reassert personal liberty through spontaneity, love and a productive existence.

This emergence of the individual and consecutive exodus of humanity from a basically intact world may best be described as a chain reaction of socio-economic, psychological and historical phenomena. For Fromm, this chain reaction is a dialectical historical process, which he discusses at length in the second and third chapters of his study. During the middle ages, he argues, this mythical "oneness" of human beings with themselves and nature was still in-

tact to a great extent. Although feudal society sacrificed "individual" freedom to an all-encompassing set of rules governing every
aspect of life, the elements of *doubt* and *insecurity* characteristic for
the "modern" being were yet conspicuously absent from human
consciousness. Every person had a "distinct, unchangeable and
unquestionable" place in the societal context. Social order,
presumably, equalled natural order. In spite of all the restrictions
imposed on the subject, Fromm asserts that there "was a great deal
of *concrete individualism in real life.*"[16]

This somewhat idealized picture of life during the middle ages is
based on Jacob Burckhardt's description of medieval society and
the spirit of the Renaissance. Even during the 1930s, however, this
viewpoint was already outdated for many historians. To be sure,
there was little or no vertical class mobility for the individual during
the middle ages. Within the three laterally divided classes--the no-
bility, the clergy and the serfs--a strict hierarchic order prevailed.
During the 1200s, urbanization began as a first and laboriously slow
move toward individual freedom. All this is true. Life within the
feudal system, however, was anything but ideal for the overwhelming majority, who were forced to work for the wealth and welfare
of their rulers. They not only carried the burden of eking out their
own minimal subsistence, but surely must also have experienced
some primitive form of alienation, as the fruits of all their labor
were re-channeled for the benefit of others. They were certainly
excluded from the accumulation of private property--which Fromm
considers "a necessary institution, at least in a fallen world."[17]
Nevertheless, the economic system of the middle ages is diametrically opposed to Fromm's "ideal" of communism. Further, it remains questionable whether life in medieval society was psychologically as secure and undisturbed as Fromm maintains. People
were certainly beset by multiple fears, superstition, even mass hysteria, and frequently plagued by neurotic disturbances. Many of
these fears were cleverly manipulated by the spiritual and worldly
rulers of the epoch, as a means of oppressing the masses.

The reader might well disagree with the slightly distorted picture
Fromm paints of medieval society, and would be well advised to

keep in mind that *Escape from Freedom* is not the work of a historian. The issue under consideration is not medieval life as it actually *was*, rather Fromm tries to delineate its social character as it *might have been*. The middle ages are used merely as a model for his theory of evolution. Two factors are primarily responsible for the subsequent destruction of medieval "freedom": the change of the economic system and its impact on the individual and social character, and, concomitantly, a second alteration of the social character caused by the Reformation and related theological and ideological influences. During the 15th and 16th centuries, commerce underwent drastic changes. Prior to that time, retail and wholesale business were not yet clearly separated. As a consequence of urbanization and the amassing of capital in the new trade centers, money became an end in itself, where it had previously been a means to the end of material subsistence. A market of supply and demand developed, and soon the dictates of the marketeer regulated economic life. Clearly, Fromm's description of the dialectics of the socio-economic process follows the theories of Karl Marx. For the sake of expedience--or prudence--he quotes frequently from the works of the British economist Richard Henry Tawney, who himself in turn is indebted to Marx.[18] For Tawney, as well as for Fromm, the emerging capitalist economy is the *first* decisive factor for the consecutive radical change in the self-perception of humanity. Security has given way to insecurity. A "natural" order of life has been replaced by an artificially imposed set of rules and values basically alien to the alleged "oneness" and unbroken totality medieval life had guaranteed:

> . . . the world has become limitless and at the same time threatening. By losing his fixed place in a closed world man loses the answer to the meaning of his life; the result is that doubt has befallen him concerning himself and the aim of life.[19]

A new form of freedom is thus born through economic change. Humanity has been driven from the paradise of the pre-commercial world--one feels acutely reminded here of Fromm's own childhood experiences as discussed above-- and must now engage in the struggle for survival dictated by the money market. Doubt, isolation, anxiety and the feeling of powerlessness are, according to Fromm, the immediate results of this dialectical socio-historical process. (Once more, it remains hard to believe that these feelings were *not* present already in medieval society. Especially the literature of this epoch, which deals exclusively with the sphere of the ruling class and disregards the much more miserable life of the masses, gives ample proof for their existence.) These character changes within the individual are reflected in the changing social character as a whole. Each person, however, has to deal with them on a personal basis in order to cope with this new, emerging social character. Adaptation appears to be the necessary consequence.

The *second* step away from "natural" or primeval freedom occurred when Lutheranism and Calvinism began to exert an ever-increasing influence on the individual and the collective consciousness. The person of Martin Luther himself is seen as an illustrative anticipation of modern, "authoritarian" character. His love-hate relationship to world authorities played a decisive role in the formation of the Protestant work ethic, which, in turn, is intricately bound to the principle of obedience. Max Weber has accurately described this phenomenon.[20] Humility and submission, as propagated by Protestantism in general and to an even greater extreme by Calvinism, became inportant facets of the new social character of early capitalism. Fromm had previously touched on the problem in his article "Selfishness and Self-Love" (1939).[21] Now he engages in a large-scale investigation of the orientation of the new bourgeois class.

Even more than Luther's submission to worldly authorities, Calvin's doctrine of predestination was instrumental in the development of a new and important character trait: the feeling of powerlessness. Moreover, since this doctrine stresses the basic inequality of human beings, it must be recognized, according to Fromm, as a distinct forerunner of authoritarian ideologies such as National Socialism. It may be added at this point that *all* racist or discriminatory traits in a given social character in the Western world have been reinforced, at least in part, by this influence. The post-Calvinist belief in the a priori superiority of the ruling white business class is one of the factors responsible for racial and sexual discrimination, as it may still be witnessed today in America and elsewhere.

Self-humiliation and self-abasement, as taught during the Reformation, thus gave rise to the individual feeling of impotence. Quite often, this feeling is internalized by modern individuals in form of an intense self-hatred. It may, on the other hand, also be externalized and lead to an aggressive, stifling and generally oppressive social character. In this environment, neither love for others nor love for one's own self can thrive. Love as the strongest affirmative, creative force in life has been treated by several of Sullivan's writings.[22] Fromm also stresses the importance of love in many of his works, beginning with *Man for Himself* (1947) and culminating in *The Art of Loving* (1956). The gradual loss of humanity's ability to love is one of the most essential stages in the evolutionary pattern described in *Escape from Freedom*. With the rise of capitalism, a new character structure emerges which is predominantly oriented toward material wealth, and progressively impoverished in terms of its ability to love. This new character structure, "resulting from economic and social changes and intensified by religious doctrines, became in its turn an important factor in shaping the further social and economic development."[23]

In the following two chapters, which make up the study's main body, Fromm proceeds to describe the inherent characteristics of this new, post-Reformation society. Chapter IV is devoted to a diagnosis of modern capitalist society from a primarily *economic* viewpoint. Two divergent aspects of freedom are experienced by the modern individual. The first, which has already been discussed above, leads to isolation, loneliness, fear and the general feeling of powerlessness. The second aspect is no less important: the post-medieval human being becomes gradually more "independent, self-reliant, and critical." Human existence is thus defined by an apparently irreconcileable dualism of bondage and mastery, i.e. the gradual shrinking of true and essential *human* substance and the simultaneous growth of technical and civilizational ingenuity. Bondage is economically furthered by the ever-increasing power of capital: "In the medieval system capital was the servant of man, but in the modern system it became his master."[24] Work, which was once necessarily a spontaneous, often satisfying activity (at least in Fromm's idealized view of medieval society), now becomes a compulsive act aimed predominantly at the accumulation of commodities and wealth. (Here, a lengthy discussion of Marx's concept of the "alienation of labor" follows, which need not be paraphrased for the purposes of this discussion.) The major factor in this development is, next to the emotional impoverishment of the individual, the steady increase of monopolistic capital. In modern capitalist society, the process of labor and manufacture of goods, which had previously been directly related to the activities of the individual worker, becomes more and more impenetrable to his or her intelligence and thus more and more "alienating."

With the strengthening of a monopolistic market sytem, modern advertising was created. The psychological impact of this ever-present influence in daily life further diminished the individual's importance. Persons whose every need and desire can be commercially manipulated are perceived, both by themselves and by the surrounding social character, as weakened and insignificant. Based on his own observations of American capitalism, Fromm arrives at the conclusion that advertising and the mass media apparatus are "methods of dulling the capacity for critical thinking" and are "more dangerous to our democracy than many of the open attacks against it . . ."[25] Interestingly enough, this part of *Escape from Freedom* already contains a full-fledged diagnosis of the manipulation of public opinion--leading ultimately to both mindless consumerism and to ethical and political indifference--which became the topic of many later studies originating from Critical Theory. Especially Adorno, in his various incisive investigations of *Bewußtseinsindustrie* (the industry of forming human consciousness), has shed light on this phenomenon. And Herbert Marcuse's much-debated book *One Dimensional Man* (1964) still remains a milestone of probing into the collective consciousness of capitalist society.

Chapter V of *Escape from Freedom* is devoted to the *psychological* aspects of the new social character. Capitalist society is seen as "being adverse to human happiness and self-realization."[26] Although Fromm, as opposed to Karen Horney, avoids the term "neurotic" as a characterization of this society as a *whole*, he concedes that the prevalent social character strongly reinforces neurotic trends in the *individual*. Both the immense pressure to succeed and the equally overwhelming pressure to conform to established but often irrational societal norms are conducive to the formation of neurotic escape mechanisms. The individual who is forced to *adapt* to a given social character without really *understanding* its implications feels more and more need of emotional safety valves. A personality stifled in its growth will therefore automatically engage in neurotic escapism.

Within the categories of "authoritarianism," "destructiveness," and "automaton conformity," Fromm describes four basic patterns of neurotic escape. Once initiated, these mechanisms are not only self-propelling forces which directly influence the greater social character, they also further cripple the afflicted individuals themselves. In his socio-psychopathology, Fromm follows closely the neurotic typology used by Karen Horney in her book *The Neurotic Personality of Our Time*.[27] The *first* neurosis described is the masochistic dependence on others and on authority. Horney uses the term "neurotic need for affection." A *second*, equally common escape mechanism is the sadistic exploitation and degradation of others, which is meant to reaffirm the self's feeling of power. In Horney's terminology this is called the "neurotic striving for power." The *third* possible neurosis is escape into destructiveness. Destructive strivings suppress the "biophilous" factors within the individual and thus within a given society in favor of the "necrophilous" tendencies. (The terms "biophilous" and "necrophilous" are not yet used in *Escape from Freedom*. Fromm still adheres to Freudian terminology here. Nevertheless, his discussion of destructiveness here is clearly an anticipation of *The Heart of Man* and the *Anatomy of Human Destructiveness*.) Destructivity is "the outcome of unlived life." Horney's category of "neurotic withdrawal" is only partially compatible with the concept of destructive-ness, as it covers only the inverted, self-inflicted forms of the phenomenon. A *fourth* and final neurotic escape is termed "auto-maton conformity." Automaton behavior or, in other words, mind-less adaptation to societal norms, is closely related to Horney's "neurotic submissiveness." This particular neurotic type appears to be especially characteristic for American capitalism, whereas the more authoritarian or aggressive mechanisms prevailed in central Europe before and during the time of fascism. It should be understood, though, that even if Horney's and Fromm's *descriptions* of neurotic syndromes are often congruous or even to a certain extent interchangeable, their approaches to therapy of these neuroses differ radically. Horney provides some insights into her own methods in her study of *Our Inner Conflicts* (1945).[28] Fromm's suggestions will be discussed below.

In the final part of his study, Fromm explores the "psychology of Nazism" parallel to an accurate analysis of the social character in America in the early 1940s. As a means of elucidating the former, he frequently quotes Adolf Hitler's autobiography *Mein Kampf*: an exceptionally illuminating document with regard to the neurotic personality of its author. Authoritarian character is defined as "the simultaneous presence of sadistic and masochistic drives."[29] National Socialist mass psychology rested to a great extent on the di-rect mobilization of these drives. Joseph Goebbels, the Nazi pro-paganda minister, is seen as a pièce de résistance in this complex machinery designed to manipulate multiple character traits. Fromm astutely observes that Goebbels himself had experienced the effect of demagoguery on his own person, and subsequently de-scribed it in his autobiographical novel *Michael* (1936). Hitler's character, the driving force of this disastrous movement, is cor-rectly diagnosed as sadistic in its orientation toward humans and masochistic in its perception of fate or destiny (*Vorsehung*). Many of the fundamental thoughts to be propounded much later in the *Anatomy of Human Destructiveness* can already be found here in a nutshell, although Fromm's description of the "authoritarian per-sonality" still remains somewhat sketchy. Obviously, he relied largely on his own empirical studies (*The Working Class in Weimar Germany*), as well as on Harold D. Laswell's inspired but tentative investigation of the socio-psychological factors involved in National Socialism.[30] He does not yet, however, achieve a fully convincing historical and socio-economic explanation of the fascist syndrome.

Far more persuasive is the book's final chapter on "freedom and democracy." Now, the author turns to the less overt but equally disquieting effect exerted by the total commercialization of life on the human self and, consequently, on the social character of America at that time. In a step-by-step analysis showing how the dictates of rampant commerce infiltrate everyday life, Fromm comes to grips with the emotional destitution of individuals in an affluent and seemingly individualistic society. The *illusion* of individuality, as it is fostered by the mass media, is in the final analysis nothing more than incessant persuasion to conform. Every commodity is for sale and has its market value: social and professional skills, in order to be appreciated, have to be "sold" with the correct sales pitch. Consequently, spontaneity is stifled and basic emotions like "cheerfulness, and everything a smile is supposed to express, become automatic responses which one turns on and off like an electric switch."[31] Genuine feelings are often almost totally suppressed. Modern psychotherapy--here Fromm deals an undisguised blow to the orthodox Freudian school of analysis--has more often than not become an auxiliary agent for the prevailing social character. Betraying their true, therapeutic function of *freeing* the individual from neurotic compulsions, psychotherapists and psychiatrists instead seem to do their utmost to make the patient *adapt* to societal norms. Consequently, they further the ultimate deformation of the individual by inducing conformity at all costs, instead of effectively impeding progressive neurotic deformation. Analogously, educational institutions, even on the elementary level, already systematically stifle independent thought. Original thinking, like genuine emotion, is rapidly being replaced by a marketable surrogate. This ersatz for intellectual creativity is to be found in a deluge of more or less unrelated "facts": "The pathetic superstition prevails that by knowing more and more facts one arrives at knowledge of reality."[32] Had Erich Fromm had the opportunity to assess the public education system in the United States as it is now, forty-eight years after he wrote these lines, he would surely have been at a loss for words. Even the fig leaf of obsessive fact-accumulation has long withered away. Today, the nation's hopes are raptly focused on the computer, the "magic helper" who will eventually save students and teachers from the painful task of thinking altogether.

Freedom, according to Fromm, has become perverted to the point that fact and fiction, relevant information and willful mind-pollution can no longer be told apart. Proponents of this new, totally commercialized type of freedom are the media. Newscasters report the "bombing of a city and the death of hundreds of people" with the same inane intonation they use for soap and wine advertisements. The listener thus feels less and less connection to the true importance and respective proportions of his environment. Political decisions and social developments of the greatest import can no longer be distinguished from the trivia of consumerism. At the same time, individual vision--not only in terms of *external* perceptions, but also of an inner sense of balance--becomes more and more fragmented: "In the name of 'freedom' life loses all structure; it is composed of many little pieces, each separate from the other and lacking any sense as a whole."[33] Human desires can be artificially stimulated or suppressed at random. Lacking the true impetus of natural creativity, the individual in monopolistic capitalism is little more than a mindless, emotionless automaton: a puppet drawn by the invisible strings of indoctrination and conformism.

Fromm goes one step further in this diagnosis. Through the progressive loss of its perceptible identity as a human self, the individual is ultimately driven to conform even more fervently. Only excessive conformity to the social character assuages nagging self-doubt and even self-incrimination. And only through total conformism can the modern human being avoid the stigmatization of being "different" from the group. In conclusion, Fromm puts forth the question what "freedom" really means for modern individuals. His answer: humanity has managed to shed all shackles and restrictions that formerly prevented the individual from "doing and thinking as he sees fit." A previously unimaginable state of "freedom from" the miseries of life imposed on earlier epochs and generations has been achieved. A void has been created that should be filled with a new kind of freedom, the "freedom to" create, and lead a life consonant with human nature. But this vacuum remains as yet unfilled. Human beings could, at least theoretically, enjoy this new freedom, if they still had an awareness of their emotions, thoughts, and desires. But this natural awareness has been replaced by the need to conform to "anonymous authorities." The original, human self has been ousted by a prefabricated surrogate. Power and initiative as appreciable individual qualities have vanished. In their place, powerlessness reigns. In seeking a concrete example of this situation, today's reader might be reminded of certain commercials for soft drinks which insinuate that the consumer's "freedom" hinges on the choice of one beverage over another. The illusion of power created by systematic deception of the powerless masses could not be better illustrated. And powerlessness, in turn, increases the individual's desire to conform. Individual and social character, it can be concluded, have formed a vicious circle which reciprocally reinforces detrimental and neurotic orientations.

The evolution of humanity, as delineated in *Escape from Freedom*, leads evidently to a deadlock. What appeared at first glance to be progress turns out to be a slow but irrevocable process of human desintegration. Fromm's summation of the two predominant socio-economic systems of the early 1940s--the authoritarian fascist state and the capitalist democracy--is dismal. It is an utterly discouraging socio-pathology, in which progress seems impossible, humanity's self-inflicted dilemma inescapable. The diagnosis itself would seem to preclude any prognosis of dynamic character mutations as emphasized in Fromm's characterology, since such mutations only "facilitate societal changes at a time when the greater political and social circumstances are favorable to those changes."[34] As they are analyzed here, neither the social character of the authoritarian state nor that of the monopolistic capitalist system can be conducive to "positive" mutations.

Is there a solution to the problem? Despite all, Fromm's final answer on this question is affirmative, yet hardly convincing on all counts. The lost "freedom to" *can* be re-established "by the realization of his [man's] self," by the decision of each individual to be his or her true self. How might this be accomplished? Fromm postulates a renewal from within, the first step of which would be the individual's return to *spontaneity*. Spontaneous action and feeling are seen as the primary liberating agents absconded but not entirely lost in the human self. Once a spontaneous relationship to the own self and to others has been established (an idea which prefigures not only Fromm's ethical theory as expounded in *Man for Himself*, but also the popular book *The Art of Loving*), the individual will be able to relate more naturally to a second important sphere: work. Work "as creation" will release human beings from the bondage of alienation. These changes within the individual character--which will in time presumably alter the social character as well--must be met simultaneously by greater socio-economic transformations. Fromm makes a strong plea for a planned economy, an economic structure based not on the irrational principles of manipulation and exploitation, but carefully designed to provide for the common welfare. Before this goal can be realized, one major obstacle must be tackled: "the elimination of the secret rule of those who, though few in number, wield great economic power without any responsiblity to those whose fate depends on their decisions."[35] By means of this two-pronged effort--evolution from *within* and social change from *without*--Fromm hopes to restore life in its beauty and dignity, to re-gain its true meaning in form of "the act of living itself." The observant reader, when first opening the book, will notice an allusion to this revolution of consciousness in its Talmudic motto: "If I am not for myself, who will be for me?" Compressed into this one line is Fromm's own leitmotif: the eternal hope for humanity's inherent potential to realize life as fulfillment and exploration of the human self. The question remains, however, if and how this great goal can be achieved.

Even in 1941, the utterly unrealistic quality of these suggestions must have been evident to many readers. Fromm propagates a voluntary change of individual and collective consciousness within a societal order solidly based on the alienation of work and exploitation of the labor force. If modern capitalism were able to do away with mass production of goods (the primary force of alienation in the manufacturing process), and with the categorial division of capital from labor (by means of profit sharing, etc.), it would simply cease to be capitalism. A different socio-economic structure would emerge. Obviously, *this* change of the status quo would not be possible without major upheavals. Further, though Fromm accurately describes the systematic manipulation of both individual and social character, he seriously underestimates its totality. Given the case that certain individuals or groups might in fact be willling to participate in this change of consciousness, or, for that matter, given the existence of individuals who still retain some of the natural human qualities described above, they would still be a minority. Their mode of life would necessarily clash with the predominant social character. Tensions arise whenever individuals find themselves in total contradiction to their environment. These conflicts usually result--as Fromm himself well knew--either in neurosis, in isolation of the individual/group concerned, or, most likely, in total or partial resignation and thus adaptation to external norms. The rapid rise and subsequent decline of the student and peace movements of the 1960s and 1970s in the United States provides striking verification of this hypotheses. All in all, Fromm's radical and incisive critique of monopolistic capitalism does not result in practicable solutions. Instead, it resorts to an almost mythical vision of salvation. The image of capitalism--as Fromm describes it--pulling itself out of the quagmire by its own bootstraps is appealing, but not convincing.

Escape from Freedom, Fromm's first and also one of his most controversial books, met with both acclaim and harsh criticism. In a very complimentary review, Fromm's friend E. Schachtel comes to the conclusion: "In unfolding the particular role that this force [i.e. the striving for freedom] plays in modern man . . ., Fromm has made a most outstanding and challenging contribution to the social and individual psychology of modern man."[36] Judging from the fact that Schachtel's review appeared in the *Zeitschrift für Sozialforschung*, one may well conclude that Horkheimer as the periodical's editor must have also been impressed with the relevance of this publication for the work of the Institute. Other reactions, especially from Protestant quarters, were less favorable. J. Stanley Glen, one of Fromm's most outspoken critics, rejects his doctrine of self-realization as a feasible way out of bondage: "For it appraises the human predicament too cheaply and in its concern for the universal man loses sight of the personal."[37] Similarly, John H. Schaar expresses the fear that humanistic self-liberation as suggested by Fromm will ultimately lead humanity "into deeper slavery, the slavery of the social."[38] For conservative critics, "the" social invariably means a progressive economic system leaning toward socialism. In brief: a change of the status quo, always anathema for this school of thought. In professional pschychiatric circles, the study's reception, at least in the initial phase, was practically unanimously negative. Reviewers such as Thomas Harvey Gill, M.F. Ashley Montagu, and Patrick Mullahey[39] were sharply critical of its unorthodox methodology, as well as of Fromm's innovative Neo-Freudian-Marxist approach.

For today's student of Fromm, the fact remains that this pivotal work contains many--if not all--elements of his thought, and is his first provocative foray into the field of applied psycho-sociological criticism. Brilliant insights into the extremely complex interplay between individual character traits and social character as a whole combine with impressive analyses of the given socio-economic apparatus of the time. Many resultant disturbing contradictions notwithstanding, the book culminates in a noble, utopian vision of the ideal state populated by free and self-reliant beings. As such, it is a paradigmatic illustration of Erich Fromm's often contradictory thought--a hallmark of *his* greatness and *his* limitations.

Working from this impressive fundamental survey of the human condition in the 20th century, Fromm's ensuing oeuvre sets out to explore in depth three distinct facets of human existence: (a) the *human soul* and *the subconscious*; (b) various aspects of *political and social life*; and (c) the *practice of living*. This last group of texts, the most popular of all, attempts a synthesis of the internal and exterior factors at work in the formation of human consciousness.

Allowing for a certain amount of oversimplification, Erich Fromm's major studies of the years to follow may then be divided roughly into the three above-named categories (the dates of publication are given here for the sake of clarification, although they also appear elsewhere in this study):

a)   *Man for Himself* (1947); *Psychoanalysis and Religion* (1950); *The Forgotten Language* (1951); *Sigmund Freud's Mission* (1959); *Zen Buddhism and Psychoanalysis* (1960); *Marx's Concept of Man* (1961); *The Heart of Man* (1964); *You Shall be as Gods* (1966); *Greatness and Limitations of Freud's Thought* (1979).

b)   *The Sane Society* (1955); *May Man Prevail?* (1961).

c)   *The Art of Loving* (1956); *Beyond the Chains of Illusion* (1962); *The Revolution of Hope* (1968); *To Have or to Be?* (1976).

Beyond this scheme, a special place is held by *The Anatomy of Human Destructiveness* (1973). This text is unquestionably Fromm's weightiest and most impressive exploration of a particular character trait. Moreover, it stands apart through its technical and preponderantly "academic" approach to the topic.

This three-fold division is indicative for the predominant orientation of Fromm's research interests throughout several decades. The first group of books explores various aspects of human ethics, the psychological and emotional organization of the human soul and the closely related (from Fromm's viewpoint) issues of religion, myth and the subconscious. If the latecomer *Greatness and Limitations of Freud's Thought* may be temporarily set aside for practical purposes, Fromm engaged in this linear pursual of his *major* re-

search interests for a time-span of almost forty years: from his
early essays to the final and most heartfelt work *You Shall be as
Gods*.

The second, much smaller group of texts--some additional related articles and briefer contributions will be mentioned later--
reflects his direct intervention in American political life during the
1950s and 1960s. *The Revolution of Hope*, althought categorized
here as a more practically oriented book, resulted directly from his
own political activities in the later 1960s during Eugene
McCarthy's presidential campaign. The texts listed under (c) may
well be regarded, finally, as spinoffs from the respective theoretical
works. *The Art of Loving* provides a practical guide to the humanist
ethics explored particularly in *Man for Himself*. *Beyond the Chains
of Illusion* summarizes, on a rather personal basis, Fromm's own
reception of Freud and Marx. And *To Have or to Be?* describes two
vastly different modes of life which may be traced back through *all*
of his works devoted to human characterology. The book attempts
a controversial synthesis of character analysis, economic theory,
and ethics and must therefore be regarded as one of its author's
most important statements on the totality of human existence. All
Fromm's studies devoted to the practical aspects of life represent
crucial points in his development as a thinker. Admittedly, the grid
provided here is somewhat rough, but it should nevertheless serve
the reader as a basic orientation for the following discussions of the
oeuvre.

5

Psychoanalysis, Ethics, and Religion: Toward a Humanist Credo (1944-1950)

As much as his theory of social character and the synthetic societal diagnoses propounded in *Escape from Freedom* provide the cornerstones of Erich Fromm's socio-psychological work, the core of his thinking has, from the very beginning, always been directed toward the exploration of the *inner* human being: its potential for good and evil, for creation and destruction. In the mid-1940s, his attention shifts noticeably toward religious and ethical character analysis. Much of this renewed research interest in religious questions is certainly due to the relationship with his second wife, Henny Gurland (1902-1952). Fromm had met Henny Gurland and her eighteen-year-old son Joseph in New York, after they had emigrated via Spain and Portugal from Nazi-occupied France. Henny Gurland had separated prior to her emigration from her first husband, who was later detained by the German occupational powers. In Marseilles she had met Walter Benjamin and, together with him and a group of other refugees, fled from the National Socialist invasion. When they reached the Spanish border town Port Bou, Spanish officials denied them immigration. The reason: persons "sans nationalité" were no longer allowed to travel through Spain. In utter desperation, Benjamin committed suicide during the night of 26/27 September, 1940. This splendid thinker and highly vulnerable man thus became, almost within arm's reach of safety, one of the countless victims of Nazi brutality. His brilliant Marxist theory of art and literature is still extremely influential today.

During her subsequent flight to Lisbon, Henny Gurland is said to have received a spinal injury which was to become the ultimate cause of her death.[1] On 24 July, 1944, she married Erich Fromm. She was an extremely talented woman, who shared his interest in various character orientations and, on the basis of her own religious orientation, encouraged him to explore ethical and mystical thought. She must also have been instrumental in furthering his leanings toward Zen Buddhism: a tendency which first becomes apparent in the works written after the mid-1940s. It should be mentioned in passing that Henny Fromm's brother-in-law was the renowned Moscow-born economist and political scientist Arkadij R.L. Gurland, who was employed between 1940 and 1945 as a research associate at Horkheimer's Institute of Social Research. Gurland was, during his stay in the United States, one of the most outspoken opponents in the Institute's ranks to the USSR party line. After the war, he accepted a professorship at the Berlin Academy for Political Science.

With the publication of *Escape from Freedom*, Fromm rapidly became a controversial public figure in American intellectual life. Against his own volition, he was regarded as a guru by many who shared his criticism of monopolistic capitalism and its societal ills. At the same time, he was a much sought-after speaker in the academic community. His reputation as an academic teacher of psychoanalytic theory and practice was finally--despite his lack of medical schooling--firmly established. From 1945 to 1947, he taught at the University of Michigan. In 1948, he was appointed adjunct professor of psychoanalysis at New York University. For the winter semester 1948/49, he was selected for the extremely prestigious position of Terry Lecturer at Yale University, an honor he shared with C.G. Jung (who served in this function in 1937). His book *Man for Himself* had appeared one year prior to this appointment. In Yale, then, Fromm co-taught a seminar on social character and anthropology with Ralph Linton. His primary lecture series, however, followed the course established in *Man for Himself* and offered an in-depth exploration of the interrelations between psychoanalysis, ethics, and religion. It was published in 1950 as

Psychoanalysis and Religion.[2] The title of the study itself offers an intriguing allusion to C.G. Jung's Terry lectures, which appeared in print under the title *Psychology and Religion* twelve years earlier.[3] During the late 1940s, Erich Fromm's academic career reached a first impressive peak. And, although his publication list as yet included only three book-length studies, he had secured for himself a wide readership far beyond the limits of academia.

In late 1949, Henny Fromm's health had deteriorated to the point that a change in climate seemed imperative. After Fromm's resignation from Bennington College in 1950, the couple moved to Mexico City, where they lived at Gonzales Cosio 17 until Henny Fromm died in 1952. In 1951, Fromm was appointed professor of psychoanalysis at the National Autonomous University of Mexico. Later, he also assumed the directorship of the Psychoanalytical Institute of Mexico. He held both these positions until he retired in 1965. During the 1950s and 1960s, Fromm commuted regularly between Mexico and the United States. While in Mexico, his primary research interest remained focused on psychoanalysis and socio-psychology. During his frequent lengthy stays in the United States--which included an appointment as professor of psychology at Michigan State University (1957-1961) and an adjunct professorship for psychology at New York University (1962-1970)--he gradually became more involved in politics. All of his later writings on social criticism evolve from the firsthand evidence he gathered in North America. In Mexico, Fromm also met Annis Freeman (born 1902), who became his third wife on 18 December 1953. Annis Freeman was born in Alabama and had lost her first husband while living in India. After staying three more years in Mexico City, the couple moved in 1956 to Cuernavaca, a small, wealthy town southeast of the capital. There, the Fromms resided in their own house until 1969.

These were the biographical events surrounding the continued formation of the foundations for Fromm's religious and ethical works. The ethical guidelines derived from his early immersion in Talmud study were discussed above. When he renounced orthodox Judaism in 1926, Fromm briefly became interested in Buddhism.

This infatuation, however, faded quickly. Only after he met Henny Gurland did he plunge into a wealth of philosophical and mystical literature, all of which deeply influenced his thought for the decades to come. After Zen Buddhism--which will be dealt with later in some detail--the triad of Aristotle, Master Eckhart, and Benedictus de Spinoza is of primary importance. At first glance, this seems to be an audacious combination indeed. But its importance for Fromm can quickly be summarized. In his *Nicomachian Ethics*, Aristotle presents one of the first non-theological ethical conceptions in world history. Productivity--an absolutely central term in Fromm's own ethical canon--is based for Aristotle on the "activity of the soul." Happiness can only be achieved through an active spiritual encounter between the individual self and the world as a whole. Every noble and sublime experience is the result of relatedness, whereas inertia is regarded as detrimental to both spiritual and intellectual growth. For Aristotle, ethical standards evolve directly from scientific norms. Virtue is ultimately defined as activity, and there is no clear demarcation line between physical, intellectual and emotional activity in Aristotle's concept. This--admittedly brutally abridged--excerpt from the *Ethica Nicomachea* may suffice to demonstrate the common denominator between Fromm and Aristotle: human character, particularly in its ethical substructure, is seen as a *dynamic* entity. Only through incessant activism may perfection of the soul be attained. In Aristotle's wake, Fromm re-adjusts his psycho-kinetic characterology to allow for the construction of a humanistic concept of ethics.

As opposed to Aristotle, the Thuringian Dominican Johannes Eckhart, provincial of his order in the whole of Saxony, propagated a theistic faith. A proponent of idealistic mysticism, he postulated that God--the reason, beginning, and end of all creation--ultimately eludes human knowledge. The world, according to Master Eckhart, is the materialization of God's will, and serves as a constant source of divine self-revelation. Human beings, in turn, may progress toward God by means of speculation, intuition, or introspection. Eckhart's unorthodox definition of human interaction with the deity brought him into conflict with the clergical hierarchy of his time (his cryptic definition of the *Godhead* still remains elusive to modern theologians). His conception of mysticism, however, as far as it impinges on Fromm's thought, does not deviate seriously from the medieval mainstream of the movement. Mysticism in the tradition of Bernard de Clairvaux and the Parisian school of St. Victor generally relies on a three-step pattern in its approach to God: the *via purgativa seu negativa* (the purging of the flesh and consciousness of worldly effects), the *via illuminativa* (the gradual illumination of God's essence in the mystic's soul), and the *via unitiva* (the final stage meant to initiate *unio mystica*, or mystical union, of the human soul with the deity). Eckhart and his successors Johannes Tauler and Heinrich Seuse founded the German school of mysticism. European mysticism remained extremely influential up to the pre-Enlightenment period. Even Spinoza's rational theistic philosophy still contains certain mystical elements. For the reader, it must be fairly obvious that mysticism as such and the teachings of Master Eckhart in particular stand in contradiction to the ethical dynamism and activism of Aristotle. For Fromm's eclectic mind, however, the two spheres of influence are not at all mutually exclusive. To the contrary, they augment each other fruitfully and contribute to a holistic concept of the human self.

A few words on Spinoza's philosophy must suffice for the purpose of this overview. Spinoza, a pantheist thinker, maintains that ultimate truth is self-revealing. The one and only *substance*--nature or God--manifests itself in innumerable forms. Reason is the only way to achieve reliable knowledge. He attempts to base his ethical system on scientific methodology in *Ethica more geometrico demonstrata* (*Ethics* [1677]; literally translated the title means: "an ethical system demonstrated along the lines of geometry"). For Spinoza, true perfection of the human self may be achieved in a state of union with nature. And nature equals God ("Deus sive natura"). Human freedom is attained by the constant development of intellectual--and thus ethical--powers which enable the individual to truly love God ("amor intellectus Dei"). Human happiness results from the progression to ever greater perfection. Conversely, sorrow indicates that the human soul has slipped into a state less than perfect. For Fromm, the central passage from the *Ethics* reads as follows: "To act absolutely in conformity with virtue is, in us, nothing but acting, living and preserving our being (these three things have the same meaning) as *reason* directs, from the ground of our own *profit*."[4] In other words: full realization of *all* human potential is the ultimate goal of living itself.

What emerges from this brief outline of the cornerstones in Fromm's ethical and religious system is, even for the indulgent reader, an extremely eclectic and definitely bewildering composite. In its heterodox combination of rational and mystical elements, this system is also strongly reminiscent of Fromm's methodology in socio-psychoanalysis, which welds together exact observation and free-wheeling speculation. Similarly, Fromm's foundation of humanist ethics combines the seemingly uncombineable: the *dynamism* of Aristotle with Eckhart's *meditation* and the pantheistic *rationalism* of Spinoza. The following discussion of *Man for Himself* and *Psychoanalysis and Religion* attempts to shed some light on the complex interaction of these heterogeneous schools of thought and their gradual amalgamation.

Man for Himself has been called by Rainer Funk its author's "central work."[5] Considering the far-reaching impact the study had on *all* of his later texts, this assessment may well be correct. For the first time, Fromm admits to the limitations of a purely intellectual or "reasonable" approach to the human self. A new aspect of irrationality emerges, although still tentatively, which will be explored in more detail in later works. Particularly his most popular book, *The Art of Loving*, proves to be a direct derivative of the psychology of ethics explored in this earlier study. But the book not only anticipates many later developments, it is in itself a linear continuation of Fromm's characterology as explained in *Escape from Freedom*. There, the individual and collective character traits of contemporary humanity are described and analyzed from a socio-psychological point-of-view. Now, Fromm turns to the *intrinsic* forces at work, from the macrocosm of society to the psyche of the human self.

Once more, *Man for Himself* follows a three-step pattern. After a brief explication of "the problem"--i.e. the book's focus and the methodology it employs--the first part is devoted to a definition of "humanistic ethics" and to the historical factors involved. An intricate connection between ethics and psychoanalysis is then developed. The second part and main body of the book describes various human character orientations in great detail. And in the final part, Fromm turns to the discussion of numerous aspects evolving from his ethical characterology. A brief postscript entitled "The moral problem of today" concludes the book. Already in the first chapter ("the problem"), Fromm touches upon the central idea of his whole ethical system: the "character structure of the mature and integrated personality," which he terms "the productive character."

True to his established form, Fromm again does not overwhelm his reader with a sleek and concise style. To the contrary, the text contains numerous repetitions and terminological infelicities. It is cumbersomely organized and makes for altogether difficult reading. In retrospect, one can not but wonder at its immediate mass-appeal, which may, at least in part, hav been due to its riding on the coat-tails of the bestselling *Escape from Freedom*. For the sake of expediency, Fromm's concept of *humanistic ethics*, as it emerges from the study's first part, can be briefly summarized as follows:

1. There is a long-standing tradition of humanistically oriented ethics. This tradition, for Fromm, begins with Aristotle's ethical activism (or, depending on the critic's viewpoint, vitalism), and is finally absorbed by Spinoza. The latter insists that true realization of a being's substance must by necessity lead to ethical perfection. Karl Marx, Herbert Spencer, and John Dewey propagated a similar view: what is *beneficial* for human nature must by nature be *good*. Conversely, actions detrimental to the self must be regarded as unethical. A humanistic approach to ethics, consequently, must be based on the knowledge of human nature and of those elements which are consonant with its constructive development.

2. As opposed to authoritarian ethical concepts derived from "irrational" authority, humanist ethics is *a-authoritarian* by nature, i.e. it recognizes as final authority only human nature itself. (The distinction between a-authoritarian and anti-authoritarian will be discussed later in this chapter.)

3. From this postulate, a two-fold definition of humanistic ethics follows:

> *Formally*, it is based on the principle that only man himself can determine the criterion for virtue and sin, and not an authority transcending him. *Materially*, it [humanistic ethics] is based on the principle that "good" is what is good for man and "evil" what is detrimental to man; *the sole criterion of ethical value being man's welfare.*[6]

For today's readership, passages like these are annoying in their exclusively male-oriented terminology. The bulk of Fromm's oeuvre, despite his early interest in Bachofen and the principles of matriarchy and also his association with Horney, *is* centered on the male viewpoint. This orientation is certainly due to the lasting influence of Freud, who thought, all in all, very little of the female psyche. In terms of its content, the second, material aspect of Fromm's above-cited definition betrays some reminiscences of Freud's later writings on ethical subjects, whereas the first, formal component is clearly anti-Freudian. Fromm is fully aware of the utopian dimensions of this humanistic ethical system. In fact, he makes a brief but interesting reference to utopian models in general, which he regards as "not meaningless," but rather greatly conducive to the "progress of thought."[7]

4. A powerful critique of Freud's "naturalistic" and intrinsically authoritarian approach to psychoanalysis is, finally, one of the central arguments in Fromm's plea for an a-authoritarian, humanistically motivated alliance between ethics and psychoanalysis. Freud's theory of the Super-Ego is correctly classified as the result of the ethical relativism displayed in some of his writings. It follows that the Super-Ego, or human conscience, must be seen as internalized authority. Humanistic ethics re-defines Freud's "genital character" as the "productive" character orientation. As in his earlier writings,

Fromm again adheres to a dynamic character definition. Character is not, as Freud assumed, the product of certain instincts, rather its formation is based on social and cultural experience or, in Sullivan's terminology, "interpersonal relations." Therefore, the human self must be regarded with Sullivan (who followed the theory of George Herbert Mead) not as an entity in its own right, but *a dynamic organism composed of a predetermined biological structure* which is then *molded according to the given environmental conditioning*. In Fromm's application of this theory, economic factors are rightly given special consideration.

A lenghty and sometimes diffuse description of the *conditio humana* comprises the main body of *Man for Himself*. After dispensing with ethical orientations based on a utilitarian principle--be it the material enrichment of the individual in capitalist society or the "greater" good of the collective in totalitarian systems--Fromm recapitulates his dynamic concept of character. This the reader already knows from *Escape from Freedom*. A remarkable new aspect is now introduced in form of a modification of Freud's libido theory. The ontogenetic definition of libido is replaced by a socio-psychological term: *character orientation*. Character as a dynamic unity reflects both the individual's experiences within the given social context (=assimilation), and a person's relatedness to the outside world (=socialization). Two clearly distinct types of character orientation are then described: *nonproductive* and *productive* orientations.

Fromm devotes considerable effort to his "negative" characterology, in which four different nonproductive orientations are distinguished. While the orientations described as follows are prototypes or "ideal" phenotypes, actual individuals usually display a blend of two or more characteristics.

a) The *receptive* orientation. Receptive personalities show a general tendency to passivity and submission. They are prone to obey any kind of authority and tend to engage in relationships where their dependence on the domineering partner is firmly established. Instead of taking independent action, they invariably place their hopes in a "magic helper"--some device or gadgetry which holds the promise for improving their lives. Modern psychology has come to describe the positive traits of this orientation as "gentle lobed." In *Sigmund Freud's Mission*, Fromm classifies Freud himself as a modification of this type.

b) The *exploitative* orientation. Exploitative personalities share with their receptive counterparts the premise that "the source of all good is outside, that whatever one wants to get must be sought there, and that one cannot produce anything oneself."[8] In general, they have a strong drive toward the accumulation of material wealth. They are inclined to take profits from others by means of force or cunning, rather than to work for a specific goal. The exploitative orientation is based on the use and abuse of others: human beings are generally appraised according to their potential usefulness and ultimately regarded as objects or means to an end.

c) The *hoarding* orientation. Here, possession is the ultimate motivating factor. Hoarding personalities have little or no regard for life itself and living creatures. Their highest values are order and security. It may be added that Fromm accurately describes in this type the frequently encountered self-declared "conservative," whose fascination with law and order is nothing else than deeply rooted insecurity and an innate inablility to cope with the influx of new ideas. Potential change in their own modes of existence and/or in greater society is met by defensiveness or by lethargy. In terms of their predominantly passive temperament, hoarding types are peripherally related to representatives of the receptive orientation, without, however, sharing their potential for emotional warmth. The hoarding orientation clearly anticipates what later will be called the "necrophilous" character (cf. *The Heart of Man* and *The Anatomy of Human Destructiveness*).

d) The *marketing* orientation. This final nonproductive character orientation is, according to Fromm, rapidly becoming the prevalent type in American society. Everybody seems to be obeying the market's dictates. Every professional skill, even every emotion is ultimately for sale. Personalities are shaped into marketable commodities, and the mass media produce a constant flow of "desired" personality patterns. Persons of the marketing orientation are all too ready to conform to these examples, even at the price of eventual loss of any discernible individual personality facets. Under the guise of "equality," individual characteristics and feelings are attacked and ultimately wiped out: "Today, equality has become equivalent to *interchangeability*, and is the very negation of individuality."[9] Human relationships are, at best, a superficial pastime for the marketing personality. The potential of the self, conversely, remains underdeveloped and stunted in its growth. Summa summarum, this particular orientation is best defined by the striking *lack* of relatedness and of individual personality traits. Chameleon-like, it demonstrates a constant interchangeability of attributes in order to remain acceptable to the given environment, i.e. the marketplace.

The reader will easily recognize the affinities of these four nonproductive character orientations to the four neurotic escape mechanisms explained in *Escape from Freedom*. They correspond with each other as follows:

	neurotic escape patterns		*character orientations* (nonproductive)
1.	masochistic dependence on others	↔	receptive orientation
2.	sadistic exploitation of others	↔	exploitative orientation
3.	destructiveness	↔	hoarding orientation
4.	automaton conformity	↔	marketing orientation

Equally obvious is the proximity of the receptive and the hoarding orientations to Freud's pregenital types, respectively the oral and the anal type. A drastic modification of the Freudian typology lies in Fromm's direct application of his negative characterology to societal interaction and to the given economic system.

In his previous study, Fromm had relegated masochistic and sadistic neuroses (and the frequently encountered sado-masochistic mélange) predominantly to authoritarian states in pre-fascist and fascist Europe. The same applied, to a certain extent, to the "destructive" neurosis. Now, in *Man for Himself*, all four character orientations are clearly derived from the observation of American society. Further, in opposition to Horney's socio-pathology, he had earlier repudiated the assumption that society *as a whole* must be seen as a conglomerate of neurotic syndromes. On this aspect, *Man for Himself* is much less clear-cut. (Fromm's article "Individual and Social Origins of Neurosis" [1944] had already demonstrated a dualistic re-orientation of his earlier view.[10]) Even if it does not proclaim the inevitability of the development of these four nonproductive orientations from the given social character in modern capitalist society, the book's general thrust leaves little doubt on this point. In particular, Fromm's ensuing descriptions of various blends of these orientations are fairly convincing as such. They accurately describe the prevalent types in a modern capitalist society based on the accumulation of money and the consumption of goods. All of the main characteristics of these different orientations are even circumscribed in economic terminology. The receptive (=oral) orientation is seen as *accepting*; the exploitative orientation is classified as *taking*; the hoarding (=anal) orientation is generally *preserving*; and the marketing orientation appears to be *exchanging*. Acceptance of goods and finances, as well as their being taken from one party for the benefit or detriment of another, are basic mechanisms of economic exchange. And exchange, still speaking in economic terms, is the opposite of preservation. Fromm's terminology leaves little doubt in the reader's mind as to the economic roots of his negative characterology. The question follows: are certain economic conditions bound by their very design to produce *exclusively* nonproductive character orientations? And if so, how can this chain reaction of economic-psychological-ethical deformation be halted in its tracks?

A brief digression will be in order at this point. From the ethical characterology developed in *Man for Himself*, it becomes apparent that Fromm--given the societal panorama of the United States in the immediate post-war period--had certainly arrived at an accurate, if somewhat primitive, description of the prevalent individual and collective behavioral patterns of that time. More than that: He perspicaciously *anticipates* developments he could not possibly have gleaned by even the most astute observation. Present-day conditions in capitalist societies prove Fromm's diagnosis even to be prophetic. The receptive orientation with all its weaknesses (Fromm mentions, among other things, the lack of character, opinions, and principles, as well as a streak of gullibility and senti-mentality[11]) has become the predominant consumer mentality. Today's consumer--at least in his/her ideal incarnation--is a new so-cial species that cannot be outdone in terms of submissiveness to advertising and market propaganda. He/she may be duped into buying about anything that promises a better mode of living, any "magic helper," any presumable increment in pre-fabricated iden-tity. In most instances, this orientation--which need not be ana-lyzed in further detail--merges with the marketing orientation. The end result of this match is a perfectly pliable, eminently manipula-ble being who willingly abandons all individual thought in order not to be "different." This individual has lost most or all individuality and derives temporary satisfaction from the fulfillment of rapidly changing, artificially created needs; a conforming "automaton" (to use Fromm's own term) whose self-appreciation hinges mainly on possessions and on the emulation of certain idols, i.e. "TV person-alities," the rich and "beautiful" people, members of royalty, etc. In addition to the mind-deformation induced by the mass media, es-pecially television, a new medium has most recently been created that perfectly exemplifies this phenomenon: video games and video-screen entertainment. Any objective observer of this device can easily notice its effects on the personality of the naive "player": a pseudo-relationship develops between person and machine, cre-ating a "new and improved" surrogate for human interaction, which further suggests to the "player" that he/she has total control over this interaction. In fact, the "player" could not be more powerless. With the increasing dependence on the magic screen, any rudimen-tary capacity for human exchange rapidly dwindles away. So much for the new breed of a receptive/marketing character orientation.

Fromm's descriptions of the hoarding and the exploitative orientations are equally applicable to certain representatives of the economic and political power structure. By no means does this apply exclusively to capitalist societies. To the contrary: the political apparatus of socialist and communist countries might be an even more intriguing object for the application of this theory. In general, any bureaucatic power structure whose main purpose is the retention of the respective status quo invites further study. But this is not the point of Fromm's theory, at least not yet in *Man for Himself*. The capitalistic hoarding orientation combined with its exploitative counterpart may be found today particularly in members of the military-industrial complex. There is a distinct trickle-down effect involved in preserving the respective negative traits (aggressiveness, egocentricity, rashness, possessiveness etc.) in the hierarchic ladder of commerce, from the seemingly allmighty chairman of the board all the way down to the "aggressive" salesperson. As much as the former is in a real position to make decisions of economic consequence resulting in tangible profit, the latter at least *believes* that he/she is an equally indispensable member of the same team. Military and political leaders of the superpowers have in the recent past become more and more obsessed with the concept of maintaining the "balance" of power. In their obsessive retention of the strategic and political staus quo, they provide striking examples for the hoarding orientation. The most bizarre manifestation of this orientation and its predominant characteristics (suspicion, obsessiveness) is doubtlessly the international arms race and the hoarding of nuclear weaponry capable of destroying the earth several times around. Regarding internal economic policies, American capitalism today seems not only determined to retain the present situation, but intent on turning the clock backwards to an even more inequitable distribution of goods. Again, a rampant hoarding drive on the part of the privileged is at the heart of this trend.

In brief: the characterology of nonproductive orientations as described by Fromm seems more real and more omnipresent today than ever before. Herbert Marcuse, in his diagnosis of the "one dimensional" human being who inhabits a one dimensional society, reaches very much the same conclusions. His sociological method, however, is much more sophisticated than Fromm's ethical characterology.[12]

The *productive* orientation, on the other hand, is the epitome of Fromm's humanistic ethics and stands in clear opposition to the nonproductive ones. Its definition is largely a continuation of the concept of spontaneity as developed in *Escape from Freedom*. Every human being, according to Fromm, is capable of productivity. The essential precondition for this orientation is love. Forms of productive love include "*care, responsibility, respect*, and *knowledge*."[13] Love must be based on a conscious, intelligent decision to love and will ultimately activate the productive and dynamic forces within the human self. The connections of this focal point in Fromm's ethical system to Aristotle's ethical activism, the spiritual love of God as exemplified in mysticism, and the rationalistic approach to love and nature in Spinoza's ethics are obvious. Don Hausdorff, one of Fromm's most perspicacious critics, correctly observes the proximity of his approach to that of Martin Buber.[14] Buber, too, is greatly indebted to Master Eckhart's mysticism, and the center of his ethical system is a similar conception of "wholeness." Nevertheless, Buber remains consistent in his theological thinking, whereas Fromm's view is atheistic.

Productive thinking--based on spontaneous relatedness to the self and the other--leads the individual to active participation in societal processes. Both objective and subjective insights result from this approach: a picture of the whole as well as a clear but compassionate estimate of its parts. Characteristically, Fromm begins his discourse on relatedness with a story of Buddha's discovery of the "fourfold truth," and concludes it with quotations from Max Wertheimer[15] and Karl Mannheim,[16] two influential thinkers of his own time. His eclecticism is once more, to say the least, impressive. The productive character orientation clearly anticipates the "biophilous" character of *The Heart of Man*. It also re-appears much earlier as the focal perspective of *The Art of Loving*.

At this point, Fromm returns to the aspects of *assimilation* and *socialization*. The following graph once more illustrates the two stages in the development of character orientation as they emerge from *Man for Himself*. Assimilation, as Fromm defines it, must be seen as involving primarily the character orientation toward things, whereas socialization concerns the inter-personal sphere:

CHARACTER ORIENTATIONS

I. NONPRODUCTIVE

ASSIMILATION →	SOCIALIZATION →	BEHAVIORAL PATTERN
1. Receiving (accepting) →	Masochistic (submissive) →	symbiotic ⎫
2. Exploitative (taking) →	Sadistic (domineering) →	symbiotic ⎬
3. Hoarding (preserving) →	Destructive (aggressive) →	withdrawn ⎫
4. Marketing (exchanging) →	Indifferent (regressive) →	withdrawn ⎬

II. PRODUCTIVE

ASSIMILATION →	SOCIALIZATION →	BEHAVIORAL PATTERN
Engaged in Productive Activity (=Work) →	Love and Relatedness →	reasoning, caring

---

He does *not*, as could be expected, attempt to answer the questions raised previously: why does a particular socio-economic system tend to produce particular character orientations? And could this causality--if indeed there is a causality at work--be broken by means of a different socialization process? Instead, the book's main part concludes, somewhat anticlimactically, with the statement that there appears to be an "endless number of variations" in character blend and orientation.

In its reluctance to tackle these absolutely central questions lies the book's most striking weakness. Fromm, in effect, leaves his reader totally up in the air by failing to examine the inherent potential for *actual* change in both adaptation and socialization. Recent experiments in various Western European countries have amply demonstrated that character orientation in children and adolescents *can* be effectively directed toward a more humanistic, a-authoritarian outlook on life. But, as one of his sharpest critics, Mauro Torres, points out, Fromm deprives his own humanistic vision of a relevant application to real society, in which most mortals will never be touched by grand ideas, but only by chaotic and often deforming reality.[17] As in his earlier study, *Escape from Freedom*, Fromm proves himself an outstanding diagnostician. His approach to ethical therapy, in contrast, is reluctant and inconclusive.

The final section of *Man for Himself* deals with various problems of humanistic ethics, which can be briefly summarized here. The creation of a truly humanistic concept of ethics, according to Fromm, is dependent on three factors: 1. The individual, through "subjective dissatisfaction with a culturally patterned aim,"[18] must be ready for radical reorientation. 2. Further, the socio-economic basis for this change must be present. 3. Finally, rational insight must underlie any concrete steps toward betterment. Especially the third condition can only be met by a reconstruction of human consciousness. Authoritarian religion and hierarchically oriented socialization have been instrumental in forcing individuals to internalize external authority. Once more, Calvin and Protestantism receive much of the blame. Patriarchal society in general, and parental authority in extreme forms (Fromm mentions Kafka here, as well as Sophocles' *Antigone*) have expelled the human self from potential autonomy. Heteronomy has become an intrinsic part of human existence. Humanistic conscience, in order to reverse this situation, would have by definition to be oriented primarily toward the *self*.

Neglecting one's self should arouse more guilt than, for example, disappointing one's parent. It follows that happiness, within the realm of humanistic ethics, is nothing more nor less than living in accordance with one's self: "Happiness is the criterion of excellence in the art of living, of virtue in the meaning it has in humanistic ethics."[19] This postulate should not be misunderstood, though, as a plaidoyer for a purely hedonistic approach to life. As much as faith must be revived in its true and a-authoritarian meaning, life and work have to be re-directed toward productivity: the precondition of happiness. In addition to Aristotle and Spinoza, Kant's Categorical Imperative lurks somewhere in the background of this argumentation. In simple terms, Fromm's ethical formula boils down to the assumption that every human being living in accord with her/his own self will automatically find harmony with the greater community of individuals. At the end of this gradual process of human revitalization--Fromm does not explicitly say it, but the implication is there--a truly humanistic community of beings will emerge. This theory is anything but new, and it still remains open to debate.

Again, there is no practical answer to be found in this study as to *how* galloping ethical impoverishment may be stopped in its tracks. The book's appendix, fittingly entitled "the moral problem of today," arrives at the dismal conclusion that we "have become things and our neighbors have become things." From this sad state of human ethics results an all-pervading feeling of powerlessness--a phenomenon first diagnosed by Fromm in his article "Zum Gefühl der Ohnmacht" one decade prior to the publication of *Man for Himself.*[20] In a final apotheosis, Fromm throws the ethical malaise of our time back into the reader's lap, challenging "man" to take life and happiness seriously and to summon the courage to be "himself" and be "for himself." In the face of the foregoing pages' wealth of insights into the human psyche and of Fromm's truly noble concept of a humanistic ethical system, the book's flat conclusion must disappoint its reader. Instead of a feasible *solution* to the ethical dilemma of capitalist sociely, it presents an *aporia*. Any evolution of human consciousness or awakening of a humanistic conscience--

these being the ray of light at the end of the tunnel--are irrevocably blocked by the very factors responsible for the deformation of character from (potentially) productive to nonproductive. Working from the assumption that Fromm's overall diagnosis is basically correct, the only answer to the given ethical dilemma would be revolution. But there can not be a revolution of the mind alone--political and economic changes of the greatest consequence would have to follow. An a-authoritarian foundation of ethics is certainly not sufficient to achieve this goal. Human authority, as Fromm depicts it, is as much a part of the deformative chain reaction as is the economic system. Consciousness and the truly productive ethical orientation must therefore, in order to *actively* resist non-rational authority, become *anti*-authoritarian. Revolutionary change of the status quo might only be instrumented through a general reorientation towards active protest against "wrong" authority. Fromm consistently dodges this issue. Will his reader be able to face it?

Psychoanalysis and Religion (1950) is a direct continuation of the humanistic concept of ethics as presented in *Man for Himself*. After his dissertation *Jewish Law*[21] and the article "On the Development of the Dogma of Christ" (1930),[22] which belongs to the group of fundamental studies published in Horkheimer's *Zeitschrift für Sozialforschung*, Fromm had written only one brief essay on the subject of religion during the 1940s. It is entitled "Faith as a Character Trait," and was originally published in Sullivan's journal *Psychiatry*. Thereafter, it reappeared in the final part of *Man for Himself* in practically unmodified form.[23] Now, at the end of the decade, he returns with new insights to the theme of religion. As mentioned above, the influence of his second wife, Henny Gurland, played a decisive role in the re-awakening of his interest in this topic.

An additional factor responsible for this re-orientation in his thinking may surely be found in the greater historical and political circumstances of the post-war era. The end of the war had brought victory over fascism and National Socialism: the political systems which embodied, for Fromm as for many others, authoritarian de-

formation par excellence. But victory did not lead to an improvement of the socio-economic conditions within American society,
nor to an international movement toward peace and demobiliza-
tion. To the contrary: Cold War was incipient, and the nuclear
threat to humanity became increasingly virulent almost overnight.
Leo Löwenthal, one of Fromm's former colleagues at the Institute
of Social Research, expressed in an interview much later the disappointment felt by many American intellectuals over the political
realities which followed the Second World War: "This was not victory won by a new political philosophy and morality over an evil society, but the victory of the superior military apparatus of the
United States." Fromm must have been similarly sobered by the
post-war developments. In this light, his temporary abstinence from
direct social criticism as apparent in his ethical and religious works
must also be regarded as a sign of withdrawal, if not resignation.
Metaphorically speaking, he returns, at least for some years, to the
mythical origins of his own thinking. Fromm never abandoned the
Judaeo-Christian tradition, even when he argued--paradoxically--as
an atheist. And the ultimate promise of humanity's redemption is
the teleological backbone of this tradition.

Psychoanalysis and Religion carries, in its second edition, the
characteristic motto: "What matters is not the difference between
believers and unbelievers, but between those who care and those
who do not care." As opposed to both Freud and Marx, who denounced religion as a means of oppression, Fromm takes a position
somewhat reminiscent of Jung--his predecessor as a Terry lecturer
in 1937--inasmuch as he maintains that the human unconscious is
directly related to religious experience as such. In contrast to Jung,
however, he does not accept the premise that this religious experience must be concomitant with the self's surrender to a "higher
power," i.e. God or the unconscious. The book retains to a great
extent its original lecture format, and may therefore be regarded as
an instructive preservation of Fromm's academic teaching method-
ology--about which there is little or no testimony, even in the texts
written about him by his immediate disciples. Interestingly enough,
Fromm the lecturer displays a practically identical style to Fromm

the popular writer. *Psychoanalysis and Religion*, although on a much smaller scale, follows pretty much the same stylistic and structural methods found in *Escape from Freedom* and *Man for Himself*. It uses their proven three-step pattern, within which arguments are deployed in the same discursive and peripatetic fashion.

In analogy to the two forms of ethical character orientation described in the study's predecessor, two diametrically opposed forms of religious experience are now defined. *Authoritarian religion* is based on the recognition of and subsequent submission to an authority or being vastly superior to human existence. Once more, Fromm returns to his dismissal of Calvinism and related denominations known to the reader from *Escape from Freedom*. Authoritarian theology evokes the same character orientation as autocratic political power. It might be called, in free paraphrase of Fromm's arguments, a metaphysical variation of the *Führer* principle. *Humanistic religion*, conversely, can be found in the teachings of Isaiah, Jesus, Socrates, Spinoza, as well as in "certain trends" of the Judaeo-Christian tradition and, remarkably enough, in the cult of Reason established by Robespierre and St. Just during the French Revolution of 1789. According to Fromm, the most striking humanistic religion (which will again, for the purpose of this study, be called a-authoritarian) is Buddhism. Especially Zen Buddhism, an esoteric sect within the larger Buddhist faith, is exclusively oriented toward the human self. No knowledge other than that arising from the self is valid for Zen. Life is a virtue *in itself*, an end sui generis and not a means to an end.

At this point in the study, Fromm quotes for the first time in his entire works the teachings of Daisetz Teitaro Suzuki, the then foremost authority on Zen in the United States and the author of the successful publications *Manual of Zen Buddhism*,[24] *Living by Zen*,[25] and *Studies in Zen*.[26] Suzuki was at that time an influential cult figure in American intellectual circles. He taught at Columbia University and was also Karen Horney's teacher of Zen. The term "teacher" may be misplaced here, as Suzuki himself maintains that Zen can neither be "taught" nor "learned," it can only be *absorbed* by the individual. At any rate, Horney, together with several friends, later travelled to Japan, where Suzuki served as their guide to various Zen monasteries. And it was also Suzuki and Richard De Martino--a professor of philosophy and religion at Kyoto University--with whom Fromm taught a workshop in 1957 on Zen and psychoanalysis in Cuernavaca. The seminar resulted in the publication of *Zen Buddhism and Psychoanalysis*, which will be discussed in the following chapter.

In Psychoanalysis and Religion, Fromm attempts to delineate the psychoanalytic approach to religion as a way to understanding the *"human reality behind thought systems."*[27] This human reality, the core of the self, can surely not be found when individuals merely assimilate to external rules and conventions. Consequently, the aim of humanistic psychotherapy *and* the credo of humanistic religion cannot lie in facilitating adjustment to any form of authority. Both religion and psychoanalysis must take a firmly a-authoritarian stand. And both share the ultimate goal of making the individual gain or regain the ability to love. Once more, the continuity of Fromm's thought from his establishment of a humanistic ethical canon in *Man for Himself* to this exploration of heterodox religious concepts becomes obvious. It is the same train of thought that leads up to the more practical vademecum *The Art of Loving*, to be published six years later. And once more, the important issue of a-authoritarian versus anti-authoritarian orientation is shirked. Fromm elegantly evades the question by implying that once irrational authority has been recognized as such, it will be of no further consequence for the formation of consciousness. The objection must again be raised that a potentially detrimental influence on the psychological apparatus, even after it has been classified as detrimental, will not simply disappear. It still must be reckoned with as a damaging force and will continue to exert its power--at least on others less enlightened. The courage to be human, so often invoked in Fromm's writings, cannot stand alone. In order to be effective, it must go hand in hand with an equally courageous, and if necessary rebellious, protest against those institutions and ideologies deemed inhuman.

The centerpiece of humanistic religion is what Paul Tillich termed "the ultimate concern." Fromm calls this experience an attitude of "wonder" which results from individual self-realization. Wondering is considered "the most significant therapeutic factor" in psychotherapy and, at the same time, a religious feeling of "oneness not only in oneself, not only with one's fellow men, but with all life and, beyond that, with the universe."[28] The feeling described here equals *unio mystica*--the ultimate state in mystical immersion--as well as the state of satori (=illumination and, concomitantly, the knowledge of one's own being) in Zen. In *You Shall be as Gods*, Fromm calls this phenomenon the "x-experience." The intent of both religion and psychoanalysis in their a-authoritarian, humanistic efforts is therefore to empower the subject to break through his/her shell, the "organized self" or the ego. From there, contact with the unconscious may be established and, in turn, eliminate individuation. The loss of individuation then initiates the religious experience and the feeling of oneness with the "All," the universe. Schematically, this process could be demonstrated as follows:

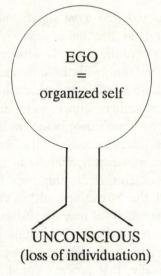

EGO
=
organized self

UNCONSCIOUS
(loss of individuation)

↓ ↓ ↓ ↓ ↓ ↓ ↓
RELIGIOUS EXPERIENCE
=
feeling of oneness with the All

Apart from the modern categories of the unconscious and of individuation, this movement through three consecutive stages of higher illumination or immersion of the self is strongly reminiscent of the *viae* of mysticism, as outlined above.[29] Only the ultimate goal is a different one. Where the christian mystic seeks union with the deity, humanistic religion aspires to gain full command of the "self" and, from there, to experience universal presence.

In this slim volume, Fromm makes a first and at times confusing attempt to come to grips with what might be called a religion without God, without a metaphysical or transcendental entity: a totally anthropocentric religion in the most literal meaning of the word. In particular, his notion of a humanistic consciousness--both in terms of its "sources and perhaps the implications"[30] --remains nebulous and requires further investigation. His later writings on the subject progress arduously in the same direction. They will be examined in the following chapters. It should be kept in mind, though, that a religious concept which dispenses with the intangible but ever-present center of a higher being, equals (at least within the boundaries of Western tradition) a paradox: *religious atheism*. A comparable paradox emerges, at first glance, from an approach to psychoanalysis which declares itself independent of established societal norms. Traditionally, scientific disciplines have always exercised the prerogative to establish norms and guidelines. Fromm's proclamation that the vocation of psychotherapy does *not* lie in the rehabilitation of the "sick" individual according to society's requirements is controversial, to put it mildly. He replaces the etiology of psychic illness as previously defined--i.e. any form of deviation from cultural and ethical behavior patterns--with a new etiology: humanity is prone to become mentally ill as long as it conforms to nonproductive assimilation and socialization processes. These processes by necessity block access to the self and, further, the feeling of oneness with both the own subconscious and the "all." A radical approach to both religion and psychoanalysis indeed. At its root lies Fromm's controversial and highly idiosyncratic definition of freedom, which was explained in the preceding chapter. The understanding of both his new approach to a humanistic religion and his humanistic re-appraisal of psychoanalysis, therefore, hinges on the reader's willingness to accept Erich Fromm's socio-psychological concept of freedom. Needless to say, Fromm's humanistic vision has been sharply criticized, even called a "reactionary ideology" in its "hostility toward the two greatest adversaries of our bourgeois society: scientific psychoanalysis and dialectic materialism."[31]

6

Forgotten Languages: Fromm's Dream Theory. Studies on Zen, Freud, and Marx

During the years he lived in Mexico--from 1950 to his final move to Switzerland in 1973--Erich Fromm reached the zenith of his productivity as a writer. Sixteen books appeared in print during that timespan, not to mention numerous articles in journals and anthologies. Within an incredibly short time, Fromm also managed to found a psychoanalytical institute at the National Autonomous University of Mexico. From 1955 until his retirement in 1965, he served as the director of this Mexican Institute of Psychoanalysis. He remained attached to it even after 1965 as an honorary professor. At the end of the year 1956, Fromm was instrumental in creating the Sociedad Mexicana de Psicoanálisis (Mexican Society for Psychoanalysis). Many symposia and lectures of this Society were held at his own home at 9 Calle Neptuno in Cuernavaca. One of the most prominent among those events was the seminar on Zen Buddhism and psychoanalysis, which took place in Cuernavaca in August, 1957, and was attended by the then eighty-seven year old Daisetz T. Suzuki; it eventually led to the publication of *Zen Buddhism and Psychoanalysis* (1960). Fromm's field study on the *Social Character in a Mexican Village*, further, is only one of the more practically oriented ventures he undertook in Mexico. Fromm spent approximately four months of each year in the United States. Most of that time was devoted to teaching assignments at the William Alanson White Institute. Between 1952 and 1961, he also commuted between New York and East Lansing, where he taught psychology at Michigan State University.

His next book publication, *The Forgotten Language* (1951), resulted directly from a postgraduate seminar at the White Institute and from a series of related undergraduate lectures he delivered during his final years at Bennington College. A brief look at the text testifies to the indulgence of Fromm's postgraduate students in clinical training at the White Institute. Even if one regards it as a sequence of loosely organized lecture notes, the book makes for disappointing reading. In the canon of Fromm's works as a whole, it stands out as one of the weakest and least convincing publications. The text is poorly organized and annoyingly repetitive. More than one fourth of its pages consist of direct quotations from other works, or of paraphrases of dreams and mythology. Footnotes are carelessly executed and often full of misprints. To give only one example: Fromm's friend and colleague Schachtel--one of the few psychoanalytical authorities he consistently cites at that time--appears as "Schnachtel" in one note. German titles are misquoted throughout. All in all, this is a slipshod, hastily whipped up concoction of unrelated parts.

Amazingly enough, this extremely weak title has thus far drawn little fire even from Fromm's more astute critics. Despite its debatable quality, the study must be discussed in some detail. For it sheds some light on two hitherto largely obscure areas of Fromm's work: first, it presents a fragmentary but nevertheless stimulating theory on the relevance of dreams and myths and their meaning for the human self. And second, Fromm's own approach as an analyst emerges at crucial points in the text. Regarding the latter aspect, Fromm was frequently and sometimes cuttingly criticized by his fellow analysts for the lack of factual observation and clinical data his studies displayed. Not only his friend Clara Thompson noted his reticence in this area. Specialists like Karl Menninger and J.A.C. Brown charged him openly with flagrant omission of vital information.[1] Moreover, he was often challenged on the grounds of his failure to quote recent psychiatric/psychoanalytical literature. This particular observation can be backed up by any objective survey of his work. The lack of technical references may, as Don Hausdorff generously suggests,[2] be due in part to the readership Fromm addressed--composed predominantly of educated laymen, not of professional analysts. In several of his writings, including *Social Character in a Mexican Village*, he emphasized that revealing details from his practical work would ultimately lead to the invasion of his patients' privacy. This is certainly a valid point. On the other hand, his various bibliographies indeed fail to indicate that his interest in new academic publications was anything more than scant. The observation may be allowed that Erich Fromm surely spent considerably more of his time writing than reading up on the subjects he wrote about.

The Forgotten Language's excursion into the realm of dreams, fairy tales, and myths may be seen as an extension of both Fromm's temporary withdrawal from direct social criticism in the wake of his post-war disillusionment, and of his exploration of the human self which began with *Man for Himself* and branched out into intensified study of various aspects of the unconscious around 1950. Characteristically, as all of his works are intricately related to each other, the spheres of dream and myth can not be clearly separated from either Fromm's humanistic ethics or his atheistic mysticism. He sees myths and dreams as further stations on the journey inward: approximations of the unattainable and elusive center of human nature. Fromm ventures the theory that symbolic language is "the only universal language the human race ever developed"--an assumption that would be equally acceptable to C.G. Jung or to more recent scholars such as Susanne K. Langer. The Talmudic proverb "Dreams which are not interpreted are like letters which have not been opened" bespeaks a drive toward understanding these unconscious activities which is as old as humanity itself.

Dreams are, for Fromm, a conglomerate of *symbols*. (He does not use the term "allegory" at this point, which would be appropriate. Instead, he prefers a more direct, "logistic" approach, as will be shown.) Three types of symbols must be differentiated: the *conventional*, the *accidental*, and the *universal*. Everyday language is a system of interrelated conventional symbols. Language is influenced and changed by cultural and historical factors and trends. As a product of the process of civilization and a means of socialization, language and conventional symbols represent an area of concern throughout Fromm's work. Accidental symbols, secondly, are of particular relevance for his dream theory because of their pre-dominantly private meaning. They may occur in every person's life, where certain places, words, actions, gestures, or things take on a special "symbolic" meaning related exclusively to this individual's experience. It follows that, in order to understand one individual's dream world, the analyst must be sufficiently acquainted with the patient's biographical background, as well as his/her resources of accidental symbols. Fromm's emphasis on this "private" language possessed by every human being already indicates his deviation from Freud's more objective and impersonal approach to dream analysis.

Universal symbols, finally, are "rooted in the experience of *every* human being."[3] Fromm mentions the constantly changing symbol-ism of fire, water, and the physical world. Facial expressions of moods and feelings are also seen as universally symbolic. And it is only through the understanding of those symbols that the full meaning of dreams may be decoded. In his definition of the *nature* of dreams, Fromm deviates from both Freud--the grandfather of modern dream analysis--and from C.G. Jung. For him, dreaming is a much less irrational function than for Freud. In contrast to Jung, on the other hand, he emphasizes the *personal* quality of dreams. He maintains that "*dreaming is a meaningful and significant expres-sion of any kind of mental activity under the condition of sleep.*"[4] Dreamers, says Fromm, are in no way less reasonable than persons awake. To the contrary, the world of dreams (=the unconscious) may often function in a more intelligent and coherent way than daytime perceptions (=the conscious). Both illuminate two differ-ent modes of existence located in the same mind. For any disciple of the more orthodox schools of dream interpretation, this is a very provoking statement indeed. Fromm goes one step further:

... the state of sleep has an ambiguous function. In it the lack of contact with culture makes for the appearance both of our worst *and* of our best; therefore, if we dream, we may be less intelligent, less wise, and less decent, but we may also be better and wiser than in our waking life.[5]

This puzzling remark has a dual implication. First, it implies that cultural/societal deformation, i.e. any of the nonproductive character orientations described in the preceding chapter, will most likely "drop out" of the individual's subconscious during sleep. Consequently, direct access to the dreamer's self might open up: an entrance door usually closed during the waking hours. This thesis is based on the traditional tenets of dream interpretation and might be regarded as the more "orthodox" component in Fromm's theory of dreams. The second aspect implied, however, breaks radically with tradition by assuming that in the dream world, an individual might be *more insightful* than in conscious thought processes. Here, for the first time in his works, Fromm displays a leaning toward cultural relativism which is to become much more pronounced in his later works. A new, often unacknowledged "layer" of his thinking emerges in form of a piercing pessimism toward the cultural/civilizational process as a whole. If a person may in fact reach deeper and "better" insights--note both the intellectual *and* the ethical implications of the statement--in the state of sleep, reality as such must obviously be regarded as an inferior and deformative sphere. This cultural pessimism, which can be derived directly from his dream theory, stands in apparent opposition to his otherwise characteristic faith in humanity's potential to attain a better future. In the final analysis, this contradiction in his thinking can not be resolved.

Various dream analysts, as well as lengthy excerpts from Freud's and Jung's dream interpretations (which need not be belabored here), are quoted to back up this rudimentary theory. In most instances, the given dream experiences can only make sense to the analyst who is familiar with the analysand's personal situation. All this boils down to the postulate that, at least for Fromm, no predetermined pattern or model of dream analysis is feasible. Both accidental (=private) and universal (=supra-personal) symbols engage in a complex interplay to make up the individual's dream reality. The reader becomes aware at this point how closely the dream theory is tied in with its author's characterology and the dichotomy between ontogenetic (=biologic and rooted in human nature) and sociogenetic (=supra-personal) factors, as well as the bifurcation of the resulting character orientation.

Release of the subconscious stress and anxiety syndromes at work on the patient through the process of dream analysis takes patience and experience. In his 1965 dialogue with Richard I. Evans--a very revealing document in several respects--, Fromm calls dream interpretation "the most important instrument we have in psychoanalytic therapy."[6] He goes one step further when he describes this technique as an equivalent to accurate, scientific observation of facts.[7] For many of today's analysts and psychiatrists, this may be a very questionable viewpoint. And Fromm's own frequent technique of free-handed association in the process of dream analysis can be labeled spontaneous, at best. Sometimes the results, as they emerge from *The Forgotten Language*, are much more multivalent than Fromm admits.

The book's final chapter turns to a re-interpretation of various myths, the fairy tale of Little Red Riding-Hood, and Franz Kafka's novel *The Trial*. Here, Fromm is at his most controversial. One can attest considerable validity to his reappraisal of the Oedipus myth, which he had already published twice before.[8] In contrast to Freud, he takes into account *all* parts of Sophocles' trilogy: *Oedipus Rex*, *Oedipus at Colonus*, and *Antigone*. The prevailing theme of these dramas as he sees it is *not* Freud's incestuous mother-fixation, but rather the conflict between father and son. Sophocles' texts are re-examined on this basis as the direct expression of tensions inherent in a patricentric society. Once more, Fromm refers back to his early studies of Bachofen's theories on matriarchy. He uses this scholar's interpretation of Aeschylus' *Oresteia* as a struggle between the old matrimonial order and the new patriarchal *Weltbild* as a stepping stone for a radical revision of the whole Oedipus complex. As can be expected, Freud with his much narrower approach falls by the wayside, like Laius, the slain king of Thebes and biological father of Oedipus.

Little Red Riding-Hood and Kafka fare worse than Oedipus. The former is seen as a girl on her way to sexual maturity. In this adventurous interpretation, the red bonnet stands for menstruation, and the dangerous woods through which she travels for a world full of sexual threats. Suddenly the seducer enters in the guise of a wolf, and the "cannibalistic" act of sexual intercourse ends in the devouring of the female. The wolf, in turn, is punished for his attempt to assume the role of a pregnant woman--one remembers that he has ingested both the grandmother and the girl--and killed by means of inserting stones, "a symbol of sterility," in his belly. Quite in contrast to the Oedipus myth, the female emerges the victor in the fairy tale. This is one of the few contributions in Fromm's whole works to the nature of sexuality in general and to female sexuality in particular. If any insight follows from his variations on the theme of Little Red Riding-Hood, it must be the conclusion that he has given the subject little, if any, serious thought.

Equally towering heights are reached by Fromm's re-interpretation of Kafka's novel. During the trial, Josef K. presumably becomes aware of the greed and "sterility" of his prior life. And at its conclusion, he realizes at last his inherent powers for love, friendship, and faith. Literary critics, who have wrestled for decades to find the "right" interpretation of Kafka's hermetic parable, surely did not breathe a sigh of relief with the appearance of Fromm's "definitive" explanation of the novel's meaning. Hausdorff dryly remarks that "literary exegesis is not his [Fromm's] specialty."[9] One must wholeheartedly agree to that.

A last question remains in connection with The *Forgotten Language*: what exactly does it reveal about Fromm's practical approach to psychoanalysis? There are strong indications that his technique must have followed the tradition of free association founded by Georg Groddeck, Sándor Ferenczy, and Sullivan. He insists on the active participation of the analyst in the analytic process; this stands very much in opposition to the "detached" stance required by Freud. The analyst, says Fromm, must internalize his patient's fears and delusions, must in fact experience them himself in order to initiate effective therapy. In Sullivan's terms, he must become a "participant observer" or, as Fromm reformulates the idea with a truly artful play on words, an "observant participant."[10] In his dialogue with Evans, he further explains his own modus operandi. Transference in the Freudian sense (i.e. the complex process of interrelation between analyst and patient, in which the latter frequently "transfers" his feelings toward a parent to the analyst and, through this mechanism, becomes dependent on him or her), should be changed from a one-way street to a dynamic interchange involving *mutual* transference.[11] Although Fromm was not an advocate of Rogers' non-directive method,[12] he worked in the same direction by encouraging his patients to respond to his own responses. By jarring the patient out of the given behavioral pattern, he hoped to elicit and activate critical willpower. On a more general level, Fromm ventured that the patient's feelings and thoughts must be present--or must have been present at one time or another--in the analyst's self. By curing the patient, he states, the analyst will also cure himself.[13] Fromm was a confirmed opponent of shock therapy, which in the meantime is no longer generally practiced. He had equally strong objections to group therapy. His verdict on this approach is quite facetious: "I can not but suspect that this is psychoanalysis for the man [!] who cannot pay twenty-five dollars."[14] Apparently psychoanalysis, in his opinion, was the rightful privilege only of the well-to-do.

Departing from his re-interpretation of the Oedipus myth in *The Forgotten Language*, Erich Fromm embarked eight years later on *Sigmund Freud's Mission*, a full-scale appraisal of Freud's relevance for contemporary psychoanalysis. In the meantime, he had published his bestselling book *The Art of Loving*, which will be discussed below in chapter nine of this study. He had also engaged in a heated debate with Herbert Marcuse who, in his book *Eros and Civilization* (1955) and in the epilogue published separately in *Dissent*, had accused Fromm of an indirectly affirmative view of societal deformation. Fromm's social criticism and his "revisionism" of

Freud's theories, according to Marcuse, take refuge in the realm of "defunct idealistic philosophy." Marcuse's sophisticated attack on Fromm pinpoints the same contradictions mentioned earlier in this study, namely Fromm's irrational hope for a solution of the human dilemma *despite* all societal evidence to the contrary.[15] In this controversy, the label of Freudian "revisionism" particularly irked Fromm. To a certain extent, his annoyance was justified, especially regarding the frequently encountered rather primitive condemnation of *all* so-called revisionists in one fell swoop. Fromm, Horney, and Sullivan, as well as many others in this loosely associated group, differed enormously in their individual approaches, despite certain common ground. Fromm was perfectly aware of these differences, and pointed them out repeatedly in his writings, most succinctly perhaps in the conversation with Evans.[16] He always went out of his way to stress that his own socio-psychological approach was not intended to reverse any of Freud's basic premises or to contradict them in toto. He was frequently classified as a "neo-Freudian," which seems perfectly appropriate. But even this noncommittal label was not totally acceptable to him. Erich Fromm liked to see himself as "somewhat like a pupil and translator of Freud who is attempting to bring out his most important discoveries in order to enrich and to deepen them by liberating them from the somewhat narrow libido theory."[17]

Throughout his lifetime, Fromm appeared reluctant to completely step forth from the overpowering shadow of the founder of modern psychology, even while others accused him of "cunningly distorting the entire works and person"[18] of Freud. Not only Fromm's direct criticism of Freud, but all of his work on this authority should be read in the light of his ambivalent vacillation between tradition and innovation. His two book-length studies on the man and his work, *Sigmund Freud's Mission* and the latecomer *Greatness and Limitations of Freud's Thought*, are both self-vindications against the accusations of "revisionism" and honest attempts to come to grips with one of the most outstanding figures in the intellectual history of modern times.

The smoldering controversy between orthodox and unorthodox disciples of Freud flared up with the publication of Ernest Jones' three-volume biography *The Life and Work of Sigmund Freud* in 1955.[19] Jones not only attacked meritorious analysts like Otto Rank and Sándor Ferenczy for their deviations from the master's rules, he displayed in general an almost total lack of distance to his subject. Fromm, who felt that the climate in psychoanalytical circles was rapidly deteriorating, reacted in a review entitled "Freud, Friends and Fiends. Scientism or Fanatism?" and later re-published as "Psychoanalysis--Science or Party Line" in his essay collection *The Dogma of Christ*.[20] He challenged Jones' bias as an expression of "party-line" thinking and noted his failure to provide analytical insights into Freud's own personality. It is one of the aims of *Sigmund Freud's Mission* to provide a detailed analysis of Freud as a person and as a product of his environment. Although the book is, according to Hausdorff, "one-sided much of the time" and probably "put together rather hastily,"[21] it must be acknowledged as a perceptive and courageous statement.

Freud, as Fromm diagnoses, was in many ways a product of enlightenment. His unflagging faith in reason and his conviction that truth will be found, even under adverse circumstances, testify to his intellectual heritage. Emotionally, however, he was an extremely insecure person who felt easily threatened or even betrayed. His quarrels with Alfred Adler and Josef Breuer, and his irrational reactions to Wilhelm Fliess' and C.G. Jung's criticisms betray both his deeply rooted insecurity and his desire for dominance over and acceptance from others. Fromm stresses his courage as the most outstanding positive feature of his character. On the negative side, Freud had little capacity for genuine love or selfless emotion. In a very sophisticated (and, tongue in cheek, strictly "orthodox") application of the Oedipus complex, Freud's utter dependence on his mother emerges as the key to the whole organization of his adult life. From *this* vantage point, his problematic assessment of the female psyche takes on a new, biographical dimension. Fromm quotes the classical statement made by Freud in reply to the question whether sexual equality would be desirable: "This is a practical impossibility. *There must be inequality* and the superiority of the man is the lesser of two evils."[22] His almost ludicrous helplessness toward women in general culminated in the proverbial remark made in a conversation with Marie Bonaparte: "The great question . . . which I have not been able to answer . . . is, what does a woman want?"[23] Regarding sex and, on a much broader plane, pleasure per se, Freud's view always remained puritanical and at times outright hostile.

A strong authoritarian trait is described as the basis of his character orientation. Predominantly receptive in his attitude toward others, Freud was extremely dependent on the men who surrounded him. Personal relationships invariably began to crumble at the first indication of a difference in opinion. Many of them disintegrated irrevocably. For documentation regarding Freud's character, Fromm relies frequently on his subject's own well-known work, *The Interpretation of Dreams*. By means of this "intrinsic" approach, he circumvents the questionable validity of circumstantial evidence, i.e. second-hand documentation, and, at the same time, tries to avert any reproach of unfavorable bias. An ambivalent picture emerges from his analysis. On the one hand, Freud is given due credit as an innovator and intellectual revolutionary of the first order. On the other, his personality appears as a puzzling composite of weakness and dependency which stands in stark relief against his self-evaluation as a messiah and spearhead of world reform.

Perhaps the most intriguing part of the study is the final chapter devoted to Freud's religious and political convictions. Political conservatism is the foundation of his division of humanity in leaders and followers. Both his political views *and* his approach to psychoanalysis are ultimately rooted in nineteenth-century capitalism. His theories on sexuality, according to Fromm, must be seen as a "deepened and enlarged version of the economist's concept of Homo economicus."[24] In particular, his libido theory, though "supposedly biological, has a curiously 'economic' aspect."[25] Fromm's postulate of this intrinsic relationship between the Victorian age's moral restrictions and its given socio-economic conditions as it emerges in Freud's thought must be seen as the book's most controversial thesis. Clearly, Fromm recognized that Freud's description of sublimation, mutatis mutandis, is nothing less than a reproduction of the social character of nineteenth and early twentieth century bourgeoisie. The common denominator of both lies in the conservation of psychic energy (=sublimation) and the hoarding of capital (=the economic guideline of certain phases in the development of capitalist economy). As a final blow to Jones' cultistic approach, Fromm describes Freud's vacillation between brilliant insights and "hopelessly opinionated" convictions. He remained, in many ways, a captive of his own time. This part of Fromm's critique doubtlessly warrants additional discussion. But that would lead beyond the realm of this study.

The reaction to Fromm's provocative book in American psychoanalytic circles was swift and vigorous. He was tacitly expelled from the International Psychoanalytic Association, of which he had been a member since the early 1930s. He was ostracized from local professional organizations. Not many reviews of the book appeared; it was generally greeted by silence. Most notable among the few objective reactions is the essay by Hilde L. Mosse, which attests "great merit" to the study.[26] In the same issue of *Psychiatry*, in support of Mosse's perceptive review, Gregory Zilboorg speaks up in defense of Fromm's independence. He takes the American psychoanalytic groups and organizations to task for their doctrinaire attitudes. This trend, he observes, "is bound to pay heavy tribute to the art of politics, to the struggle for power, to egocentric sensitivities, and to promotional drives."[27] All this certainly held true. Nevertheless, Fromm in the meantime was deeply shocked by his colleagues' open display of unbending hostility and by their total lack of professionalism. It was not until twenty years later, in his last published book *Greatness and Limitations of Freud's Thought*, that he once more attempted a re-appraisal of Freud and a self-appraisal of his earlier theories on the subject. A brief distillate of this work appeared in 1970 under the title "Freud's Model of Man and Its Social Determinants" in the collection *The Crisis of Psychoanalysis*.[28]

Fromm's second study on Freud makes no radical divergences from the first one. Subtle shifts of emphasis and various nuances, however, should be briefly mentioned. He now pays particular attention to a redefinition of "truth," and gives Freud considerable credit for revolutionizing the concept. In Freud's enlarged view, truth is no longer an empirical or moral phenomenon. Rather, essential truth is frequently located in the subconscious, and not necessarily related to a person's professed convictions. Suppression and rationalization can not only be stumbling blocks on the path toward truth, but also intrinsic parts of truth itself. In addition to his previously described critique of the Oedipus complex, of narcissistic behavior patterns and the problems of transference, Fromm once again engages in a lengthy discussion of dream interpretation. As opposed to Freud, who insisted on the predominantly irrational nature of dreams, he reiterates his theory from *The Forgotten Language* that dreams may be more rational and insightful than daytime perceptions. He tackles Freud's concept of dream censorship and arrives at the conclusion that the analyst's task must be to distinguish between "irrational" and "rational" dream symbols. His critique of the instinct theory, which concludes this study, need not be elaborated on at this time, as it runs like a red thread through most of Fromm's writings, beginning with his article "Die gesellschaftliche Bedingtheit der psychoanalytischen Theorie" (1935)[29] and culminating in later texts such as *The Heart of Man* and *To Have or to Be?*

At the very end of his critique of Freud's theory on death instinct, Fromm lands a heavy blow against those of Freud's followers who did not dare to modify his teachings, rather became builders of a Freudian "movement." He refers to these researchers as mostly "pedestrian" minds, who needed the safety of a canonized thought system. And this canonization led ultimately to Freud's posthumous petrification as an object of a cult which rejected any dynamic or creative re-appraisal of his ideas.[30] One might well compare Fromm's highly perceptive evaluation of the founder of modern psychoanalysis with his equally ambivalent love-hate relationship to American capitalism. Both count among the inherent dichotomies of his thinking. *Greatness and Limitations of Freud's Thought*, the last book published during Fromm's lifetime, was apparently intended as the first installment of a larger, three-part opus on psychoanalytical theory and practice. The trilogy could not be completed due to Fromm's failing health.

As mentioned earlier in this chapter, Erich Fromm developed a strong interest in Zen Buddhism during the 1950s and 1960s. In the course of his relationship with Daisetz T. Suzuki, he strove toward an amalgamation of Zen and psychoanalysis. One tangible result of this interest is the anthology *Zen Buddhism and Psychoanalysis*, which was published three years after the symposium on this topic in Cuernavaca. The volume contains contributions by Suzuki himself, Richard De Martino, and Erich Fromm. Other participants of the seminar included Maurice Green, James Kirsch, Ira Progoff, David Schecter, Edward S. Tauber, and Ben Weininger. For the sake of brevity, only Fromm's essay will be discussed in this context. It should be mentioned beforehand that Fromm remained a student and an adherent of Zen for the rest of his life. He admitted that he never reached the enlightened state of satori, the mystical union with the self which is the ultimate goal of Zen's self-immersion. Nevertheless, he saw in Zen a road to a mystical realization of his own personality. After he settled in Switzerland, he became acquainted with the German Buddhist monk Nyanaponika Mahathera, who opened further vistas to him in his deeper exploration of Zen.

In his appreciation of Zen, Fromm works from the premise that Eastern religious systems, due to their a-authoritarian nature, must paradoxically be regarded as more suited to Western rational thought than their Western counterparts. Analogously to mysticism in the tradition of Master Eckhart, Zen requires an inner cleansing process ("to make oneself empty") as a first step toward self-immersion. Making oneself "empty" may be compared to the *via purgativa seu negativa* of European medieval mysticism. It liberates the individual from societal influences, and at the same time initiates the process of de-individuation. This approach, says Fromm, is related to the aim of psychoanalysis, i.e. to render the unconscious conscious, or, in Freud's terms, to transform Id into Ego.[31] In the context of his lecture, Fromm achieves a sharp definition of consciousness and "the unconscious." He rejects the somewhat artificial division of the two spheres as strictly separate entities and concludes instead that "the" unconscious does not exist on its own terms. Neither does "the" conscious: "There are degrees of consciousness-awareness and unconsciousness-awareness."[32] This keen differentiation leaves the two realms separated only by a permeable membrane. The distinction is also of importance for the understanding of Fromm's later works on psychology and religion, particularly *The Heart of Man* and *You Shall be as Gods*.

Both Zen and humanistic psychoanalysis share common ground in their orientation toward *being* and their rejection of the *having* mode so deeply rooted in Western capitalist mentality. The essay, it may be noted, contains in a nutshell most of the central ideas of the later study *To Have or to Be?*[33] Unity with one's self is the essential goal of Zen. And it is, at the same time, the desirable result of effective, humanistically oriented psychotherapy. In his description of this elusive concept of "unity," Fromm for once does not discuss those factors which prevent most individuals in modern society from achieving it. He suggests, however, that unity may be attainable *beyond* alienation or, conversely, that alienation is even a necessary prerequisite in the quest for the human self:

> that unity which can be arrived at only after man has experienced his separateness, after he has gone through the stage of alienation from himself and from the world, and has been fully born.[34]

One can easily recognize what attracted Erich Fromm to Zen Buddhism. The brief passage quoted issues a strong promise for the ultimate salvation of human existence. As opposed to Judaeo-Christian religions, in particular the orthodox Judaism that provided the formative environment for Fromm's own intellectual development, this salvation promised by Eastern religion is divorced from any eschatological framework and located directly in the human self. The there*after* is replaced by the notion of the there*in*. Hope is no longer bound to a transcendental vision, it can be fulfilled--at least potentially--in the here and now. Struggle as he might with his own construct of an atheistic mysticism, i.e. a humanistic religion *without* God, he came closest to this goal in his interpretation of Zen Buddhism. Theologians might argue that a mystical journey inwards which does not seek an apparition of the deity at its end will lead to a void or to nihilism. For Fromm, the opposite is the case. In fact, his estimation of Zen remains, as Hausdorff observes, "totally un-critical."[35] He not only fails to observe the obvious "egocentric leanings"[36] in this Eastern mysticism. The equally strong escapist tendencies inherent in *any* mystical mode apparently eluded him as well. Torres censures Fromm on two counts for embracing Bud-dhism: not only is meditation traditionally a "rich man's sport," but Buddhism itself has contributed for centuries to the continued op-pression of the enslaved classes, since it encourages resignation and escapism as preferable to social change.[37] Reality's hard edges can be forgotten in the realm of total self-immersion. In effect, the *via purgativa seu negativa*, or Zen's "emptying" of the self, seems to of-fer an escape from even the propagated state of "freedom to"--from active participation in the creation of a new, more benevolent hu-man and social order.

An equally meaningful encounter with the self is presumably achievable through the psychoanalytic illumination of the uncon-scious. If indeed "the content of consciousness is mostly fictional and delusional,"[38] if society, through all its powers of indoctrina-tion, saturates our consciousness with false assumptions, the only refuge left lies in the unconscious. In this respect, Zen and psy-choanalysis can engage in fruitful cross-fertilization. Their com-mon focal point is situated in the rejection of, i.e. *retreat* from wrong and irrational authority. The Zen master incorporates, as does the humanistically oriented analyst, "rational authority." Ul-timately, both strive to free the subject from dependence on "any" kind of authority. The reader can only puzzle over this extremely provocative statement which, at least at first glance, appears to be totally inconsistent with Fromm's customary stress on rationality.

Does he indeed, at this point, resignedly assume that human nature can be developed to full potential only *outside* the realm of conscious perception? Concomitant with this retreat from the fallacies of the conscious, a total retreat from society itself would appear as the logical consequence (an avenue open, it might be noted, only to the wealthy in any event, and not to the lowly wage-earner). This ambiguous undercurrent in Fromm's thinking has been touched upon already in the foregoing analysis of *The Forgotten Language*, and it continues to provide food for thought and controversy. Retreat into the unconscious, that much can be positively deduced from Fromm's essay, may often have been the only avenue of self-realization to which he really subscribed. The escapist and elitarian tendencies of this thesis are undeniable, and will be discussed later in some detail.

De-repression, i.e. bringing the unconscious within reach of the conscious, may lead to the "experiential realization of humanism."[39] De-repression, for Fromm, also means self-liberation from repressions and rationalizations, rejection of illusions, fictions, and lies. It must be seen as a process of awakening. At its end stands the liberated human being, whose freedom will no longer be restricted, either by the self or by others. As one realizes the inevitability of this inner emancipation, one will presumably become part of the inner revolution of humanity. Both paths, that of humanistic psychoanalysis and that of Zen, may differ in their methods. Their goal, according to Fromm, is identical.

When he published *Sigmund Freud's Mission*, Erich Fromm entered a long and mutually inspiring association with the publisher Ruth Nanda Anshen. Anshen, who edited the important series *World Perspectives*, subsequently served as his agent and main advisor for various publications. *Marx's Concept of Man* (1961), however, his next important book--in fact one of the supporting pillars of the whole opus--was written upon the instigation of Frederick Ungar, an émigré himself, member of Fromm's own generation, and a mediator between European and American cultural life. It took considerable courage for both publisher and author to publish a study on Marx at the peak of the Cold War period. For Fromm, an extensive work on this author who was so profoundly formative for his own thinking, must have been a pressing issue for quite some time. Side by side with *Sigmund Freud's Mission*, his treatment of Marx pays homage to the one other most influential thinker in his life.

Marx's Concept of Man contains, in addition to Fromm's fundamental essay, an excellent English translation of Marx's *Economic and Philosophical Manuscripts* (dating from the 1840s) by the British Economist T.B. Bottomore. Suffice it to say here that the *Manuscripts* are extremely illuminating and should of course be recommended reading for everyone interested in Marx the thinker, in particular to politicians presumably conversant in Marxist theory but generally ignorant even of its most basic tenets. Fromm's primary focus in this book, then, is also theoretical (though the study ties in closely with his political writings and will also be mentioned in Chapter 8, devoted to his statements on current political and social issues). His revival of the "forgotten language" of Karl Marx--arguably the most influential philosopher of modern times--is, along with his work on Freud, a keystone in his exploration of the human condition.

Fromm's discourse on Marx frankly announces its basic intent of rectifying an often grotesque misrepresentation of Marxism in the Western world. Particularly in the United States, he argues, widespread ignorance of this subject has been further augmented by willful distortion and propaganda. Stalinist terror has been flatly equated with the application of Marxist theory. This premise was exploited especially during the Cold War period and throughout the bizarre witch-hunting initiated by the House Unamerican Activities Committee and the subsequent ultra-patriotic anti-Communist hysteria led by Joseph R. McCarthy. The astute reader, being aware that history has a tendency to repeat itself, may feel reminded in this context of certain activities of the "new right" during the 1980s. Misconceptions about Marx are, however, not the sole property of capitalistic nations. They are equally prevalent in the communist camp.

The book's initial chapter arrives at the conclusion that both the Soviet Union and the People's Republic of China have, as much as their Western adversaries, made the wrong *use* of Marx's theories. Especially the Soviet regime, for which Fromm obviously has no sympathy whatsoever, "conceived of communism--or socialism--in the spirit of capitalism."[40] Brutal oppression of human rights and humanistic strivings, as exercised in the USSR, stand in direct opposition to Marx's actual idea of communism. Fromm's condemnation of the USSR and China is so vitriolic that one can not help but wonder whether much of the information about these countries at his own disposal was really extracted from reliable evidence, and not from the same domestic sources he attacks for their ignorant bias against Marx.

But this is not the central issue here. He rightly questions the true motivations behind the hostile American public opinion of the USSR: is that vociferous indignation indeed directed against violations of humanitarian principles--or must *any* system that abandons "private property" be anathema to capitalist societies? Certainly this is an intriguing question, today more so than ever. Fromm corrects the notion that communism and socialism are fundamentally opposed to *any* private property, pointing out that personal possessions as such have never been condemned by Marx and Engels.[41] It may be added that in all existent socialist countries the possession of goods related to one's own life is not an issue challenged by the state. By "private property," Marx (and with him Fromm) mean the huge amassment of economic power (=capital) in the hands of very few individuals or groups: exactly the foundation on which monopolistic capitalism rests. It is self-evident that those in control of capital are, at least to a large extent, concomitantly in control of the educational system and the mass media, and thus in a position to shape "public opinion" almost at whim. Nonetheless, the fairy tale that private possessions like furniture and clothing are snatched away in socialist or communist countries has become an essential part of American anti-communism. The myth originated and is kept alive by those who possess immense wealth--thus divesting the majority of the population of any economic power--and would in fact stand to lose their vast influence if a drastic change in socio-economic conditions should occur. Mindless repetition of this fictitious notion by the many is strictly a product of mass indoctrination.

Although somewhat lopsided in its stress on the *early* writings of Marx (and also Engels to some extent), Fromm's appraisal is nevertheless persuasive. He draws the portrait of a messianic-humanistic reformer who shed the shackles of 19th century German idealism to create a new concept of humanity. The basis for this concept is a synthesis of humanistic and naturalistic methodology. Fromm strongly supports Marx's postulate that humanity is the autonomous maker of history. On the other hand, the direct interrelation of this postulate with economic theory and the formula commonly known as "dialectic materialism" receive much less attention. Fromm is primarily concerned with the *humanistic* rebel, and not with the *economic* revolutionary.

The first step in his explication of Marx's thought is a sweeping survey of various philosophical schools regarding the roots of human consciousness or, respectively, the distortion of true perceptions through ideology and rationalizations. In this intellectual tradition of the West, Marx is linked closely to Spinoza's rationalism, Hegel's dynamic concept of history, and, ultimately, Freud's exploration of human consciousness. Marx--no less a product of enlightenment than Freud--maintains that historical change and progress can be instrumented only through a constant educational process: humanity as the creator of history must be both educator and the recipient of a new education which responds to the perpetual changes in societal circumstance. What emerges from this social dynamism as propagated by the younger Marx may be called, in slightly simplistic terms, a *dialectic intellectualism* reminiscent of Hegel, but primarily concerned with humanity's active and autonomous role in the historical process. (The term "dialectic intellectualism" is not used by Fromm; it is introduced at this point as an attempt to clarify the young Marx's roots in both enlightenment *and* idealism.) It follows logically to ask *how* historical change may be brought about. Fromm rightly insists that Western democracies owe their present status to acts of political revolution. He mentions the "Glorious Revolution" of Oliver Cromwell, the French and American revolutions, and the unsuccessful German revolution of 1918. As acts of liberation from an exploitative and decaying political system, they are comparable to the Russian revolution of 1917. It should be understood, though, that the latter was *not* a precondition to the Stalinist totalitarian state. Regarding the question of force, Fromm perceptively observes that "indignation against the use of force, as it exists in the Western world today, depends on who uses force, and against whom."[42]

From these historical considerations, the essay turns to Marx's understanding of human nature. Marx's thinking, says Fromm, gradually emancipated itself from its origins in German idealism, especially from Hegel's influence. At the same time, however, it held true to its humanistic core. Primitive materialism--in the colloquial sense of the word--has never been propagated by Marx (nor by Engels). To the contrary, the central component of his thought is the distinction between productivity and a nonproductive existence. The affinity between Fromm's own ethical characterology and Marx's concept of human nature, as it is perceived in this essay, becomes apparent at this point. For Marx, a human being is alive through productivity and through relatedness to the outside world: by realizing inner powers and "grasping the world with these powers."[43] Lack of productiveness, conversely, means that a person is dead for all practical purposes. Fromm explicitly stresses the phenomenon of *love* as a centrifugal force in this humanistic concept. As opposed to the relatedness to material objects predominant in capitalist systems, humans must find a new, spontaneous relationship to each other. Only communism, according to Marx and to his interpreter, can liberate humanity from its enslavement to things (the German term *Verdinglichung* is a more accurate description of this state of mind). The central sentence of Fromm's essay reads as follows: "Communism as a fully developed naturalism is humanism and as a fully developed humanism is naturalism."[44] Fromm's tendency toward circular hermeneutics, once more, becomes apparent in this statement. His distinction between the modes of *having* and

being--or, in economic terms, capitalism and humanistic commu-
nism--prefigures his study *To Have or to Be?* Capital, he argues,
represents from an anthropological viewpoint an outdated mode of
existence, the past. Conversely, labor, when it finally becomes liberated from exploitation, is a direct expression of life. It stands for
humanity's future. The question remains: what exactly is the
meaning of "communism" in the philosophy of Karl Marx?

Again, for the sake of prudence, expediency, or both, Fromm
deliberately excludes the views of the older Marx from his discourse. In his later writings, Marx is both evidently disappointed by
the results of recent historical developments and much more realistic in his outlook on socio-economic conditions. This development
of his philosophy toward a purely materialistic viewpoint, which included a more mechanistic concept of human psychology, is not adverse, however, to a strong humanistic undercurrent present in *all*
of his works. In other words: the author of *Zur Kritik der kapita-
listischen Ökonomie* (1859; *The Critique of Capitalist Economy*) and
Das Kapital (1867/94) is no less ethically motivated than the author
of the *Economic and Philosophical Manuscripts.* Marx's intellectual maturation, however, was not the issue for Fromm, and it
would thus be senseless to trace it here. Fromm deals extensively
with Marx's concept of alienation (*Entfremdung*), which he originally derived from Hegel. Alienation is the principal adversary of
human productivity. For Marx, alienation results primarily from
the division of capital and labor, i.e. the means of production and
human productivity. Alienated labor and private property (=capi-
tal; *not* the goods directly related to personal life) perpetuate
alienation of humanity as a whole: from nature, physical life, and
from a full and fulfilled mental and emotional existence. *Human*
needs for spontaneity and relatedness atrophy and are gradually replaced by *artificial* needs. The individual in capitalist society is
spoonfed one artificial need after the other, thus increasing her/his
bondage to the earning of money and, ultimately, bringing
dependence and/or indebtedness which may lead to financial ruin.
Marx could certainly not foresee the intricate network of credit
(=dependence - indebtedness) on which virtually the entire eco-

nomic system in the United States would rest a century later: a house of unprecedented proportions built on sand. Consequently, his theory of alienation and economic bondage must be regarded as prophetic in many respects.

Communism, in the Marxian meaning of the word, would restore a rational and just order in the division of capital and labor. Through socialism, the necessary prerequisites for human freedom and productivity can be established. Socialism, says Fromm, is for Marx the means to an end, and not a teleological concept in the development of history. Paul Tillich, who is quoted at this point in Fromm's study, saw in Marx's understanding of socialism "a resistance movement against the destruction of love in social reality."[45] From there, Fromm has little difficulty defining socialism as an idea present in the mainstream of many humanitarian movements, beginning with Christian Chiliastic sectarianism and leading up to eighteenth century enlightenment. By nature, socialism therefore stands in opposition not only to monopolistic capitalism, but also to the totalitarian bureaucracy of the Stalin and Krushchev regimes. There is little doubt that Fromm's exegesis holds true for the works of the young Marx. Nevertheless, Marx was a disciple of Feuerbach, and even his early writings already display, in addition to their critique of bourgeois ideology, a clear and unflagging materialism. This aspect, however, gets remarkably short shrift in Fromm's essay. Although the term "philosophical materialism" is mentioned, nowhere is it sufficiently explained. Fromm's concept of Marx as a whole is paradoxical, since Karl Marx ultimately emerges as an *idealistic materialist*, a contradiction in terms.

Fromm could have avoided some of the pitfalls inherent in his study with a less sweeping and generalizing approach. Paul Tillich, Aldous Huxley, Zeno, Seneca and Cicero, as well as many other great thinkers of the Western tradition are thrown into the debate, with little or no effect on clarifying Marx's position. Second, as is customary for Fromm, his terminology lacks concise and clear-cut differentiations. Had he approached his topic in a more detached and disciplined way, the impression of lopsidedness would have been avoided. At the same time, Marx's socio-economic theories could have provided the needed counterweight to balance the over-emphasis on his humanitarianism. Even in his later article, "Marx's Contribution to the Knowledge of Man,"[46] Fromm fails to totally avoid this lack of symmetry. And third, he makes hardly any allowance for the continuity of Marx's development. Chapter 7 of the book makes a lonely attempt to link up the "young" and the "old" Marx in one deep breath. This effort is bound to fail, and the study as a whole ends on a somewhat unconvincing note. Fromm concedes that later Marx's "language became less enthusiastic and eschatological,"[47] but he does not go into the actual transformation of his humanistic and dialectic intellectualism to the full-fledged theory of dialectic materialism. Fromm must have sensed that a well-rounded conclusion was missing, for he tries to provide it in the final chapter with a brief description of Marx as a person. Here, the devoted husband, loving father, and loyal friend come to the forefront. Karl Marx is eulogized as the incarnation of "Western humanity," a pioneer of truth and social justice of "an unquenchable courage and integrity." All this is certainly borne out by biographical studies on Marx. Most likely it was not known to Fromm's larger readership and therefore, though it holds no surprises for scholars, constitutes valuable information for lay readers with a distorted conception of Marx the man. The same applies to the book's several appendices, containing various documents from Marx's own pen and testimonials of some contemporaries. Particularly touching is the "Confession" written by Marx for his daughter Laura.

Despite the criticisms outlined above, this study is to be seen as one of Fromm's central works. It holds a wealth of insights and amply demonstrates its author's honesty and courage. Even its shortcomings are revealing, as it explains in great detail one essential segment of Fromm's own thought: *his* concept of Marx. Moreover, it splendidly achieves its goal of rectifying many prevailing fallacies and misconceptions about this philosopher. In 1979, the volume was already in its twenty-seventh printing. The readership it has reached and is still reaching is, ergo, enormous. Nevertheless, even the most influential single book can provide but a modest counterforce to the massive and practically unanimous effort of educational institutions and mass media in the United States to spread the most grotesque denunciations of Marxism, in the 1980s as much as in the 1960s. It may be noted in passing that Ernst Bloch and Georg Lukács, two other influential thinkers of this century who aimed at a revitalization of Marxism, stood on much common ground with Fromm in their appreciation of Marx. Apart from his political writings, in which he relies heavily on certain Marxist postulates, Fromm returns to Marx one year later in *Beyond the Chains of Illusion.* In this study, he attempts a highly personal synthesis of Freud and Marx.

7

The Heart of Man. Deeper Probings in Characterology and Religion (1964-1970)

During the 1960s, Fromm displayed an increasingly active interest in current politics. He was particularly concerned about the escalation of the Cold War through the Cuba crisis and beyond, and about the insanity of the nuclear arms race in general. His observations, gleaned from both the aggressive policies of the superpowers and from the internal climate in the United States during this period, had an immediate impact on his continued studies in characterology. In his article "War Within Man: A Psychological Inquiry into the Roots of Destructiveness" (1963),[1] he uses for the first time the terms "biophilous" (i.e. life-oriented) and "necrophilous" (i.e. death-oriented) to distinguish between two diametrically opposed tendencies inherent in human nature. This article serves as a stepping-stone for his next large-scale publication, *The Heart of Man*. The book, in turn, must be seen as a linear continuation of Fromm's characterology as discussed in chapters four and five of this study. Indirectly, it builds upon the foundations laid in *Escape From Freedom*, and more directly it presents a logical extension of the theory of human character orientations as developed in *Man for Himself*. At the same time, as Fromm himself stresses in his foreword, *The Heart of Man* is a "negative" counterpart to the popular text *The Art of Loving*. And finally, as his penultimate major statement on the destructive traits in human character, it is not only a forerunner but also an immediate prerequisite to the understanding of his most extensive exploration of this topic in *The Anatomy of Human Destructiveness*, published nine years later. Once again, the organic growth of his thought processes and the close interrelatedness of his oeuvre as a whole come into focus. The volume originally appeared in Ruth Nanda Anshen's series *Religious Perspectives*, in which, among others, works by Karl Barth, Helmut Thielicke, and Paul Tillich had been published previously. In the meantime, it has been re-issued as a paperback bestseller. Comparable in its importance to *Man for Himself* and *Marx's Concept of Man*, this incisive work still deserves a wide readership. More than two decades have passed since it was first published, but it has lost little or none of its freshness and relevance.

Quite in line with his other writings on the subject of characterology, Fromm's tone in discussing negative character traits is much more sober than in his statements on positive character. The latter frequently take on an effusive and quasi-messianic quality which falls flat for those readers who, on the basis of ample historical and societal evidence, remain skeptical about humanistic revivalism. Between the lines of *The Heart of Man*, some traces of the cool and detached scholarly style developed during Fromm's association with Horkheimer's Institute of Social Research remain. Even in this respect alone, the book foreshadows the frequently uncompromising diction of The *Anatomy of Human Destructiveness*.

Again, a three-step-pattern is employed in this investigation. Part one, comprised of chapters one and two, presents a general description of human nature per se. Fromm first enumerates concrete societal evidence for a "present-day mood of violence," as expressed in the continuation of the Cold War, the accumulation of nuclear armament, the rise of juvenile delinquency, and, last but not least, the assassination of John F. Kennedy. Rhetorically, he poses the question whether humanity is headed toward a "new barbarism"--and whether a re-vitalization of humanistic tradition is at all conceivable. The continued modification of Freud's thought, he claims, necessitates a new philosophical approach: that of a "dialectic humanism." This formula is reminiscent of the methodology displayed in *Marx's Concept of Man*. In order to clearly demarcate his own "dialectical" approach from contemporary existentialism, Fromm presses an unnecessary and on the whole both vicious and ignorant attack against Sartre and Heidegger, the proponents at that time of existentialist philosophy.[2] (In many ways, his own thinking *is* in fact related to existentialism. Guyton B. Hammond correctly states that it "is no violation of Fromm's position, then to include him within the existentialism movement. . . ."[3] Fromm did not, however, recognize these affinities himself.) Having thus dispensed with any competitive philosophies and duly emphasized the uniqueness of his own viewpoint, he zeroes in on the fundamental question of this study: whether the Hobbesian statement on humanity's wolf-to-wolf relationship (*homo homini lupus*) might be a truthful description of human nature.

Western history, Fromm ventures, has been a series of man-made disasters, beginning with the Renaissance. The present state of "moral bankruptcy" originated with World War I and continued through the regimes of Hitler and Stalin up to the bombings of Coventry and Hiroshima. Responsibility for this catastrophic decline in human values lies not with the extraordinary villain or sadist as such, but with the *ordinary human being* imbued with extraordinary power. Which part of human nature must then be held responsible for the individual's moral degeneration and destructiveness? Fromm names three distinct drives: "love of death, malignant narcissism, and symbiotic-incestuous fixation."[4] If all three of these phenomena are sufficiently strong within a given character, they will join forces to form the "syndrome of decay," i.e. the necrophilous orientation which causes individuals to wreak destruction purely for its own sake. Standing in opposition to this pathological condition, the "syndrome of growth," i.e. the biophilous character orientation, has love for life as its main characteristic. In contrast to the narcissist, the biophilous character feels love for *all* fellow human beings and may therefore achieve independence, i.e. freedom from incestuous fixations. This basic description of the two diametrically opposed character orientations is followed by a lengthy digression on non-pathological types of violent behavior. Fromm mentions the six varieties of playful, reactive, revengeful, compensatory (i.e. violence as an expression of the feeling of impotence), sadistic, and primitive (i.e. tribal "blood thirst" etc.) violence. His list could be augmented ad libitum. Modern behaviorists and researchers in the tradition of Konrad Lorenz would undoubtedly take issue with his description of comparatively "sane" violence. For the purposes of this study, the point is moot.

Part two--the book's main body--presents in three chapters a systematic characterology of the necrophilous orientation. An incident from the Spanish Civil War serves as a basic illustration. Since it is in fact highly illuminative, it may be briefly recounted. General Millán Astray, who had already been crippled in combat, delivered a speech at the University of Salamanca in 1936, and concluded his peroration with the paradoxical motto "Viva la muerte!" (Long live death!). Miguel de Unamuno, the splendid writer and a member of the "Generation of 98," the University's rector at that time, denounced this evocation as repugnant and necrophilous. The Fascists promptly put him under house arrest. In Fromm's customary peripatetic and often circumlocutory approach to his various topics, this passage stands out for once as a well-chosen introduction. Fromm then develops the concept of necrophilia--not in the meaning of a sexual deviation, but as a character orientation toward death, the anorganic, and all things lifeless--working from Freud's anal-sadistic character and the "death instinct" he described in great detail as part of the human psyche. Fromm modifies Freud's ideas considerably, describing necrophilia as a pathological phenomenon, and *not* as an intrinsic part of human psychological structure.

Three prominent examples of necrophilous personalities are provided, namely Hitler, Stalin, and--surprisingly enough--C.G. Jung. As opposed to the two dictators, however, Jung was apparently able to "balance" his necrophilous orientation through creativity, brilliant insights into the human psyche, and his vocation, which was to cure the ill. He did not engage in destruction. Hitler, on the other hand, is used frequently throughout the book to illustrate the various preconditions responsible for the formation of necrophilous personalities. It should be pointed out, however, that Fromm's analysis of the leader of the National Socialist movement remains sketchy and tentative as yet. To cite only one example: he refers to an unconfirmed report from World War I claiming that Hitler, at the sight of a decayed corpse, fell into a trance-like state on the battlefield, and was unable to avert his gaze. This is definitely not incriminating evidence, as many shell-shocked soldiers reacted in similar ways to comparable situations. Even if one has never directly experienced the utterly senseless mutilation of humans in war, the deep shock felt by eyewitnesses has been described in reports, documentation, and literary texts ad nauseam. One might even try to refute Fromm's theory from the standpoint that--provided the report is basically true--Hitler's reaction must rather be considered "normal," and not at all necrophilous, as it displayed nothing of the *indifference* to suffering typical for this particular character orientation. At any rate, it was only in *The Anatomy of Human Destructiveness* that Fromm was able to present a full-fledged character analysis of Adolf Hitler.[5] And even there, as in *The Heart of Man*, some doubt must linger in the reader's mind regarding Fromm's claim that the Führer's self-orchestrated *Götterdämmerung* and suicide at the collapse of the Third Reich were in fact *logical* consequences of his character structure. They may just as well be seen as the deeds of a desperate man who had lost all sense of reality and, like a cornered rat, did away with himself while trying to pull a whole nation with him into the abyss.

Also mentioned here, though much too briefly, is Adolf Eichmann, the unemotional engineer of organized genocide. Hannah Arendt, another great humanist and influential thinker of our time, has studied the phenomenon of Eichmann in great depth and engaged in controversial exchange on this subject with Gershom Scholem.[6] Surprisingly, Fromm does not refer to the sensational Eichmann trial in 1961 and to its international aftershocks. Indeed, he ignores Arendt, who arrives at many insights on totalitarianism similar to his own. Instead, he delves into the physiognomic and

phenotypical aspects of necrophilia. The personality he describes
has dead-looking skin, and an unpleasant facial expression as if in-
haling a "bad odor." Orderliness and pedantry are part of this basic
outlook on life. Especially the latter characteristics are reminiscent
of the "hoarding" orientation described in *Man for Himself* and analyzed in chapter five of this study.

Everyone familiar with the theory of physiognomics, which originated in its more modern incarnations with Johann Kaspar
Lavater's *Physiognomische Fragmente zur Beförderung der Men-
schenkenntnis und Menschenliebe* (1775/78; *Physiognomic Frag-
ments for the Betterment of Knowledge of Humans and Philanthropy*) and which ultimately led to such bizarre hybrids as the
Nazis' racist physiognomic "science," will not be overly impressed
by these exterior criteria for the diagnosis of necrophilia. In truth,
some of a person's facial characteristics may well betray the inner
self. Equally, physiognomic appearances may also be patently deceptive. The reader should recall the beaming Hitler, surrounded
by blondhaired youngsters and very much the good uncle in appearance. Many press photographs have captured this well-
cultivated image. Stalin, who as a person gave the deceptive impression of being stolid, friendly, and even-tempered, was
frivolously called "Uncle Joe" in the supposedly secret code used in
communications between Churchill and Roosevelt. The Western
leaders must surely have had an inkling that appearances were
misleading, and that their ally was anything but the good-natured
Georgian peasant he pretended to be. Among present-day politicians and world leaders, the ready smile often betrays little or
nothing of the paranoia, aggressions, and potentially necrophilous
traits revealed by actions. These critical remarks must suffice for
the moment to relativize Fromm's physiognomic theory. The subject will be treated later in more detail.

Fromm's description of the biophilous orientation is largely a reiteration of the productive character outlined in *Man for Himself*,
and in many ways a condensation of the gist of *The Art of Loving*.
Following the example and the teachings of Albert Schweitzer, one
of this century's most outstanding philanthropists, he relates bio-

philia to a humanistic ethical foundation. On this basis, the biophilous character is capable of preserving life, of creativity, and
"wondering". The quasi-religious experience of wondering was first
described in *Psychoanalysis and Religion*[7] and is now expanded in
The Heart of Man. The formula "Good is all that serves life; evil is
all that serves death"[8] is re-stated in this context. It runs like a
leitmotif through Fromm's writing and might be called the credo of
his vitalistic ethical concept in a nutshell. Both necrophilous and
biophilous orientations are derivatives of Freud's life instinct
(which is sometimes also called the principle of *Eros*), and of his
death instinct[9] (this has been labelled with the Greek word
Thanatos [=death], although not by Freud himself.) The dialectic
opposition of the two basic human instincts--which Freud never
unequivocally resolved--must be seen, according to Fromm, as the
"most fundamental contradiction which exists in man." In the final
analysis, it reflects the basic dichotomy of human existence per se:
the unbridgeable gap between life and death.

Interestingly enough, Fromm's religious background and mystical tendencies notwithstanding, he demonstrates at this point in his
essay how deeply his thinking is committed to materialism. He
concedes, as he has in all of his prior writings on the subject, that
humans are constantly threatened by their awareness of death.
Life and death are, by definition, mutually irreconcilable. Ludwig
Feuerbach, the first modern materialist thinker, called death "the
one great rift in creation". This is unambiguous in meaning: there
is everything on this side of the rift, and nothing on the other. Ontologically speaking, there is only life and the absence of life in materialistic philosophy. A third alternative in form of a life hereafter
is not provided. This *awareness* of death, says Fromm, must be distinguished from a *drive* toward death. Whereas the former is a
constituent of human nature, the latter must be recognized as a
"malignant" phenomenon and therefore be relegated to the area of
psychopathology. The life instinct consequently is seen as the
"primary potentiality in man; the death instinct a secondary potentiality."[10] From the viewpoint of materialist philosophy, it is a foregone conclusion that physical life must be preserved at all costs.

Conversely, the willful destruction of this one and only property
given to a human being must be regarded as a philosophical paradox, and, from a psychiatric viewpoint, insane. In light of Fromm's
persistent emphasis on the value of life per se, one can't help but
speculate on his actual indebtedness to Feuerbach's thought. Beyond this central notion, other parallels in both thinkers' works
meet the eye, such as the uniqueness of every living organism, and
the particular stress on each species' primary source of fulfillment
(i.e. productivity, creativity etc.). Characteristically, Fromm does
not often readily reveal his sources. There are only a few instances
in the whole of his oeuvre where Feuerbach is even mentioned in
passing. This does not mean, however, that certain elements of this
thought have not been absorbed and re-shaped in Fromm's work.

When Fromm modifies Freud's empirical and detached approach by relegating the death instinct to the clinical sphere, he argues from a materialistic standpoint. He does not, however, con-
fine himself to the mere *description* of a syndrome. To the contrary, he leaves little doubt in his reader's mind that he considers
the necrophilous orientation not only a mental illness, but also the
expression of something "evil." The ensuing discussion of the
necrophilia syndrome becomes bifurcated: Fromm amalgamates a
psychoanalytic approach with a simultaneous *ethical* evaluation of
the phenomenon. As before in his seminal study *Man for Himself*,
he demonstrates that psychoanalysis and ethics, at least in his
opinion, can not be plausibly separated.

Ethical and analytical considerations are, by definition, located
on different epistemological plateaus. But for Fromm they are but
individual parts of the same totality: the human self. Many a psy-
chotherapist would frown at this holistic conception. If mental illness is stigmatized a priori by means of moral and/or ethical condemnation, it can hardly be treated effectively. In fact, the moral
stance characteristic for Fromm's thinking as a whole--and equally
typical for his former colleagues of the Institute of Social Research,
particularly Horkheimer and Adorno--becomes for once, for the
purposes of clinical therapy, a liability rather than an asset. Mental
illness has been virtually bedeviled throughout the centuries. Pa-

tients have been tortured or burned on the stake in order to "cure" them or exorcise the devils that possessed them. Only modern psychoanalysis and psychiatry, namely researchers of Freud's and Kraepelin's stature, finally managed to do away with the age-old equation of illness and evil. They established an empirical framework for diagnosis and therapy, admittedly based on speculation, but nevertheless offering a working foundation for the scientific exploration of mental illness. Fromm, or so it seems, reinstates the stigmatization of disease through the back door of his two-pronged approach to the pathological *and* the ethical dimensions of necrophilia. The results of his description of necrophilia remain therefore, from a strictly clinical point of view, questionable. Psychiatric authorities like Karl Jaspers[11] and Nikolaus Petrilowitsch[12] have described similar phenomena within a more objective and scientific framework. Even if the exact distinction between psychiatric methodology and Fromm's unique application of Critical Theory is not the issue of this analysis of *The Heart of Man*, a certain caveat for the more scientifically oriented reader appears to be in order.

After his detailed description of both the necrophilous and biophilous character orientations, Fromm turns to the all-important question: what particular factors might be responsible for the formation of these radically divergent orientations? It need not be emphasized that both types (cf. the typology of nonproductive orientations in *Man for Himself*) are rarely encountered in "pure" forms. Actual human beings usually display a predominance of either necrophilia or biophilia within a blended character structure. By tackling this question of their origins in society and socialization, Fromm takes up the task he left unfinished in *Man for Himself*. He must have felt that he had, in this study published seventeen years earlier, left his reader somewhat in limbo, particularly with regard to the causalities at work in character formation and their potential remedy. The following discourse then demonstrates both the continuity of his thought, and the keen observation he had devoted in the meantime to the societal panorama as a whole.

For the development of a predominantly *biophilous* character orientation, three essential preconditions are named. But prior to their analysis, Fromm rightly stresses the eminent importance of child-rearing as a guiding foundation for *all* future developments of the adolescent and the adult. The family is the primary and most essential factor in socialization. Warmth, affection and the absence of fears and threats are vital for the upbringing of a biophilous personality. One might add, from today's viewpoint, that most authoritarian structures have long since crumbled, at least in the typical American family setting. They have been replaced, however, by a potentially much more dangerous attitude: utter indifference. Any moderately astute observer of average family life in the United States in the 1980s will readily reach the conclusion that acute repression has frequently given way to total laissez-faire; that loving, emotional warmth and care have been ousted by overall indifference, both on the parents' and the childrens' parts. One can hardly be astonished if this emotional depletion of the family cell eventually results in the emergence of a new generation of absolutely self-centered barbarians. Fromm gave this subject considerable thought, but the socio-historical changes of the past two decades, it appears, lend his theory of biophilous child-rearing the flair of the noble, but obsolete vision.

Within the societal context as a whole, three factors are deemed conducive to the formation of biophilia as a character trait. 1. Economic scarcity has to be replaced by an *abundance* of the goods necessary to sustain physical life. 2. Injustice must be abolished in favor of a prevailing order of social *justice*. Fromm does not refer to the given jurisdictional system. He addresses rather the question of the exploitation of one social class by another and its logical consequence, the imposition of "conditions on it [the exploited class] which do not permit the unfolding of a rich and dignified life. . . ."[13] 3. The third condition is already known to the reader from both *Escape from Freedom* and *Man for Himself*: *freedom*. Once again, the concept of freedom is two-fold. It includes both the abolition of political oppression and the freedom for the individual to become engaged in a creative and fulfilling life. "Freedom from" must go hand in hand with "freedom to." Much of this argumentation is also taken from *The Sane Society* and *The Art of Loving*, and will be re-examined from a different angle in chapters eight and nine below. Suffice it to say at this point that the three-step pattern outlined above is reminiscent of the optimistic pre-enlightenment utopian tradition in the vein of Plato, Thomas Morus (*Utopia* [1516]), the socialist Tommaso Campanella (*The City of the Sun* [1623]), and Francis Bacon (*New Atlantis* [1660]). More modern writers in the dystopian--i.e. the "negative" utopian--tradition, such as Aldous Huxley, George Orwell, and Evgenij Zamiatin, have been much more skeptical in their dismal visions of humanity's possible future organization.

And indeed, social reality in the 1980s is not apt to generate much hope for the biophilous orientation in either capitalist or socialist systems. In the former, abundance certainly prevails for the few extremely rich and for the broader, more affluent upper-middle classes. Has material affluence been instrumental in instilling a life-oriented mentality? Certainly not in many individuals. To the contrary, material possessions have taken on an ever-increasing autonomous value, to the point where there is little room left for humanistic values. In fact, financial wealth and the pursuit of an ever greater accumulation of goods frequently tend to cripple human emotions. The second condition, social justice in form of a more or less even distribution of finances and commodities, has not been realized in most capitalist nations, especially not in the United States. There are millions of people untouched by the nation's abundance. Many are starving and de facto brutally exploited by social conditions on which they have little or no influence. As for the third condition, capitalist societies apparently fare much better in terms of "freedom from" actual reglementation and the violation of human rights than do their socialist counterparts. They are not in better shape, however, regarding their "freedom to." Conformism, the ever-present influence of the mass media, and an almighty network of market dictates have reduced many individuals to "automaton conformity" as described in *Escape from Freedom*. The "marketing orientation" (vide *Man for Himself*) prevails on the entire front. There seems little hope indeed for the successful development of biophilous orientations, at least in any significant numbers relative to the given population.

Turning to the factors responsible for the formation of the *necrophilous* character, Fromm discusses briefly but lucidly the civilizational conditions prevalent in European and North American industrialized nations. A new personality type has been created there which may be called "the organization man," "the automaton man," or "homo consumens." This typology is clearly reminiscent, once more, of the nonproductive orientations detailed in *Man for Himself*. Society as a whole demands an almost exclusive reliance on and relatedness to things. Violence is not only a sanctioned political tool, it is also a constant ingredient in the media's presentation of both information and entertainment. Violence, so to speak, has become part of our lives, and is thus not only unquestioningly accepted, but actually enjoyed--at least vicariously--by millions. Entertainment programs in the visual media, as well as in pop music designed specifically for adolescents, abound with the most grotesque expressions of violence. Brutality seems to have become the one and only effective means for many to achieve their "kicks." Needless to say, a general numbing of the senses and loss of an actual grasp of the consequences of *real* violence is the end result of this development.

The following brief summary of these socio-psychological factors deserves to be quoted verbatim:

> Briefly then, intellectualization, quantification, abstractification, bureaucratization, and reification--the very characteristics of modern industrial society, when applied to people rather than to things, are not the principles of life but those of mechanics. People living in such a system become indifferent to life and even attracted to death.[14]

Individual and social narcissism are necessary consequences of these societal deficiencies. The narcissistic person is infatuated with himself/herself and incapable of truly relating to others. Individuals who suffer from narcissism regard themselves as the center of the universe. Rational judgment is invariably overruled in their minds by egotism and prejudice. Criticism, even constructive advice, is anathema to the narcissistic character. (It is interesting to note that in the past decade or so, the term "critical," which is basically free of value judgment, has taken on ostensibly negative or pejorative connotations in colloquial American usage. To call someone "critical" ipso facto seems to imply that this person is an incurable malcontent and can not be satisfied even by the utmost effort.) Narcissism is definitely a factor in the constant process of re-defining everyday language. Fromm cites various historical examples for this syndrome, from Caligula and Nero to Stalin and Hitler, which are certainly illustrative. Much more relevant, though, for modern societal diagnosis is the reaction of the average person to a "critical" remark.

This excursion leads directly to the ensuing discussion of "social narcissism," a phenomenon to which Fromm had given considerable thought already in the 1930s (cf. his field study *The Working Class in Weimar Germany*), even if the term itself is not yet mentioned in the earlier works. Narcissistic cathexis--i.e. the libidinal energy present in a group--is frequently responsible for large-scale aggressions displayed by a given society. Hitler's Germany with its racist hysteria leading to the holocaust comes to mind. The same mechanisms are at work in any society where racism or the oppression of certain groups are virulent. In addition to the racial discrimination still prevalent in the United States, Fromm cites fanatical Western anti-communism--an extremely dangerous and irrational syndrome. With regard to the actual pathology of group narcissism, the roots are to be found, analogously to individual narcissism, in the absence of objectivity and sound rational judgment. An example is supplied here in form of the "poor" whites' prejudice against Negroes, which is nothing more than the attempt of one underprivileged group to achieve a false sense of superiority by discriminating against an even less privileged "minority." Surely, the example is not altogether well-chosen, as it fails to explain racism and sexual discrimination exercised by the wealthier classes, where its occurrence is certainly no less frequent. In general, Fromm does not fully come to grips with the pathological causalities of collective narcissism, at least not through his actual documentation. He is correct, however, in the conclusion that narcissistic groups are eager to identify themselves with pre-fabricated idols and, particularly, with political leaders. Personalities who are extremely narcissistic in their own character orientation are consequently best equipped to fill the needs of a nation afflicted by the same syndrome. In brief: "...there are always gifted half-psychotics at hand to satisfy the demands of a narcissistic mass."[15] The political apparatus in the United States has long recognized this narcissistic drive for identification of the voting public with their leaders. Political programs, rational arguments, and reasonable promises for a change of course therefore are hardly the issue in the modern political arena. Since the 1960s, especially in the presidential campaigns, images have been created for the purpose of mass identification and more or less successfully sold to the public. An election hinges not on the candidates' *rational* alternatives and clear programmatic differences, but rather on their ability to spend money for mass-dispersion of an identifiable *image*. A striking example for the validity of Fromm's thesis is provided by the 1984 presidential elections. Political action committees (PACS) spent the staggering sum of $15.3 million for Ronald Reagan, as opposed to a pitiful $621,000 for Walter Mondale. The outcome of this election amply demonstrates that politics, in a vastly narcissistic societal environment, have become a commodity for sale.

If Fromm does not yet manage to pinpoint the pathology of group narcissism (an issue he will re-examine in later writings), he at least accurately describes its symptoms. Seen as a whole, his theory of individual and collective character formation--the centerpiece of his entire work, as well as the core of *The Heart of Man*--displays a wealth of brilliant insights and cogent reasoning. It takes a prominent place in the intellectual history of this century. Even one of his more fervent critics, John H. Schaar, concedes that it must be regarded as "an excellent instrument of description and analysis. This part of his work represents one of the most successful of all attempts to bridge different levels of analysis and combine different styles of approach to social problems."[16] Again, there can be no question with regard to the validity of Fromm's diagnostic approach to characterology. He analyzes the illness of human destructiveness with the utmost incisiveness. What about the cure?

Narcissistic tendencies, as far as they are present in the character structure of individuals and nations, might be employed for a more constructive end. Fromm proposes that the *object* of these fixations could be changed. If *all* of humanity became the object of group narcissism, instead of a given race, nation, or political system, the situation would change drastically. Aggressive tendencies inherent in narcissistic group behavior could be eliminated and replaced by a supra-national, all-encompassing productive fixation of the human species on its own potentialities. In this case, however, narcissism as such would simply cease to exist. It would be replaced by humanism, just as "irrational" authority would give way to "rational" teachings. Fromm's argument is therefore not a valid one: his solution rests on a contradiction in terms. Moreover, the very presence of narcissism would prevent such a change in libidinous fixation. Similarly, his suggestion that the educational systems "of all countries" should stress the achievements of humanity as such, instead of the greatness and glory of one particular country, is utopian at best. Once more, it is narcissism or, in more popular terminology, rampant patriotism that precludes such a fundamental change in educational policies, desirable as it might be. Fromm must surely have been aware of the deficiencies in public education in the United States even during the 1960s, and of the parochialism of the information dispensed in the classroom. Things have not changed for the better in the meantime. Patriotism, conformity, and an early adjustment to mindless consumerism rank high on the priority lists of many curricula and educators. Fromm sees an effective remedy for collective narcissism in "furthering critical thought, objectivity, acceptance of reality, and a concept of truth which is subject to no fiat and is valid for every conceivable group."[17] This is certainly true, but utterly unrealistic under the given circumstances. In recent years, various groups on the state and national level, under the flag of the "moral majority" and the leadership of single-minded conservatism, have revived the practice of censorship in school libraries throughout the United States. Phyllis Schlafly, one of the strongest opponents of sexual equality in this country, urges parents to boycott curricula stressing an egalitarian view of the genders. These are only two examples of the *actual* reactions of a narcissistic society to the free dissemination of unorthodox, non-conforming, or controversial thought. Narcissism, on an individual or on a collective basis, does not cure itself voluntarily. To the contrary, it is self-propelling to a great extent, and only a severe shock may halt it in its tracks. Those European countries which, through extreme forms of group narcissism, have participated in genocide and mass destruction during the Second World War, have been effectively shocked into awareness by the catastrophical consequences of their actions. Blind and militant patriotism (as distinct from the perfectly natural love for one's own homeland) has been one of the components in the narcissistic behavioral pattern of both Eastern and Western European nations responsible for the military confrontations of the past. This phenomenon is rarely encountered any more in Europe, as humanity may have learned at least *one* lesson in the shambles of utter defeat.

In chapter five of *The Heart of Man*, Fromm turns to a brief examination of symbiotic-incestuous fixations, the third condition responsible for a necrophilous character orientation. He presents a modification of Freud's theory that children are sexually fixated on the parent of the opposite gender. For Fromm, "incestuous symbiosis" may be totally devoid of sexual connotations. It does, however, include extreme dependency on the "mothering person," to use a term coined by H.S. Sullivan. This surrogate "mother" can be present in form of blood relations, family, tribe, or any such group. Inability to free oneself from this self-inflicted bondage will render an individual helpless. The pathology of "incestuous ties" then develops. It must be remarked that the term "incestuous fixation" as such is not well-chosen. In his attempt to preserve at all costs one of Freud's methodological pillars (if only as a terminological device), Fromm loses track of his own arguments. Moreover, he manages to confuse his reader. The syndrome he attempts to describe has little or nothing to do with childhood sexuality. Rather, it is a particular variation on stunted growth, i.e. the reluctance of an individual to grow up and assume responsibility for the structure of her/his own life. In comparison to narcissism, which primarily precludes *intellectual* maturation, the so-called incestuous fixation inhibits *emotional* independence. Once more, as was the case in his analysis of narcissism, the actual pathology of this condition is not fully clarified. Fromm will return to it in more detail in *The Anatomy of Human Destructiveness*. But even there, this relic of his Freudian training is not convincingly integrated in the whole of his negative characterology.

As far as *The Heart of Man* is concerned, it must be noted that after his previous explorations of the human character orientation in *Escape from Freedom* and, more important, in *Man for Himself*, Fromm attempts for the first time to relate the "positive" (=biophilous) and the "negative" (=necrophilous) character traits to each other and to a common center. His designation for the mutual ground held by both orientations in their incipient stages is the "normal." Surprisingly enough, no definition of this postulated norm is supplied.

In the following graph, the development of both orientations is illustrated:[18]

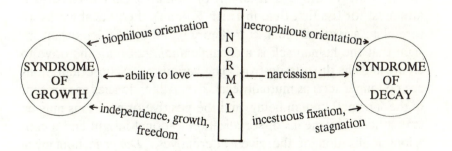

For the purpose of summarizing the foregoing discussion of the societal causalities involved in character formation, the illustration below may be useful:

CHILD-REARING	+	SOCIAL CONDITIONS	=	CHARACTER ORIENTATION	→	RESULT

Love, warmth, affection, absence of fear and threats	abundance of goods social justice freedom (from oppression and to create)	preserving, creative, loving, capable of "wondering" = x-experience	B I O P H I L I A
oppression irrational authority, fear	alienation, reification, exploitation, bureaucratization, relatedness to things, narcissism	love of death and things, malignant narcissism, symbiotic-incestuous fixation	N E C R O P H I L I A

Much of the characterology presented in this study is yet in an experimental stage. Nevertheless, the book is certainly not a mere "rough draft" of the later *Anatomy of Human Destructiveness* as it attempts, for the first time in Erich Fromm's theoretical works, to formulate a *synthetic* character theory based on the important insight that the human self is a dynamic *duality* of both the drive to create and the drive to destroy. The various character orientations are no longer seen as mutually exclusive. All tendencies are present in the "normal" human being, and the positive orientations may be strengthened by means of socialization, rational insight and a conscious realization of the given alternatives. *Dialectic* humanism therefore replaces the more static descriptions of human characterology which preceded *The Heart of Man*.

The book's third part is fittingly devoted to the important distinction between freedom, determinism, and "alternativism." The key to understanding Fromm's dialectical approach to characterology lies in the word *alternativism*. He recognizes human nature as a conglomerate of contradictory, even diametrically opposed, elements: the instinctual equipment and the powers of reason and awareness. Only the human self, as opposed to all other biological species, is able to transcend the strictures of instinct. Only human consciousness can become *"life aware of itself."*[19] Not the inherent dichotomies in human nature and the resulting variety of character orientations, says Fromm, are the "essence" of human existence. That essence is located rather in the dynamic *conflict* between those dichotomies. Therefore, the history of humanity is propelled by the dialectic interaction of two conflicting forces: the drive toward life and the disposition toward death. The ultimate decision resolving this conflict lies both in the individual and the societal forces instrumental in character formation.

At this point, Fromm engages in an interesting distinction between the *essence* and the *goal* of human nature. If the essence is indeed life's awareness of itself, which in turn could constitute the "normal" self, then the maturation of the human character toward its natural goal--the biophilous orientation--would be a foregone conclusion. Moreover, this essence of human nature might even be accessible to scientific research, whereas the respective goals of its development would depend exclusively on external, i.e. cultural and socio-economic factors. A change in the extrinsic forces at work would automatically alter the goal of human nature. This intriguing concept, as Hammond observes,[20] is not pursued in *The Heart of Man*. Fromm does return to it, however, in *To Have or to Be?*, albeit in somewhat modified form. In the earlier study, he is still primarily interested in the dialectic opposition of biophilous and necrophilous forces within the human self and in a synthetic resolution of this conflict.

One possible resolution of this dialectic process lies, as Fromm puts it, in the "regressive" answer. Regressive orientation leads the individual into dependency and irrationality. If regressive trends are encountered in the majority or the whole of a given society, "we have the picture of a *folie à millions*"[21] or a narcissistic group orientation. Fromm does not answer the question *how* these regressive impulses should be prevented from taking over the reins of individual or collective character. He carefully avoids mentioning the possibilities of either repression or sublimation, and it may well be true that he "as yet has no final answer to the question of the relation between regressive impulses and man's basic nature. . . ."[22] On the other hand, he postulates, a "progressive" resolution is equally feasible. Progressive orientation equals the biophilous character. The ultimate force which tips the scales one way or the other is freedom of choice.

In order to exercise that freedom, humans must first become aware of the opposing tendencies within their own nature. They must, in other words, realize their own powers of *awareness* and recognize the alternatives at their disposal. Awareness, in Fromm's definition, is multi-faceted. The concept includes *ethical* as well as *socio-psychological* and *rational* elements. Humans must therefore learn to distinguish between "good" and "evil" and to recognize the appropriate means for achieving a particular end. Equally important, they must gain insight into their own motivations, which are frequently located in the subconscious. Awareness must be tied to realistic alternatives and the consequences of a given choice. And finally, awareness must be accompanied by the will to act and the necessary self-discipline for successful completion of goals. Many choices are, by definition, mutually exclusive. Fromm insists, for example, that it is impossible to subscribe to Cold War, a "paranoid hate mentality" involving determined nuclear armament, and, at the same time, to truly want to avert eventual destruction of the human race.

Alternativism takes a middle road between freedom on the one hand and determinism on the other. Both factors are vital for the development of human and societal character organization, but only their dialectical interplay--alternativism--will lead to the full realization of human potential. To choose the regressive answer, according to Fromm, is tantamount to tragic failure: "*Evil is man's loss of himself in the tragic attempt to escape the burden of his humanity.*"[23] The choice between a life-oriented or a death-oriented mode of existence rests ultimately upon each individual. With this direct appeal to the reader, the book reaches an impressive conclusion. Don Hausdorff correctly calls it "a grim counterpoint to *The Art of Loving*."[24] But it is much more than that. *The Heart of Man*, as a sub-total of Fromm's negative characterology, provides at the same time the theoretical foundation for his political and popular writings. It should be read carefully by all serious students of Fromm's thinking, and it certainly still deserves more than the rather perfunctory attention it has received so far in research.

Between 1959 and 1969, Fromm directed a field study in a small, unnamed Mexican village on the various character orientations described in *Man for Himself* and, to a certain extent, in *The Heart of Man*. The results of this study were published in 1970 under the title *Social Character in a Mexican Village*, co-authored by Michael Maccoby. In addition to Maccoby, Fromm's co-director in the project, the research team included numerous test psychologists, the anthropologists Lola Romanucci Schwartz and Theodore Schwartz, as well as various scholars in neighboring disciplines. The study took considerable time and effort and is extremely carefully done. In many respects, it bears out Fromm's theoretical characterology. Especially the greater aspect of socialization is given extensive consideration, both in the empirical framework of the various questionnaires and in their interpretation. Socio-economic and cultural variables appear to have a direct bearing on the formation of positive and negative character orientations. Regarding the distinction between productive and nonproductive traits and their causal relationship to given societal backgrounds, this study is a very revealing document. Its relevance within the greater context of Fromm's work is, nevertheless, somewhat limited. As practically all of his work on characterology is based on the empirical evidence provided by the United States and, in particular, the densely populated industrial centers of the East, crucial cultural/civilizational elements, especially the influence of the mass media, are totally lacking in the context of the Mexican village.

This particular proving ground for his characterological theory, therefore, must be seen as a problematic choice.

Erich Fromm's final work on religion, *You Shall be as Gods*, is a linear development of his concept of *alternativism* as presented two years earlier in *The Heart of Man*. In this text, the psychological factors involved in character development are not directly addressed. Instead, the author returns to the realm of religious experience and offers what is called "a radical interpretation of the Old Testament and its tradition." Definitely, the stress must lie on the word *radical*, as Fromm's approach, according to his own proclaimed atheism, is anything but conventional, much less orthodox. In his opinion, the Old Testament is a revolutionary document testifying to humanity's age-old quest for an a-authoritarian, anthropocentric conception of God. Its central theme should be seen as: "the liberation of man from the incestuous ties to blood and soil, from the submission to idols, from slavery, from powerful masters, to freedom for the individual, for the nation, and for all of mankind."[25] Radical humanism--a term intricately related to the "dialectic" humanism of *The Heart of Man*--must be applied to our exegesis of the scriptures. Fromm postulates that all elements of his holistic concept of human nature are already present in the Old Testament: the "oneness" of all humanity; human beings' capability to fully develop their inner potential and thus progress toward inner harmony and exterior peace. Human independence may be attained by the abolition of fictions and illusions. At the end, there must be total awareness of reality. All this can be achieved only through an alternativistic approach to oneself, to life, and to society.

Incidentally, the "ungainly"[26] term "alternativism" has, within the two decades since the book's publication, found many adherents. In Western Europe, alternative lifestyles have become a viable mode of human existence. They do *not* derive their raison d'être from primitive renunciation of society's demands and rules. Alternative life is therefore not comparable to its American pseudo-equivalent (i.e. "dropping out").   To the contrary, *constructive* alternatives to conformism, consumerism, and the progressive ruin

of a natural habitat through rampant industrial pollution have been
formulated and are dynamic forces within a pluralistic societal
panorama. At least a small part of this change in human consciousness may well be due to the reception of Fromm's works and
the writings of other progressive, ecology-conscious authors.

Alternativism, developed within the context of this study in its
application to faith and religion, means humanity's gradual exodus
from bondage to a tyrannical father-figure: the God of the initial
days of creation who expelled Adam and Eve from the Garden of
Eden for a meaningless act of disobedience. Later stages include a
"covenant" between God and humanity, i.e. a rational relationship
based on mutual respect, and, finally, the negative theology of
Moses Maimonides. The latter, as Fromm does not fail to point
out, is directly related to Master Eckhart's cryptic conception of
the Godhead, an unfathomable being whose very essence becomes
apparent only through its presence. God, for Eckhart and to a certain extent also for Maimonides, remains nameless, and can not be
found through an active search effort. Only if one foregoes the
idea of a deliberate quest for God may God be found.[27] To use a
popular example, mysticism may in some ways be compared to the
search for the Holy Grail, as described in many medieval texts.
Those who engage in the arduous search for the sake of find-
ing--i.e. possessing--the Grail will never reach its location. Conversely, only the seeker who purges his soul through radical
self-examination, and whose travail is not motivated by greed for its
goal, will enter the kingdom of the Grail. Wolfram von Eschen-
bach's novel *Parzival* is the finest realization of this theme in medieval literature. Richard Wagner set it to music to illustrate the
late romantic notion that the *quest*, and not the *capture*, is the most
sublime act in human life.

Moses Maimonides, the twelfth-century scholar and one of the
most outstanding Jewish philosophers in history, supplies the following definition of the nature of God:

> Hence it is clear that He has no positive attribute whatever. The negative at-
> tributes, however, are those which are necessary to direct the minds to the

truths which we must believe concerning God; for, on the one hand, they do not imply any plurality, and, on the other, they convey to man the highest possible knowledge of God.[28]

It is not difficult to relate this "negative" theology to Fromm's atheist mysticism as outlined in *Psychoanalysis and Religion*, or to his essay *Zen Buddhism and Psychoanalysis*. In Maimonides, he finds a third alternate answer to his life-long struggle for a religion without a defineable deity. Nontheistic religious experience, the feeling he now terms the "x-experience," is the focal point of this study. He concedes that this experience is not only indispensable for human nature, it also facilitates human growth: the transcendence of irrational and narcissistic bondage, as well as the incessant striving for love and reason. This experience--the reader will recall that it appears as the capacity to "wonder" in Fromm's earlier writings--is humanity's ultimate fortress against mental and emotional impoverishment. The x-experience is an effective bulwark against alienation and reification of human existence.

It is interesting to note that toward the end of his study, Fromm returns to the orthodox Jewish understanding of the Sabbath. He had explored the ritualistic aspects and their societal ramifications in his first published article, "Der Sabbath," already in 1927.[29] Now, almost forty years later, he offers a quasi-utopian interpretation of this institution in Jewish dogma. The Sabbath, he ventures, symbolizes a state of unity and harmony between humanity and nature, as well as between human beings. Humanity refrains from work on this day, and therefore withholds itself from the process of constant change in nature and society. Time, consequently, is suspended for one day of the week, and the human self enjoys a state of timelessness reminiscent of a primal oneness with nature. In *The Heart of Man*, alternativism is described as a dialectic synthesis of both determinism and voluntarism. It enables humanity, through a *conditional* exercise of freedom, to grow and to create. Now, in his exploration of the Sabbath in *You Shall be as Gods*, Fromm for once postulates an *unconditional* concept of freedom. Only during the rites of the Sabbath can humanity be totally freed

of the duty to act and participate productively in the socio-historical process. And only the Sabbath grants a temporary
refuge from the individual's function in the greater whole of society.

This treatise on the Sabbath is the only passage in all of Fromm's
works in which the conflict between messianic teleology and social
theory is not somehow reconciled. Critical Theory in this specific
application --which requires rational thought and action on the basis of a productive, biophilous character orientation--and the
mythic longing for primeval harmony beyond socio-historical stringencies stand in direct opposition to each other. Clearly, this exis-
tential dichotomy, i.e. the irretrievably lost oneness of humanity
and nature, is the final realization in Fromm's *personal* struggle for
a non-theistic religion, a transcendental humanism which does not
need the crutches of organized religion and naive imagery. And it
is not without particular significance that his research in the realm
of religion at the very end describes a full circle, returning to its
starting point in form of the Sabbath and Jewish tradition. Standing
at the center of this circle is not God, however, but the almost desperate longing for a return of the Golden Age, a pre-historical *unio
mystica* of the human being with creation.

Between the lines of *You Shall be as Gods*, there is a poignant
sense of melancholy and loss. What becomes apparent in this work
of the sixty-six year old author is a deep undercurrent of his
thought, usually carefully hidden in the emphatic promise of a better way of life for all of humanity: a cultural pessimism more and
more noticeable in his later and last writings. Fromm certainly
does not resign himself to this negative eschatology, as did the
ageing Horkheimer when he returned to Schopenhauer's universal
pessimism. Adorno, too, took refuge in his late writings in a shattering negation of the evolutionary process (cf. his *Negative Dialectics* [1966][30]). As opposed to his former colleagues from the
Institute of Social Research, Fromm did not relinquish all hope for
a change for the better. His thinking vacillates between cool observation of the predominantly dismal societal panorama of which
he himself is a part, and mythical faith in the regenerative powers

of humanity. He does not lose this faith, in spite of all evidence to the contrary. In *Man for Himself*, he quotes a well-known phrase ascribed to Tertullian, which perfectly characterizes his own ambivalence: *Credo quia absurdum* (I believe because it is absurd to believe). He finds refuge and solace in the sphere of mysticism, which, at least for him, is situated beyond good and evil, beyond the miserable and the beautiful.

You Shall be as Gods ends on an encouraging note. Fromm calls the message contained in the Old Testament and in the teachings of Maimonides a form of radical (=dialectic) humanism: a position between the poles of determinism and unbound free will. Determinism would preclude the possibility of religious and ethical freedom, whereas totally unrestrained will can not materialize within the biological and societal strictures imposed on the individual. The synthesis of both--alternativism--will prevent the hardening of the human heart and its corruption by evil. Humans who exercise alternativism and who are able to achieve the x-experience or ultimate affirmation of life will then be able to be *like* Gods. Needless to say, they will never actually *be* Gods, because in Fromm's atheistic religious concept there is no God. The deity remains a sublime projection of the human mind: the fleeting image of eternal beauty and perfection unattainable for mortals.

Nevertheless, even during the years of the Second World War, Fromm sporadically contributed through printed statements to the shaping of public opinion on current political issues. This tendency is perfectly in keeping with the goals he proclaimed in his very early article "Politics and Psychoanalysis" (1931), i.e. to further the understanding of collective and socially relevant strivings of a group bound together by a common destiny.[3] In 1942, one year after the United States had entered the war, he published an article under the title "Should we Hate Hitler?" in the popular *Journal of Home Economics*.[4] Here, he attempts to discern between two types of hatred: the irrational, brutally oppressive emotion as opposed to its rational and reactive counterpart. One feels strongly reminded of his distinction between irrational (=repressive) and rational (=conducive to growth) authority, as first propounded in *Escape from Freedom* and further developed in many of his later writings. The concept of nonpathological violence in its reactive form also reappears in *The Heart of Man*, where its aim is described as "the service of life, not of death. . . ."[5] National socialist society, says Fromm, is the product of the social character of the "lower middle class" (the German word *Kleinbürgertum* = petty bourgeoisie would be more accurate in this context) in Germany even during the Weimar years. Sadism and destructiveness are presumably the roots of this orientation. (Here, Fromm is not consistent with his own empirical findings, published posthumously [*The Working Class in Weimar Germany*], which showed a surprising *lack* of those character traits.) At any rate, Nazism is termed a "movement of nihilism profoundly attracted by destruction."[6] One should, on the basis of a clear and rational decision, hate this movement. Further, the war could only be won by the vision of a better future: a world in which destructiveness would be eradicated and human happiness the ultimate goal.

The syndrome of fascism, long after this scourge was stamped out for good in its most virulent organized form, remained a life-long object for Fromm's sociological studies. He was, in fact, so traumatized by his experiences during the pre-fascist years that even decades later, his perceptions of the new democratic Germany--i.e. the Federal Republic founded in 1949, not the Eastern German Democratic Republic which Fromm never vis-ited--remained biased and inaccurate. In an interview given in 1964 to the journal *Look*,[7] he claimed that "the" German mentality, i.e. the mentality which produced National Socialism and the holo-caust, had remained essentially unchanged in the two decades since the war. Americans, ventured Fromm, had fallen into a trap by re-arming West Germany as a buffer zone between Western Eu-rope and the USSR. The leaders of West Germany, he claimed, had no other goal than to "dominate Europe again." During his yearly visits to Germany, he claimed, he still encountered the "same sick, hating, disturbing faces I saw during the thirties."[8] Moreover, he bemoans that an unguided, unmotivated younger generation of "nihilistic" youth dominate the German scene. For one who has witnessed these years in a fledgling democracy predominantly committed to a more humanitarian future, Fromm's statement is a grotesque distortion of facts. His hatred for the "old" Germany had blinded him to the assets of the "new." All the shortcomings of the gradual evolution of this democratic society notwithstanding, Fromm was unable to give the nation--actually two nations on German soil--credit for the attempt to rehabilitate themselves and break radically with the past. He was never able, as opposed to many émigrés and former victims of Nazi terror, to make peace with his homeland.

What becomes apparent in his political writings of the 1950s and 1960s, is a paradoxical relationship to his "second" home, the United States (if we consider Mexico the third, and Switzerland the final stations in his life). The intense love-hate Fromm felt in re-gard to American capitalism, its shortcomings and its virtues, is an everpresent, if not always obvious factor in his theoretical writings, especially in his theories on social characterology. Erich Fromm must have loved this society for all it provided to him: security, freedom from fear, professional recognition, and wealth. At the same time, he was only too conscious of the ills and injustices of the most highly developed capitalist economy on earth. As an avowed socialist and communist, albeit in opposition to all existing such organizations and states, he certainly lacked the "dispassionateness" of a detached observer. For him to witness the moral and societal disintegration caused by rampant consumerism and brain-polluting mass media, especially during the post-war period, must have been a shattering experience: an experience comparable to that shared during the 1930s by many Germans who observed the rapid ruin of all ethical norms in their own country. In some ways, this irreconcilable ambivalence toward North America--one of the unresolved dichotomies in Fromm's thought--might be compared to his attraction-repulsion relationship to Sigmund Freud, the threatening and beloved father-figure from whom he could never totally break free. On a broader plane, the same dialectic opposition of forces is characteristic for the whole of his thinking, which vacillates between dismal diagnosis and utopian hope.

Beginning with the publication of *The Sane Society* in 1955, Fromm took an increasingly active part in the American political scene. The manuscript of this book was actually finished already in 1953.[9] It reflects both the critical distance to American society Fromm had gained through his move to Mexico and his intensified political involvement. Certain aspects of the study foreshadow the central ideas expressed in *Marx's Concept of Man* and *The Revolution of Hope*, published thirteen years later. *The Sane Society* must be recognized as one of Fromm's two or three very best works. Despite its length, the volume is clearly structured and on the whole not redundant. It still makes fascinating reading, three decades after its initial appearance. A more appropriate title, however, would have been The *In*sane Society, as its bulk is devoted to diagnosis of the societal ills of capitalism.

Once more, a tripartite structure is employed. Part one raises the central question of the human situation and of basic human needs, as they either fulfilled or squashed in a given societal context. Fromm's *pathology of normalcy* is extremely exact. He diagnoses, on the one hand, a peak of civilizational progress achieved by modern-day capitalism, which would have been inconceivable to earlier generations. On the other hand, the population of this highly civilized society is subject to a constant bombardment of the "cheapest trash" by the mass media: sadism and violence are pre-dominant in entertainment, where moral censorship at the same time vigorously tries to eliminate "immorality" on the screen. The contradiction of uncensored brutality and puritanical prudishness toward sex is obvious. Basic human needs remain mostly unful-filled, and society as a whole is counterproductive to the full and mature development of the individual.

Many of the symptoms described in the diagnostic part of the book are--for the first time in Fromm's career--backed up by hard statistical data relating to suicide rates, crime and the occurrence of mental illness in the capitalist West. Alienation is the key factor to the deformation of human life. The essence of the human self is again seen in its ability to transcend nature: *"Life became aware of itself."*[10] Human needs are described in accordance with the char-acterology developed in *Man for Himself* (discussed above in chap-ter five). They are divided into five categories and need not be re-peated at this point in any greater detail. Fromm mentions the fol-lowing needs and their corresponding adversary orientation: 1. re-latedness versus a narcissistic orientation; 2. transcendence and creativity versus destructiveness; 3. rootedness and love versus in-cestuous fixation; 4. a sense of identity and individuality versus conformism; 5. a frame of orientation and devotion, i.e. an exis-tence based on reason, versus irrationality. Some modifications of this characterological pattern are presented in *The Heart of Man*--vide chapter seven of this study--but the framework for both the ethical and the societal characterology remains essentially the same.

On the basis of these theoretical considerations, the book's sec-ond part engages in a lucid step-by-step analysis of the human situ-ation in today's capitalist society. Given a certain degree of simpli-fication, Fromm's arguments may be summarized as follows:

1. The social character prevalent in contemporary capitalistic societies has created certain character orientations within these so-cieties' individual members which are essential in order to guaran-tee the functioning of the whole socio-economic structure. Work, punctuality, and order have therefore become inherent drives in

the individual or, in other words, parts of the human libidinal organization. Modern human beings are kept in a state of powerlessness by their inability to intellectually grasp the complex economic interrelations of the system as a whole: "Thus the 'freedom' of the individual is largely illusory."[11] Fromm concedes at this point in his discussion that, all its shortcomings notwithstanding, the capitalist method of distribution through the free market system "is better than any other method devised so far in a class society,"[12] as it at least *could* potentially provide a basis for the expression of individual political freedom. This appears at first glance to be a strange contradiction indeed. It will be resolved to a certain extent in the book's final part, which propagates not the *abolition* of capitalism, but a drastic evolutionary *change* in its actual implementation.

2. The principle of profit for its own sake must be seen as one of the primary causes of human alienation. As opposed to the owner of capital, who can earn tremendous profits without actually working, the wages of a worker in fact frequently stand in no realistic proportions to the efforts devoted to earning them. Fromm correctly diagnoses the root of the profit principle as greed. His definition of the capital-owner's hoarding orientation is a derivative of Freud's anal character type. The profit principle, for which those in control of capital have found many "pious justifications," is the key factor in the "use of man by man."

3. Perhaps the most important part of this analysis is provided in the theory that a strong dependency of the exploited classes on their rulers has developed in capitalist society. In a relationship where *rational* authority prevails, love, admiration, and gratitude are the logical coefficients of human interrelations. If, on the other hand, slavery is determined by *irrational* authority, hostility and rebellion might arise against the oppressor. In order to avoid an obviously painful or futile conflict between slave and master, the former frequently internalizes his hostile feelings to the point that they are replaced by pseudo-voluntary submission to and even admiration of the oppressor. Thus, the original hatred will ultimately be eliminated and the humiliation of bondage blunted to a large degree. Concomitantly, the premise is adopted that the person in

command of the economic powerstructure (=the owner of capital) *must* in fact be much more suited for the exercise of power, and the exploited (=the laborer) should not feel shame for submitting to the more powerful being. Fromm describes here for the first time in extremely accurate terms the *libidinal relationship between the rich and the poor* which exists in capitalist countries, particularly in the United States. This libidinal fixation on the exploitative classes is frequently glorified by the remark that in "free" enterprise, anybody, by means of sheer motivation and industry, can fulfill the American dream and rise from dependency/poverty to the Olympian heights of the very privileged. Reality, though, is different. The slogan that "every boy can become president" is just as misleading as the fictitious premise of unhindered mobility toward a more affluent mode of life.

4. Alienation, however, is not only restricted to the sphere of work and production. It rules equally with regard to consumption. Characterological changes have been instigated by market dictates and advertising. The *real* needs of humanity have little or nothing in common with an irrational craving for consumption stimulated continually by artificial means. The receptive orientation is the characterological end-product of this development. Any good consumer, "if he dared to be articulate about his concept of heaven, would describe a vision which would look like the biggest department store in the world. . . ."[13] Alienated consumerism, then, has a two-fold effect on the individual. First, it contributes to the lack of basic insights into the functioning of society as a whole. Independent thinking and the potential to make rational decisions are stultified. And second, it augments the principle of egotism and the atrophying of full human relationships. Further, the alienated consumer loses his or her sense of unique individuality and becomes prone to accept the mode of blind conformism. Here, Fromm takes issue with Sullivan, who had attacked his concept of the human self. For Sullivan, the self is predominantly determined by its interaction with others. Fromm rightly insists there *is* a primary and original quality of the self inherent in every person. This particular quality of the self, he ventures, becomes more and more di-

minished, to the point of actual disintegration, if it is not activated through self-awareness and productivity.

5. Anonymous authority ruling in capitalistic systems uses the principle of *conformity* to enforce its dictates. As an example of a perfectly "adjusted" mini-society, Fromm deploys extensive documentation about a housing community in Illinois (Park Forest), which was based on a stringent set of rules for behavior and social exchange. (In the meantime, countless similar developments have sprouted: people virtually flock to their conformistic confines, witness the condominium craze of the 1970s and 1980s.) The primary goal in the greater organization and, specifically, in the Park Forest development, is to be "well-adjusted."

What is the meaning of this all too familiar phrase? First, an individual must avoid at all costs being "different" from the crowd. Being different can be expressed in numerous ways. Humans, for example, need to be alone at certain times, or they might prefer the company of few over the anonymity of mass gatherings. The ability to be alone indicates that a person is not totally alienated. From the standpoint of the alienated herd, however, the loner is "different" and therefore not acceptable. Second, cultural interests and activities are stigmatized by the alienated, conforming plurality. People who like to listen to classical music or read philosophical texts dare not admit this to the crowd. Consequently, these interests are either exorcised by the drive to conform, or they become a clandestine pastime carefully concealed from the more alienated neighbors. Third, indiscriminating sociability is euphemistically labelled "outgoing." In reality, it has nothing in common with genuine human interaction. The "outgoing" person is often alienated to the point that he/she can no longer relate meaningfully to another individual. Quantity and superficiality of social contacts have eliminated mature communication. And fourth, social "adjustment" culminates in the total lack of privacy and the "indiscriminate talking about one's problems." The architecture of many such developments has made all concessions necessary to ensure the absence of privacy, both within and from without: doors are abolished in the home itself, and the aquarium-like picture windows allow for unbroken contact with one's neighbors. In sum: "Virtue is to be adjusted and to be like the rest. Vice is to be different."[14] Social ostracism is the price an individual has to pay for voluntary or involuntary deviations from the path of conformity. In addition to Henri Bergson and Max Scheler, both authors of astute observations regarding the living conditions of modern humanity, Fromm repeatedly mentions Huxley's *Brave New World* and Orwell's *1984* as insightful fictionalizations of these and similar developments. Today, thirty years after the publication of *The Sane Society*, one has to admit that the "brave new world" has in fact already arrived in numerous respects. Forest Park is now to be found all over the Western world. The symptoms of alienation as described above are more and more the order of the day.

Among the other pathological aspects of alienated life Fromm mentions, the "principle of nonfrustration" warrants special consideration. Immediate fulfillment of every whim to acquire material goods (=a temporary sense of satisfaction) is characteristic for present-day capitalism. The "fun" one can achieve today must be obtained at all costs and never be postponed until tomorrow. In general, "having fun" is almost exclusively centered around the rapid consumption of commodities and pre-fabricated entertainment. Any given moment of happiness achieved thus is, inevitably, short-lived and soon gives way to some other equally nonproductive purchase or activity. Ultimately, people are perpetually disappointed by their own lack of development and their inability to attain a lasting sense of fulfillment.

Fromm paints a dismal picture. He describes a world in which free thought and association are almost extinct, from which reason and ethical/religious values are totally absent. Work has lost all its creative potential, and the only given alternative to alienated labor is the possession of capital, i.e. the exploitation of others. Equally dismal is Fromm's perspective on the actual functioning of the democratic process. Free elections, as they are manipulated by advertising campaigns and the mass media, frequently fail to represent the will of the people. Opinion formation is the key factor to winning an election, and political representatives often have only a vague relationship to their electorate. Again, the presence of an all-powerful political machinery, comparable in its remoteness from the voting public to the management of super-corporations which is totally divorced from the individual worker, contributes to a pervading sense of powerlessness. Political intelligence, in the face of the individual's actual impotence, must wither. And if an individual is unable to act, she/he becomes ultimately unable to think.

Just as an alienating society can not be considered sane, the mental health of its individual members leaves much to be desired. From the viewpoint of Fromm's *normative humanism* it follows that ". . . the very person who is considered healthy in the categories of an alienated world, from the humanistic standpoint appears as the sickest one--although not in terms of individual sickness, but of the socially patterned defect."[15] The alienated person can be neither healthy nor sane. Happiness as a lasting condition can not be achieved, and the inevitable awareness of unhappiness is constantly repressed by the consumption of "fun." Ultimately, the two greatest dangers inherent in the given socio-economic situation are: *mindless robotism* for the individual and *war* for the whole of humanity.

R.H. Tawney, in his influential work *The Acquisitive Society*,[16] and Elton Mayo in *The Human Problems of an Industrial Civilization*[17] have described similar phenomena, not to mention Marx and Freud, who are cited frequently throughout the book. Another acute diagnostician of the societal desiccation imposed on human beings is Frank Tannenbaum, who stresses the moral obligations of the big corporations.[18] But for Fromm, the answer to the given problem can not be primarily provided by sociological and economic theory. An initial impulse must arise from the humanistic tradition in the vein of Aldous Huxley, Albert Schweitzer, and Albert Einstein. In his *Brave New World*, Huxley had stated already in 1946 that political and economic totalitarianism can only be halted in its tracks by means of a broad "popular movement" which would aim to decentralize the whole societal organization. And Albert Schweitzer, in his *Philosophy of Civilization*,[19] had observed a "tragic alliance between society as a whole and its economic conditions" which effectively represses all human and humanitarian qualities. The answer, therefore, can only lie in the liberation of humanity through a large-scale reviviscence of the tradition of humanist thought.

Part three of *The Sane Society* is aptly entitled "Roads to Sanity." For the first time in the whole of his oeuvre, Fromm presents an entire set of *concrete* suggestions for the abolition of alienation in its various pathological forms. Characteristically enough, he does not propagate revolutionary change of present conditions. Nor is his aim the fundamental destruction of the capitalistic socio-economic framework. Fromm envisions a compromise solution which would on the one hand incorporate some remnants of the present system and, on the other, establish a new state which might be called predominantly socialistic. He is perfectly correct in his assumption that economic change alone will not be effective in a radical re-orientation of society. Needless to say, in this thesis he deviates from orthodox Marxism. Fromm insists on a simultaneous re-structuring on three intricately interrelated levels: the *economic*, the *political*, and the *cultural*.

In this three-pronged approach toward the construction of a "sane" society, his own origins as a thinker in the school of Horkheimer's Critical Theory become apparent.[20] Naturally, he gives considerable thought to a viable re-organization of the present economic system. Reform has be radical in the sense that it goes to the roots (lat. *radix* = root) of the problem. Nevertheless, it should not be implemented by force. Observation, patience and active persuasion, according to Fromm are more effective tools for long-range reform. First, *awareness* of the problem has be to be created on a broad, public front. Socialism must be widely accepted as the *only* practicable form of unalienated economic life and the ultimate goal of the intended reform. Communitarian socialism, as defined by G.D.H. Cole and W. Mellor,[21] and based on the thought of early socialists like Kropotkin and Proudhon, stands in opposition to both state communism as prevalent in Eastern European countries and in the USSR and to monopolistic capitalism. Factories would be, in the system of communitarian socialism, sub-

ject to direct management by the workers. Production, distribution, and exchange would then be directly governed by labor itself.
Consequently, "every working person would be an active and responsible participant, where work would be attractive and meaningful, where capital would not employ labor, but labor would employ capital."[22]

The old argument that profit is a necessary incentive in the economic process, says Fromm, is valid only in a very limited sense.
Laziness is not a normal part of the human self, but a pathological
symptom. Moreover, one of the "worst forms of mental suffering"
is boredom. Therefore, the need for productive and unalienated
work is an integral part of human existence. When, through proper
training and the implementation of direct management, this need is
fulfilled, interest and participation of the individual worker in the
whole process of production are logical consequences. A striking
example is supplied in form of the Communities of Work which
had been installed already during the 1940s in several European
countries, namely France, Belgium, Switzerland, and the Netherlands. The results of these successful experimental projects have to
be modified to suit a larger industrial context, and then applied toward general economic change. Fromm's documentation of the
feasibility of these *Communautées du travail* is ample and unim-
peachable. The principle thrust of his argument is *not* directed at
ownership of the means of production, but *participation* in all areas
of management and decision-making. In this one aspect, his intention to salvage one of the supporting pillars of the capitalistic sys-
tem--the private ownership of capital--becomes obvious. Even
monopolistic concentrations of capital would still be possible in
communitarian (or, as he later, in *The Revolution of Hope*, terms it,
humanitarian) socialism. Many critics of the study, among them
Herbert Marcuse, have reproached Fromm on this particular issue.
And indeed, there is a strange contradiction in his concept, as it is
logically impossible to attack capitalism on its very foundations and,
at the same time, to re-admit it through the back door.

As a next step in the economic evolution, Fromm proposes the
reduction of unnecessary consumption: a step which would sup-

port both humanitarian re-organization of the social character and
a return to sanity in the individual orientation. Additional benefits
would lie in the possibility of sharing the wealth of the highly industrialized West with countries of the Third World. The humanitarian implications of this measure are obvious, and politically, it
might be conducive to the avoidance of war. Further, a basic income must be guaranteed for everyone in order to secure human
subsistence. This guaranteed income would become part of the
present social security system. Fromm does not believe that this
minimal amount necessary to fill basic human survival needs would
discourage people from working. (A more extensive discussion of
this intriguing concept can be found in the article "The Psychological Aspects of the Guaranteed Income,"[23] which originally appeared in 1966).

Political reform, ventures Fromm, must aim at dismantling the
huge and remote political apparatus which currently governs the
United States. Instead of the manipulative process of political
opinion formation, *direct* democratic representation should be organized in small communities of not more than five hundred people. This "grass roots" network would then elect representatives,
who would assemble in a true "House of Commons." Quite obviously, the commissariat government (i.e. the *Räterepublik*) as propagated during the ill-fated German revolution of 1918/1919 (and
actually instituted in Bavaria, where it ruled for a brief period of
time before it was brutally dissolved by the army) serves as a model
for this section of the book.

And finally, cultural reform must, as Fromm rightly observes, be-
gin with a radical re-organization of the school system. His
thoughts on this important area of cultural life have already been
discussed in the preceding chapter and need not be repeated
here.[24] From there, a general revitalization of individual creativity
must be instrumented. Culture and art, as much as mass enter-
tainment--"college plus football, crime stories plus Fourth of July
celebrations, with Mothers' and Fathers' day and Christmas thrown
in for good measure"--have degenerated to the point where they
are nothing but commodities for consumption. A new form of cre-

ative artistic self-experience must ultimately emerge, hand in hand with a new religious awareness. The problem, Fromm states in his conclusion, is not that "God is dead," as nineteenth-century philosophers proclaimed. It rests in the fact that "man is dead." Our only chance to revive the individual human being and, concurrently, society as a whole, lies in the implementation of humanistic communitarian socialism.

This impressive volume met with much acclaim and an equal amount of harsh criticism. Paul Tillich greeted the publication of *The Sane Society* with great enthusiasm. Other critics remained more skeptical. In psychiatric journals like *Psychoanalytic Quarterly* and *Psychiatry*, Fromm's specific criticism of Sullivan and his general assessment of current psychotherapy as an agent of social conformity were sharply censured. Today, a fair-minded appraisal of the study is much easier, as the dust has long settled on old partisan controversies. Fromm's social critique is doubtlessly at its most incisive in this publication. Moreover, many of his proposals for betterment of human existence in capitalist societies have long since been adopted, especially in Europe, by futurologists and researchers devoted to peace. If one considers the individual components of communitarian socialism, most of them are perfectly convincing and even practicable. Social democratic parties in Austria, France, Germany and in the Scandinavian countries have in fact worked throughout the better part of this century to realize the majority of these goals. In many respects, they have been successful. The problem remains, however, of instrumenting Fromm's three-fold pattern of economic, political, and cultural change in highly industrialized, media-controlled, monopolistic capitalism, i.e. in the specific context of the United States. A crusade of reason to cure all prevalent societal ills in a presumably insane, robotized society has extremely remote chances for success. Given the assumption that Fromm's social diagnosis is essentially correct, his expectation that a revolution of consciousness will self-ignite, like the cargoes of coal freighters in the past, is utterly unrealistic. The reciprocal sustenance of capital, the political apparatus, and the media--in brief: the balance of power--can not possibly be dissolved without the use of force. The military-industrial complex in particular is too monolithic and too tightly interwoven for a painless unraveling. Force, in turn, could only be the consequence of a revolutionary upheaval based on a more or less *general* awakening of revolutionary consciousness in the masses. But this revolutionary consciousness, once more given the accuracy of Fromm's very own description of the social character, is totally lacking in the actual configuration. It *can not even develop*, due to the libidinous relationship between ruling and exploited classes.

Despite this criticism regarding the realistic possibilities for large-scale societal changes, *The Sane Society* stands out as a courageous and imposing statement. Especially during the Cold War years, the climate in the United States was anything but favorable to internal dissent and to even the most tentative criticism of the American way of life. Fromm paid the price for his integrity as a thinker and for the brave attempt to voice a vision of a better future when he was further ostracized by psychoanalytical circles. Conformity--as he stated himself--has the urge to lash out viciously against those who dare deviate from its rules. He remained safe, at least, from the more obvious forms of political persecution, both on account of his prominent position in American society and due to his acquaintance with liberally oriented politicians, in particular Senator James W. Fulbright.

During the mid-1950s, at the apex of the Cold War, Fromm became a member of the American Socialist Party. For the first time in his life, he was now part of a political movement: admittedly a small group, which had never had much popular appeal and was constantly hindered in its campaigns by overt or surreptitious government interference. Together with Irving Howe, Murray Kempton, Upton Sinclair, and others, Fromm composed a party platform which originally appeared in 1960 under the title of *Let Man Prevail: A Socialist Manifesto and Program*. Later, it was reprinted in the anthology *On Disobedience*, published posthumously in 1981.[25] The manifesto asks, first, whether there is a third alternative beyond capitalist and communist "managerial industrialism" and, second, whether economic prosperity must inevitably be incompatible with the fulfillment of human needs for the masses. In a condensation of the large-scale social diagnosis presented in *The Sane Society*, it points out the irrationality of present economic life--i.e. the grossly inequitable distribution of wealth and the de-humanizing effects of consumerism. A return to the political concepts and visions of the founding fathers of the United States appears of paramount importance. Their noble ideas (which indeed could still serve today as a spiritual guideline for public life in a truly democratic society) have gradually degenerated to the utilitarian notion of "progress." A basically humanistic drive has been perverted to a mentality devoted to the production and consumption of things. Euphemisms dominate today's political propaganda: dictatorships are called "people's democracies" in the East; Western allies who are ruled by equally crass totalitarianism are termed "freedom loving people." A huge propaganda machinery is in fact able to distort all political facts and to reduce the voting public to "A Nation of Sheep,"[26] as William J. Lederer calls it in his perceptive book. Capitalism puts things (=capital) higher on the value scale than human beings (=labor). Therefore, power is identical to the possession of capital. Alienation must be the necessary consequence for all members of a capitalistic society.

Conversely, the aim of socialism, at least in its nineteenth-century formulations, is the liberation of humanity from the dictates of capital and therefore from alienation. This aim, according to Fromm, has not been achieved in existing communist countries, where a "vulgarized, distorted" socialism rules. Democratic and humanistic socialism must be the basis for the formation of a new society. Later in the manifesto, the concrete solutions propounded in *The Sane Society* are repeated in condensed form. Although this certainly might be an acceptable party platform for most labor-oriented movements, it caused considerable controversy in the ranks of the American Socialist Party. Darlington Hoopes, then the national chair of the party, reported on its polemical impact on various factions. In the election year of 1960, the party won only a negligible fraction of the vote. Fromm must have realized that the chances for organized mobilization of socialist thought were indeed nonexistent at that time in the United States. He consequently withdrew from the organization's leadership and soon left the party altogether.

Nevertheless, he did not abandon hope for an immediate change of the political climate in North America. In 1957, together with A.J. Muste, Norman Thomas, and many other like-minded pacifists, he had founded the National Committee for a Sane Nuclear Policy (SANE), an organization to which he devoted considerable time and effort. Pamphlets and open letters were printed and distributed on a national and international level. Fromm's collaborators in this effort were Roger Hagan, the sociologist Michael Maccoby, and David Riesman. In later years, SANE became a propelling force within the nationwide movement against the Vietnam war.

In 1960, Fromm published in the journal *Daedalus* a lengthy plaidoyer for gradual unilateral disarmament, based on the suggestions of Charles E. Osgood.[27] Here, he correctly pinpoints the true menace to human existence as the disintegration of moral and ethical forces *within* Western society. A real threat, says Fromm, does *not* originate from communist ideology or the military power of the Communist bloc. One should see the Soviet Union as neither a revolutionary society nor a truly socialist country, but as a conservative class structure very much comparable to Western countries. A reconciliation with the USSR should meet no major obstacles. American foreign policy, by means of constant paranoid escalation of existing conflicts, is tantamount to a provocation of nuclear warfare. As George F. Kennan observes, the continuation of this policy is literally suicidal.[28] Fromm concludes with a strong plea for voluntary, step-by-step reduction of atomic weapons. Once more, this is a courageous and very convincing statement. It does not take into account, however, the enormous importance of armament industries within the American economic structure. Disarmament, in order to become a *realistic* alternative, would mean dismantling the backbone of American industrial production and/or replacing it with equally profitable peacetime industries: a fundamental economic change indeed.

In the wake of the Berlin crisis of 1961, civil defense became a hotly debated issue in the United States. Herman Kahn, the self-styled expert on nuclear warfare, had already published his controversial book *On Thermonuclear War* in 1960.[29]   Erich Fromm and Michael Maccoby, in their article "A Debate on the Question of Civil Defense,"[30] put forth a lucid statement on both so-called civil defense and Kahn's theories. They correctly denounce the former as a benign illusion, and the latter as dangerous and irresponsible speculation. This brief article contains sufficient factual documentation to refute the hare-brained notion that "survival" would be possible in a nuclear war--or, for that matter, that such an existence would be worthwhile for the survivors. Especially in the political climate of the 1980s, where the possibility of atomic warfare has become more real than perhaps ever before, and where the most grotesque stratagems (including the use of orbital space as a potential danger zone) are being considered as possible shields against a nuclear strike, the article is exceptionally instructive.

In 1961, along with *Marx's Concept of Man*, Fromm also published *May Man Prevail?* Though this book's investigation of American foreign policy is illuminating and provocative, on the whole it lacks the coherency of its predecessor, and in fact strikes the reader as a series of haphazardly compiled individual articles. Since many of the factual observations, especially the sections on the Soviet Union and the People's Republic of China, are now outdated, the facts and insights that are still relevant can be briefly summarized here.

Fromm engages in a lengthy, although not always accurate description of the USSR's political system. He is correct in his assumption that for most Americans, this system "is a mythical entity." Incidentally, not much has changed in this respect in the meantime, as most information currently available in the United States on the Soviet Union is still a horrendous mélange of fact and fiction. Fromm ventures that the revolution of 1917 failed its purpose, as it did not fulfill its promise to install direct democracy and humanitarian socialism. Lenin's early death and the ousting of Trotsky were two decisive factors in this historical development. Stalin, then, transformed the communist movement into a managerial revolution, and created a police state founded on the regime of terror. During the post-Stalin era, terror was abolished and the political powerstructure consolidated itself along the lines of an hierarchical administrative bureaucracy. Private ownership of capital had long since been eradicated. (Here again, Fromm stresses the point that private ownership of *goods* is not reglemented by the state--a fact still widely unknown in the United States and systematically distorted in anti-communist propaganda.) Instead, all economic production is state-owned and state-operated. In Fromm's opinion, the USSR under Khrushchev--despite the fact that brutal oppression of civil rights had ceased and been replaced by stringent bureaucratic reglementation of public life--was not a socialist state. The spirit of Marx and Engels and their plea for human independence have been betrayed by the post-revolutionary leadership of the Soviet Union.

Just as the USSR is not a truly socialist state, neither can it be seen as revolutionary in its *internal* direction, nor as aggressive and imperialist regarding its *foreign* policy. World domination by means of force is definitely not its aim. To the contrary, Soviet hopes for the eventual creation of world-wide socialism are based on economic competition, i.e. the expectation that communist economy will prove to be more productive and durable than capitalist economy and will, in the foreseeable future, "overtake" it. Fromm states that " . . . Soviet thinking is evolutionary and sees as the central factor in human evolution the development of the productive forces, the transformation of one social system to the next higher one."[31] American foreign policy, which rests on the assumption of Soviet aggression, is therefore the product of paranoid delusion.

Before he presents actual solutions to the question of preserving peace, Fromm turns to various geographical "problem" areas and their potential for endangering humanity. The "Chinese problem," as he perceives it, is situated in the country's poor economy and its poverty. Both might eventually lead to war. But much more imminent, for Fromm, is the "German problem." West German rearmament is considered a first significant step toward a potentially renewed effort at German world domination.   As in the above-mentioned interview with *Look,* and in *The Revolution of Hope* (published seven years after *May Man Prevail?*), Fromm fails to come to grips with the realities of both German states.   He should have known better than to claim that in the GDR, the East German Democratic Republic, a government rules "against the will of the vast majority of the population."   In 1961 this no longer held true. Equally ludicrous is his assumption that Germany and Japan "would use their military power as an adjunct to their political ambitions."[32] His bias in this particular area may be understandable on a personal basis.   As a precondition for objective political fact-finding, it inevitably leads to grotesque misconceptions.

What concrete suggestions for the preservation of peace does this book offer? Fromm delineates five possible causes of war. 1. War might be caused by accidental malfunctioning of the complex alarm system. A false alarm could be triggered at any time, and result in wholesale destruction. 2. Irrationality in the guise of rationality constitutes another potential cause. Mutual escalation of any given crisis might result in an ultimately catastrophical "game of chicken." Bluff from one of the opponents might not be recognized as such by the other, and nuclear forces could appear imperative in order to avert the possibility of the "enemy's" first strike. 3. War could equally well result from calculations based on the insane assumption that nuclear bombardment in form of "anticipatory retaliation" would be the only given alternative. 4. Escalation in a strategic sense could, at any time, result in global cataclysm. 5. Finally, a "catalytic" war is conceivable in the case that a "third" power might interfere with the given balance of nuclear threats. This type of war could involve the superpowers quasi by accident in a nuclear exchange. The results would nevertheless be the same: world-wide destruction of tens of millions of lives.   In his deployment of these five categories, Fromm adheres to the mainstream of Kahn's research on the topic.[33] He further quotes Henry A. Kissinger's analysis of the strategy of deterrence.[34] From there, he takes Kahn to task for his basically inhuman premise that the loss of sixty to one hundred and sixty million lives might be an "acceptable" risk factor in global strategy:

> Acceptable to whom? That this kind of thinking has become so popular is one of the gravest symptoms of despair and alienation, and of an attitude in which moral problems have ceased to exist, in which life and death are transformed into a balance-sheet problem, and in which the horrors of war are minimized because peace--and that is life--is felt to be only a little less horrible than death.[35]

War, as Fromm correctly emphasizes, would be the utmost calamity for *all* peoples of the world. It can be averted if two conditions are met: a) universal controlled disarmament and b) an American-Russian agreement on the maintenance of the political status quo. Obviously, there are no economic and political conflicts between the super-powers sufficiently virulent to necessitate war. If an agreement on the balance of power *and* on the mutual acceptance of the given spheres of influence could be reached, war between the USSR and the United States should be out of the question. Both countries would be in a position to contain localized conflicts in their respective spheres of domination. Regarding North American foreign policy versus Cuba and Latin America, Fromm diagnoses that these conflict areas are more imaginary than real. If the United States would adopt a policy of non-interference in Latin America--from today's viewpoint a utopian suggestion indeed--, long term appeasement and the basis for peaceful cooperation could be achieved.

What Fromm suggests in terms of an agreement between the super-powers, as opposed to his applaudable proposal for disarmament, warrants some criticism. In fact, the solution might be, mutatis mutandis, compared to the notion of communitarian socialism of *The Sane Society*. In the earlier study, he propagates co-management as a means to implementing active participation of labor in the production process. He avoids, however, the decidedly unpopular topic of actually divesting the owners of capital of their overall control of the economic apparatus. Similarly, the modus vivendi he now suggests to the super-powers would still boil down to "dividing the cake" among the "big boys." Smaller nations would face the alternative of either complying to the given prerogatives within the respective spheres of influence, or, if they attempted to steer an independent course, suffering economic reprisals. This is certainly a more or less accurate description of the fate of many smaller states since the end of the Second World War. A *desirable* state of affairs it is not and, for many, will never be.

In 1961, Fromm and Hans Herzfeld edited a collection of articles in honor of the sixtieth birthday of Adolf Leschnitzer, a professor of German language and literature at New York City College and a well-known authority on Jewish history. Interestingly enough, Fromm's own contribution in this volume is not devoted to the practical, but the religious aspects of peace. Peace between humans and nature "is more than the absence of strife; it is accomplishment of true harmony, of the experience of at-onement and unity . . . it is the end of alienation . . ."[36] Once more, the political thinker and messianic propagator of a utopian vision of unity are inseparable in this statement.

A succession of Fromm's political concepts is presented in The *Revolution of Hope*, which will be discussed in the following chapter of this study. Fromm also gave a concise postscriptum to his thoughts on détente in his *Remarks on the Policy of Détente* (1975), an exposé instigated by Senator Fulbright and presented to the U.S. Senate Committee on Foreign Relations in the Fall of 1974.[37]

In 1965, Fromm was instrumental in the organization of an international symposium on socialist humanism in Mexico City. This resulted in the publication of an anthology entitled *Socialist Humanism*, which contains contributions by Ernst Bloch, T.B. Bottomore, Danilo Dolci, Irving Fetscher, Herbert Marcuse, Léopold Senghor, and others. Through his indefatigable work for humanitarian socialism, Fromm came into close contact with the "Praxis"-group located in Belgrade and Zagreb. Among his associates in this movement were the Yugoslav philosophers Gajo Petrovic and Mihailo Marcovic. On the occasion of his seventieth birthday, Bernard Landis and Edward S. Tauber--both former colleagues from the William Alanson White Institute and prominent members of the American Psychoanalytic Association--edited a collection of articles in Fromm's honor, properly entitled *In the Name of Life.*[38] Many of the contributions are devoted to the implementation of humanist socialism. Noteworthy among the contributors are Bottomore, Markovic, Petrovic, and the psychologist David Riesman. Prior to the celebration of his seventieth birthday, Fromm had retired from his professorship at the National Autonomous University of Mexico, and had also, in 1965, relinquished his post as director of the Mexican Institute of Psychoanalysis. Three years later, he joined the campaign of Senator Eugene McCarthy for the nomination of the Democratic Candidate in the coming presidential elections. McCarthy incorporated in many ways Fromm's ideas for constructive societal change: as a first measure he promised, if elected, the immediate cessation of all hostilities in Vietnam. His political platform was identical to a great degree to the convictions of Robert Kennedy, who was murdered before he could officially enter the race. During the tumultuous Democratic party convention in Chicago, McCarthy was defeated by Hubert H. Humphrey, who subsequently lost the presidential election to Richard M. Nixon.

Michael Maccoby conducted a statistical survey at the time which proves beyond doubt that only 27 percent of Nixon's supporters exhibited a biophilous character orientation. Rockefeller's voters fared somewhat better with 46 percent, as opposed to 77 percent of those who were ready to cast their ballots for McCarthy.[39] The survey was based on Fromm's characterology as explained in *The Heart of Man* and conducted with 160 Californians picked at random. Despite the fact that some of the criticism leveled against the survey's methodology is valid, there can be little doubt about the character orientation of those who supported a president committed to continued warfare in Southeast Asia. Subsequent historical events leading to Nixon's disgrace and ousting from office would indeed support the thesis that his own character made him the most suitable candidate for a predominantly necrophilous electorate.

During McCarthy's campaign, Fromm travelled extensively throughout the country and delivered many speeches in support of his candidate. He also worked feverishly on the completion of *The Revolution of Hope*, in hopes of publishing it still prior to the elections. All this activity severely over-taxed his strength, and he suffered a serious heart attack in the fall of 1968. He was forced to rest for almost a year. After his recuperation, he and his wife moved in 1969 to Locarno, where the couple spent the summer months of the coming five years. In Fall and Winter, the Fromms resided in Mexico, until they moved permanently to Switzerland in 1974. There, they settled at 4 Via Franscini in the small town of Muralto at Lago Maggiore.

Obviously, Fromm was deeply disappointed by the outcome of the presidential campaigns and, on a broader basis, by the relatively small resonance his own efforts at enlightening the American public had produced. Although *The Revolution of Hope*, written in 1967 and early 1968, still carries strong overtones of optimism, one has to assume that Erich Fromm's position changed rather drastically with the results of the 1968 elections. His former love-hate relationship to American society gradually gave way to resignation. During the following years, he partially disengaged himself from active participation in both North American public life and in the international humanistic-socialist movement. In part, this withdrawal into private life was due to his failing health. To a large extent, however, Erich Fromm must have realized that the time was simply not ripe in the United States for a public awakening of the spirit of peace, equality, and social justice. He must have sensed that Nixon's victory and, concomitantly, the triumph of the military-industrial complex were signals for totally different changes in the socio-economic development from those he had proposed. How radical and lasting the change in direction actually was to be became visible only more than a decade later. With the 1980 election of Ronald Reagan, the social platforms began to crumble, the welfare state was successfully dismantled, and the rich became richer, the poor poorer. In diametric opposition to everything Erich Fromm believed, George Gilder--the economic prophet of the new order of the 1980s--triumphantly states with the first sentence of his bestselling book *Wealth and Poverty*: "The most important event in the recent history of ideas is the demise of the socialist dream."[40] Luckily, dreams don't die that easily. And socialism, contrary to Gilder's assumption, is more than a dream. As Fromm so untiringly emphasized, a multitude of socialistic concepts have been part of the mainstream of the humanistic tradition for many centuries. They might well, in the not too distant future, coalesce into a dignified and unalienated modus vivendi, at least for some nations of this world.

9

The Art of Living. Fromm's Popular Writings Reconsidered (1956-1976)

In his theoretically oriented books, Erich Fromm frequently makes the point that living is more than a biological function, more than a process of struggle and maturation: living is an *art* in itself. As any other skill and any artistic proficiency, living--in the full meaning of the word--requires theoretical knowledge, as well as critical self-examination, practice, and constant striving toward mastery of the art. Beginning with *Escape from Freedom*, practically all of Fromm's studies, even the more theoretical and technical writings, follow a didactic pattern. They are designed to instruct their readers, through step-by-step examination of individual and societal characterology and various related phenomena, in the capacity for self-evaluation. By informing, they aim to raise the reader's awareness of his/her own particular place and role in a given social environment. They deliver a canon of theoretical knowledge essential for the study of the "art" of living. Erich Fromm's first and foremost vocation has always been the *teaching* of truth as he perceived it. He never made much of a name for himself as a gripping or brilliant academic lecturer. His teaching tool was predominantly the printed word. The call to teach humanity a better way of life is certainly owed to his Talmudic upbringing. But the strong impulse to combine the dissemination of theoretical knowledge with the practical and social application of intellectual concepts originated with Fromm's training in Critical Theory. In fact, his writings, as opposed to the (generally more esoteric) works of his colleagues at the Institute of Social Research, have reached an enormous audience in many countries and from literally every stratum of literate society. One can only speculate on the *effect* his books actually have on their readers. Given the fact, however, that they have appeared in extremely large printings, the assumption seems safe that Erich Fromm has influenced many minds and, moreover, must have contributed to a new outlook on life for tens of thousands. This must apply in particular to his "popular" writings, where the didactic intent is the author's primary and immediate goal.

The canon of his popular works is comprised of *The Art of Loving* (1956), *Beyond the Chains of Illusion* (1962), *The Revolution of Hope* (1968), and the latecomer *To Have or to Be?*, published in 1976. Each of these titles is a direct spinoff from the more theoretical texts produced in the immediate chronological vicinity. *The Art of Loving*, for example, expounds the productive character orientation defined in *Man for Himself* and further developed in the political study *The Sane Society*, which preceded it by one year. In addition, the loving personality Fromm describes in his all-time bestseller clearly foreshadows the biophilous orientation explored further in *The Heart of Man* eight years later. Similarly, *Beyond the Chains of Illusion*, a personal testimonial to its author's life-long involvement with Freud and Marx, must be regarded as a popularized distillation of both *Sigmund Freud's Mission* and *Marx's Concept of Man*. In *The Revolution of Hope*, Fromm builds on the foundations he laid in his political books, namely *The Sane Society* and *May Man Prevail?* He had also hoped that the book could still be published prior to the presidential elections in the United States in 1968 and that it might help tip the scales toward Eugene McCarthy. As it turned out, it appeared only in November, after Nixon had already carried the elections.

Finally, *To Have or to Be?* is clearly a didactic counterpiece to *The Anatomy of Human Destructiveness* and, at the same time, a popular expansion of the characterology presented in *The Heart of Man*. Each individual title must therefore be seen as but one piece in the greater mosaic of the whole oeuvre. Surely, every text stands on its own merits and may be read independently from the rest. A *full* understanding of Fromm's popular works, however, requires at least a peripheral knowledge of the theoretical basis of their argumentation.

Even if one considers only the four didactic books to be discussed in this chapter, both the continuity and the dynamic development of Fromm's thought come into focus. As a microcosm within the greater framework of his writings, these texts clearly demonstrate how much ground their author covered between 1956 and 1976: in terms of his own perceptions of the human condition and, even more important, with regard to his observations of historical and societal change. From the overwhelming exuberance of *The Art of Loving* and the firm humanistic credo put forth in *Beyond the Chains of Illusion*, a line of evolution can be seen which leads to the ultimately much more sober, if still optimistic *Revolution of Hope*. The last book in this series, *To Have or to Be?*, displays a decidedly realistic--in parts even grim--approach to the question of humanity's potential to change course and improve its existence. The dichotomy between humanistic hope and clear minded diagnosis characteristic for Fromm's whole production is still there. But hope has gradually diminished in strength. In the last decade of his life, Fromm became visibly ready to acknowledge the predominance and rampant increase of necrophilous tendencies in Western society. Especially when examining *To Have or to Be?*, one has to keep in mind that Erich Fromm had taken McCarthy's and Humphrey's defeat as an unequivocal indication that rapid change for the better in North American society was out of the question. Nixon's victory was tantamount to the defeat of his own hopes. And his move to Switzerland, apparently necessitated by reasons of health, was also a symbolic act. After devoting the work of almost four decades to the New World, Erich Fromm withdrew to his origins in the Old World. Did he actually acknowledge defeat for *all* his efforts? Definitely not. Even in the final years of his life, he remained moderately active as an observer and commentator of the political and social panorama. Even the physiognomic variety of the pictures taken of him during that decade is startling.[1] Some photographs reveal Erich Fromm's physical and mental suffering. But others vividly and touchingly capture an indefatigable joie de vivre, a clear presence of the humanistic outlook on life, and the transcendence of illness and resignation through the great vision he never fully abandoned.

The Art of Loving was first published in Ruth Nanda Anshen's *World Perspectives* series.[2] In the United States, the book was an immediate smashing success. Doubtlessly, many readers purchased the book on the assumption that it offered a "how-to" approach to the practice of erotic love. They found themselves either starkly disappointed or at least surprised by its contents. In the meantime, the slim volume has been translated into seventeen languages and has been sold in millions of copies all over the globe. Ironically, it never passed censorship in the German Democratic Republic, due to its misleading title. Communist countries are often even more paranoid than their capitalistic neighbors toward what is presumed to be "pornographic" material. Fromm could have avoided these misunderstandings regarding the book's content by naming it "The Art of Living"--which would have been an almost equally fitting title. On the other hand, the commercial success it achieved would hardly have been comparable.

In many respects, *The Art of Loving* is a subversive book: subversive to both commonly accepted theories on love and to a social climate counterproductive to the practice of love. Although it does recapitulate various earlier concepts--particulary the productive character orientation from *Man for Himself*--it also contains a wealth of new and provocative insights. Characteristically, Fromm approaches his topic from three vantage points: the theoretical, the social, and the practical. It is definitely worthwhile to follow the chronological deployment of his ideas. Contrary to the widespread opinion that love is primarily a problem of *being* loved, he says, its nature must be defined as the *capacity to love*. Therefore, the prevalent passive (vide the receptive character orientation as discussed above[3]) concept of love must be replaced by an active and dynamic understanding of the term. Love is not "a mixture between being popular and having sex appeal," but an art which needs intense study and training. This definition is diametrically opposed to current social trends, in particular to the market-

ing orientation which, in turn, is a keystone in the negative characterology of *Man for Himself.* The marketing character is a product
of a society devoted almost exclusively to the rapid consumption of
commodities. In this societal pattern, love has become a commodity comparable to the things displayed in shop windows; "falling in
love" often means merely that one presumes to have encountered
the best "product" available, considering the limitations of one's
own "exchange value." Love, in brief, is subject to the "same pattern of exchange which governs the commodity and the labor market."[4] Even if this statement is fully in line with Fromm's thinking
as a whole, it runs contrary to everything his reader must expect
from a book about love. Socialization in the United States has always stressed pseudo-values such as popularity and the "perfect
match" of the supposedly beautiful and successful couple. Love, in
the common usage of the term, is frequently regarded as an act of
exchange, a trading off between status and beauty or similar qualities. And indeed, if divorce rates are indicative of the many shat-
tered hopes in the perfect marriage, the North American concept
of love is mostly based on illusion. Courageously, Fromm sets out
to destroy this illusion and to replace it by truth. Love, if properly
perceived, must be learned. And the process of learning may be
divided into two parts: "the mastery of the theory" and "the mastery
of the practice."

To grasp the *theoretical* aspects of love, he argues, one must first
comprehend the basic problems of human existence. Through their
capacity for reason, humans are capable of awareness of themselves, their fellow beings, and future developments. Life--here he
restates his frequently used definition--for humans is *"Life being
aware of itself."*[5] And this awareness enables humans to experience
"separateness," isolation, or loneliness, which Fromm regards as the
cause of all anxiety. Separateness can evolve in many forms. Humans may be separated (i.e. alienated) from their own selves, from
the groups to which they belong, from nature, and from society.
Especially the last form of isolation is a dangerous threat to modern individuals. Not only does the individual who feels out of touch
with the given social environment become increasingly alienated,

to the point where actual neurosis develops. But society itself has protective mechanisms designed to prevent individual or group deviation. In dictatorial systems, regimentation, threat, and actual terror are employed to insure individual conformity and, concomitantly, the functioning of the whole structure. Democratic countries use more subtle, though no less effective means of enforcing the cohesion of the societal framework: propaganda, indoctrination and, more important, constant pressure to conform. Conformism, whether induced by force or by brain-washing, results in the curtailing and ultimate destruction of human freedom. Fromm observes correctly that the humanistic concept of *equality* has degenerated in contemporary Western capitalism to the pitiful state of "sameness." People are far from equal in terms of their rights and privileges. Regarding their drive to adapt to pre-fabricated behavior patterns, however, they are equal in the sense that everyone wants and does the same. Feelings and human interaction are largely prescribed. In particular, the ability to "get along" with everyone is stressed by conformistic societies to an absurd degree. One is reminded in this context of the Brave New World mode of living in Park Forest, as described in some detail in *The Sane Society*.[6] The answer to this highly controlled libidinal substructure of a basically love-less society can frequently be found in a state of symbiotic union, an unproductive form of human relationship which may consist of a passive, masochistic coexistence or of a sadistic domination of one person by another. Both have nothing in common with love, although they are perceived as legitimate patterns of attachment. An alternative, according to Fromm, lies in mature love, which can only develop if the individual's own self and integrity are preserved.

What, then, is the nature of love for the productive, non-alienated being? Four basic ingredients are essential: *care, responsibility, respect,* and *knowledge*. Care must be interpreted as "active concern" for the loved one, whereas responsibility implies constructive participation in fulfilling the other person's needs. Respect requires that the loved person is allowed to grow and realize her/his own potential. Finally, knowledge as the most important and complex concept of the four refers (in analogy to the Biblical use of the word) to the "act of love" itself, which permits the ultimate state in both self-discovery and in discovery of the loved one's essence. Characteristically, Fromm emphasizes that "objective" knowledge is a precondition for mature love: "I have to know the other person and myself objectively, in order to be able to see his reality, or rather, to overcome the illusions, the irrationally distorted picture I have of him."[7] The same dualistic premise of *objective* knowledge and *subjective* love applies to an individual's religious experience. One can not experience union either with a loved person or with God on the basis of irrationality alone. Both require the rational act of freeing oneself from fallacies and illusions and the decision to achieve full knowledge of the object of one's love.

Once more, mysticism and rationalism are fused in Fromm's conception of love. The combining of the seemingly incombineable does not lead to an epistemological paradox, but rather serves to bring both the dynamic (i.e. rational) and the introspective (i.e. mystical) parts of human nature into play. A holistic characterology of the loving self emerges which is directly derived from the dynamic theory of human character in *Man for Himself*. Needless to say, Fromm once again makes frequent use in *The Art of Loving* of the thoughts of Aristotle, Spinoza, and Master Eckhart: the stalwarts of his eclectic philosophy. Without actually naming his source, he also makes reference to the idea of a male-female polarity which he regards as the "basis for all creativity." Plato first described this concept in his *Symposium*. For Plato, the ultimate creative force of eros is a similar dynamic duality, which includes both desire for the loved one *and* intellectual passion. Its goal is union with the beloved and, at the same time, the creation of a new and higher entity. This *dialectic* understanding of love provides the basis for Fromm's further argument. It must also be seen as the central idea of the book.

A brief discourse on masculine and feminine character orientations follows. The former, Fromm says, has the qualities of "penetration, guidance, activity, discipline and adventurousness," whereas the latter is distinguished by "productive receptiveness, protection, realism, endurance, motherliness." He concedes that real persons do not offer these characteristics in their pure form, but rather a blend with a preponderance of either the male or the female. Many modern readers of both sexes will nevertheless take issue with (or outright reject) this stereotypical and almost laughably conventional characterology of the sexes. In the ensuing discussion of parental love, Fromm relies heavily on his debatable premise of a fundamental difference in the emotional structure of father and mother. Mother, he claims, "is the home we came from, she is nature, soil, the ocean ..." In contrast, a father "does not represent any such natural home."[8] He stands presumably for a different realm of existence: the intellectual and structural order of things, "law and order," discipline, and contact to the outside world. Motherly love is seen as unconditional, the love of a father as contingent upon his approval of the child's obedience and achievements. From the viewpoint of contemporary educational psychology, this typification of parental love is highly questionable. But Fromm's basic premise, once isolated from the gender stereotypes he uses to "prove" it, is correct: a child needs *both* uncompromising love and discipline in order to become a mature human being.

The book's central section is devoted to five different types of love: a) brotherly love; b) motherly love; c) erotic love; d) self-love; e) love for God. Brotherly love is seen as the most fundamental of all. Firmly rooted in the Judaeo-Christian tradition, the mandate "love thy neighbor as thyself" provides the centrifugal force for *all* existing forms of love. Next to it, motherly love most be seen as the soil from which a loving person grows: the essential precondition for the formation of a biophilous character. Erotic love is both exclusive--as it is centered on a one-to-one relationship--and universal, for "it loves in the other person all of mankind, all that is alive." For many readers, the second part of this definition will be hard to accept and indeed very provocative, as it fuses the humanistic postulate of philanthropy with the infinitely "private" experience of sexual intimacy. Be that as it may, Fromm perceives both emotions as ontologically inseparable and as

deriving from the same core--human essence--but as heterogeneous in their direction. In order to be mature love, he argues,
erotic love has to fulfill one condition: "That I love from the
essence of my being--and experience the other person in the
essence of his or her being."[9] This sentence may well be the central
statement of the whole book regarding erotic, i.e. heterosexual
love. Fromm does not concede that the homosexual "deviation" is
capable of attaining a union of the two poles of Platonic eros.
Homosexuals presumably will suffer the same fate as heterosexuals
unable to love, i.e. the pain resulting from unresolved separateness.[10]   Again, for many of today's readers, this may be an
unacceptable viewpoint.   Sexual love in its mature form, for
Fromm, goes far beyond the biological desire for consummation. It
encompasses a rational element (i.e. knowledge) and an irrational
or mystical component (i.e. the striving for unity) which form a
dialectic duality. The synthesis of this dialectic process, then, is the
union of the self with the other. Hausdorff correctly observes that
this fusion of mysticism and sexuality brings Fromm "much closer to
Jung than Fromm would like to believe."[11]

With respect to self-love, Fromm sharply criticizes Freud's definition of this phenomenon as a pathological form of narcissism.
One must, he ventures, be capable of accepting one's own self in
order to love another person. Self-love is not to be confused with
selfishness. True love for one's self can be extended in undimin-
ished proportions to the other and to God. At this point, Fromm
cites a central passage from Master Eckhart, which should be
quoted verbatim as it provides immediate insight into Fromm's own
concept of universal love. It reads as follows:

> If you love yourself, you love everybody as you do yourself. As long as you
> love another person less than you love yourself, you will not really succeed in
> loving yourself, but if you love all alike, including yourself, you will love them
> as one person and that person is both God and man. Thus he is a great and
> righteous person, who loving himself, loves all others equally.[12]

From there, it follows that the love of God must be an integral part
of the human capacity for love. Once again, this form of love can

not mature if its object--God--is defined by authoritarian religion or, in other words, if love equals submission.   The affinity of Fromm's a-authoritarian concept to Moses Maimonides and to the writings of Hermann Cohen is obvious here.   Fromm does not elaborate on his atheistic approach to a mystical and religious experience in *The Art of Loving*. He has devoted various books to this topic, including *Psychoanalysis and Religion* and *You Shall be as Gods*, which have already been discussed earlier in this study.

Before he turns to the practical aspects of loving, Fromm presents his reader with a succinct diagnosis of the causes responsible for the disintegration of love in present-day Western society. *Alienation* is seen once more as the key factor in the development of a fundamentally love-less environment. Through alienated labor and the consecutive atrophying of human feelings, individuals have been reduced to automatons unable to love. Instead, "personality packages" are exchanged at fair market value. Love is often presumed to be the result of sexual satisfaction. In reality, sexual happiness is the result of a loving relationship. All in all, contemporary Western society displays a "socially patterned pathology" of love and is strongly counterproductive to all mature forms of loving. As is customary for Fromm's writings, the brief social critique displayed in this section strikes the reader as remarkably perceptive. With a frontal attack on the societal malaise of capitalism, Fromm denounces commonly accepted forms of human relationships as a miserable substitute for love which is sold in various attractive packages but mainly consists of fraud and self-delusion.

The practice of love, as opposed to the widespread phenomenon of egotism à deux, is described as a five-step pattern toward mastery of the art. In order to succeed, the loving person has to exert *self-discipline*. Laziness is definitely the wrong approach to love. Together with self-discipline, *concentration* and *patience* are essential ingredients. If all these conditions are met, *supreme concern* for the beloved will follow. Shallow pastimes and entertainments should be avoided. Trivial conversation and bad company must be regarded as detrimental to one's own growth.   And finally, *self-awareness* in form of rational self-analysis must accompany the gradual process of maturation toward the full capacity to love. All this is necessary in order to overcome one's own narcissistic tendencies and to reach a mental state that includes both reason and humility. Love requires faith and courage. And it can not rest idle, but must spark an active orientation toward both the loved one and the greater whole of society. At this point, Fromm confronts his reader with the all-important question: how can love be practiced and achieved in a societal structure that is hostile toward genuine emotion? How can one love and, at the same time, prevail in a world based on the principle of egotism? In an "abstract" sense, obviously, a reconciliation is impossible: "The *principle* underlying capitalistic society and the *principle* of love are incompatible."[13] From a more practical viewpoint, however, Fromm believes a compromise might be reached. And there is always hope for constant societal change, even for eventual drastic socio-economic transformations which would liberate humanity--and love--from the bondage of alienation.

Despite its somewhat vague conclusion, the book is impressive. *The Art of Loving* is vintage Fromm at his best and well deserving of the mass appeal it has retained through the three decades since its publication. From today's viewpoint, its primary thrust--the shattering of an illusory and ultimately detrimental understanding of "love"--remains as relevant as ever. The humanistic, holistic alternative it provides might not convince everyone. Anthropologically speaking, Fromm's premise that one must love oneself as much as one loves the "other" and God is problematic. Various concepts of love--which are, after all, situated in ontologically separate levels of human consciousness--are blended altogether too seemlessly in this approach. In the final analysis, however, Fromm is correct in his assumption that *all* love springs from the same, the biophilous well of human nature: eros as much as caritas (the Christian term for the ultimate care for the fellow-human) and the longing for a transcendental being. Interestingly enough, Fromm fails to mention what is indisputably the essential root of both love and creativity--the desire for immortality shared by all humans.

Once more under the editorship of Ruth Nanda Anshen, *Beyond the Chains of Illusion* was published seven years after *The Art of Loving* in the *Credo* Series. The book carries the appropriate sub-title *My Encounter with Marx and Freud* and is meant as a pre-dominantly personal, yet didactic statement on the humanistic movement, its tradition, and its future. In addition to the text proper, the volume contains an "intellectual autobiography" (which has been quoted repeatedly in this study), and an appendix entitled "Credo." Fromm's autobiographical remarks warrant particular attention, especially in view of his chronic reticence regarding specific influences and events in his own life. The propelling force of his development as a thinker, as he perceives it, has been *doubt*.

Early in his life, he was confronted by the cataclysmic experience of the First World War, an outburst of wholesale hatred and destruction. Ready explanations and propagandistic euphemisms such as the "fight for freedom" etc. made little sense to the adolescent. He began to ponder the question whether war results from coincidence or is "a result of certain social and political developments which follow their own laws and which can be understood--or even predicted--providing one knows the nature of these laws."[14] Like many other members of his generation, Erich Fromm was shocked into social and political awareness by the war. He began to investigate individual phenomena of character orientation. Thus originated his life-long concern with Sigmund Freud's theories. At the same time, his political interest focussed on the thought of Karl Marx, the pre-eminent founding father of modern socio-economic theory. Fromm has never excelled as a theoretician alone. As opposed to Horkheimer and Adorno, whose most exquisite writings are theoretical, he has always kept an open eye on the day-to-day political and societal scene and its implications for the practical formulation of his theories. Many of his observations are directly blended into his work, and his theories on social character are intricately connected to his immediate environment and the historical events of this century. In this autobiographical preface, Fromm describes his own scientific method as accurately as possible: I think little of pure speculation . . . but believing in the superior value of *blending empirical observation with speculation* ... I have always tried to let my thinking be guided by the observation of facts and have striven to revise my theories when the observation seemed to warrant it."[15]

Fromm's intellectual autobiography is a revealing document. Various aspects of his own development are brought together in a somewhat simplistic, but nevertheless convincing pattern. Perhaps most instructive in this essay is the *absence* of certain names who have indeed been formative for Fromm's evolution as a thinker. Groddeck and Ferenczi, whose influence on the emerging, still orthodox Freudian analyst was considerable, are also omitted. Fromm makes no mention, either, of the tremendous impact Horkheimer and his circle--specifically Borkenau and Marcuse--had on his training in socio-psychology and Critical Theory at a crucial time. This list of omissions could be expanded almost ad libitum. The question must be raised at this point whether he in fact attempts to project the popular American image of the "self-made man"--a naive but altogether understandable inclination--or if there is an unconscious repression factor at work in his self-portrayal. The latter seems the more plausible explanation.

If a flaw in Fromm's own character can actually be gleaned from his writings alone, it must be seen in his reluctance to acknowledge intellectual debt to others. His eclecticism as a thinker--which has been amply demonstrated in the pages of this study--is certainly beyond reproach as such. All thinking, as we perceive it from the viewpoint of modern epistemology, is primarily eclectic in terms of the selective process that precedes the combination and subsequent formulation of potentially "new" or "original" ideas. The failure, though, to openly and readily acknowledge one's sources with all due respect to prior intellectual achievements frequently indicates a layer of doubt regarding the ultimate validity of one's *own* findings. In fact, the nagging fear of being perceived as a mere epigone within an intellectual tradition established mainly by others is often the ultimate root of such a lack in disclosure.

All this does not impinge on Fromm's intellectual integrity and honesty per se, which are beyond doubt. Nevertheless, a deep-seated insecurity can be deduced from both his omissions and, at times, even his deliberate attempts to obfuscate his antecedents by terminological smokescreens. My intention here is definitely not to analyze Fromm as a person; neither am I equipped for the task. Still, some suspicion lingers that Fromm himself might have been more receptive in his character orientation than he seemed able to admit. This recourse to his own characterology could be helpful in explaining both the tacit renunciation of formative influences and, moreover, his ambivalent relationship to Freud. As he himself stated, insecurity is the motivation of this character trait, not self-aggrandizement--which would be incompatible with Fromm's basic humility, as well as with the whole of his humanistic approach to life.

A critical "mood," Fromm states, is the foundation of modern thought. Together with Einstein, Marx and Freud are named as the vanguards of modern time. The importance of the former far outweighs that of the latter, and for Fromm, a re-vitalization of the humanistic tradition in the West must be founded on the theories of Karl Marx. He cites Marx's favorite mottoes, which he might as well claim as the premises for his own thought: *de omnibus est dubitandum* (everything must be subjected to doubt), and *nihil humanum a mihi alienum puto* (I believe nothing human to be alien to me). Both Marx and Freud taught humanity the essential "art of doubting." Both were spearheads in the large-scale attack against illusions which served the purpose of awakening humanity to the actual state of reality. Awakening from a dream-like state, then, is the first step toward changing reality, so that illusions are no longer a requirement for coping with it. Marx, Engels, Ferdinand August Bebel (the leader of the German Social Democratic Party in the 1870s and 1880s), the French socialist Jean Jaurès, Rosa Luxemburg, and Lenin were the proponents of a humanitarian socialistic movement designed to reshape social reality according to human needs. Freud, whom Fromm calls a "liberal reformer," was instrumental in the evolution of *individual* change. His aim was the liberation of humanity from unconscious and subconscious fears and threats. Regarding both societal improvement and individual

emancipation, the essential tool is "to penetrate through the surface of past or present behavior and to understand the *forces* which
created the pattern of behavior."[16]

Much of the following discussion of Marx and Freud is a survey
of Fromm's previous efforts, namely *Sigmund Freud's Mission* and
Marx's Concept of Man, and need not be repeated here. In general,
the study is rather repetitive and even loquacious in parts. Its substance, though, is an illuminating *direct* juxtaposition of the two
thinkers most influential in Fromm's own life. Some noteworthy
aspects will be discussed in the following brief analysis.

Marx emerges as the infinitely more progressive thinker than
Freud. Where the former had an unflagging faith in humanity's
capacity for progress toward perfection, Freud remained ambivalent in his outlook on societal evolution. Progress was always a
mixed blessing for him. For Marx, alienation is the fundamental
sickness of all mankind. Therefore, self-realization can not be
achieved without abolishing alienation. Discussing Marx's concept
of alienation through labor and the dictates of the market, Fromm
casts a particularly harsh indictment against the "entrepreneur" or,
in a broader perspective, against the mode of life typical for merchants. Creating new commodities and the corresponding artificial
needs in one's fellow humans, he says, is little more than pandering
to their weaknesses and most vulgar feelings. For those familiar
with his own childhood, these sentences carry a double entendre, as
they describe not only the marketing orientation typical of capitalist businesspeople, but also the somewhat demeaning form of existence in which Fromm's father Naphtali saw himself caught. An
almost schizophrenic image of the merchant who has to provide for
his family and the would-be rabbi is invoked between the lines of
an outright condemnation of business life. That Erich Fromm, four
and a half decades after he left his parental household in Frankfurt,
still felt so strongly with respect to the alienating influence of trade
and commerce on the small merchant is an exceptionally illuminating facet in his biography.

Every neurosis, states Fromm, is in the final analysis the product
of *alienation*. With this argument, he returns to the central ideas of

Escape from Freedom. Freud, despite his occasional excursions into the realm of social neuroses, remained primarily interested in the pathology of the individual or the pathological interaction of individuals on a small scale. In contrast, Marx's ultimate concern was societal pathology. He held the social organization as a whole responsible for the pathological deformation of its members. Hence, it needs no further emphasis that Fromm's own socio-psychological method and particularly his theory of the social character are predominantly indebted to Marx, and that Freud's impact on this keystone of his work is secondary, albeit by no means negligible. Once more, the essential dichotomy of the social character in present-day capitalistic societies is stressed: its potential for a humanistic revival on one hand, and the detrimental drive toward repression of individual growth, as well as toward large-scale aggression (i.e. war) on the other.

The remedy for this predominance of destructive traits within the social character lies in a general re-orientation toward *constructive interaction* and *productive work* as postulated by Marx. It is interesting to note that here, as in some of his previous writings, Fromm cites the example of Goethe's *Faust* as "the most outstanding expression" of the humanistic concept of the "ever-striving" man. He had grappled with this greatest drama in nineteenth-century Western intellectual tradition repeatedly without, however, arriving at a convincing interpretation. And yet, it *is* possible to read the drama from the viewpoint of messianic, humanistic socialism. Here is a sketch of the interpretation Fromm must have had in mind but remained unable to formulate.

Faustus, the ageing medieval philosopher and universal genius, engages in a pact with Satan--Goethe calls him Mephistopheles--in order to achieve ultimate insight into universal order and access to all pleasures of the flesh. Mephistopheles will serve him unconditionally up to the point where Faust ceases to strive and rests in contentment. At that time, his soul will be claimed by the devil. God himself sanctions the covenant. In the first part of the tragedy, Faust becomes guilty by seducing Gretchen, who satisfies his lust for youth and beauty. The tragedy of his egotism ends with

the death of Gretchen (who is saved from damnation through re-
pentance) and the departure of a sobered Faust to the realm of
mythology, which provides the setting for part two. Faust's union
with Helen of Troy--the symbolic marriage of ever-striving German
idealism and the beauty of Greek antiquity--produces a son, Eu-
phorion. His early death indicates that the mystic union of classi-
cism and romanticism is short-lived at best. At the end of his life,
Faust finally becomes blind. Blindness to things, paradoxically, enables him to see and gain awareness for the human community. His
last words are devoted to productive, altruistic work and to the idea
of freedom and humanity. In his ultimate moment of self-realiza-
tion--where he indeed is ready to cease striving--Faust is redeemed.
In a sense, he loses his wager with Mephistopheles. On a transcendental plane, however, he remains the victor in the struggle
between "good" and "evil," lassitude and striving; his soul is claimed
by God.

The humanistic concept of the drama and its direct relevance for
Fromm's fusion of activism and mysticism is all too obvious. Moreover, the end of part two certainly lends itself to an interpretation
focussed on the strong undertones of religious socialism: Faust is
saved because he has realized, in his final hour, that true creativity
can only be achieved in the service of *all* humanity. Fromm
doubtlessly sensed the potential of this outstanding literary creation as a demonstration of his own personal humanistic-socialistic
credo, but he never came to terms with the enormous complexity of
Goethe's text.

The second part of *Beyond the Chains of Illusion* is devoted to
Fromm's theory of the social character. With the term "resistance,"
he defines one particular motivating factor within individual and
collective action: a "socially conditioned filter" through which specific thoughts are channeled and/or repressed. Subconscious
mechanisms may either inhibit or propel certain actions without
ever becoming clear to the respective person or societal group.
Consequently, people tend to forget what they *want* to forget or to
repress. Sullivan's term "selective inattention" is used to further
illustrate this phenomenon. In the words of C. G. Jung, the "social

unconscious" is a dynamic factor present in every social organization and to a large extent responsible for its libidinal substructure. If manipulated by propaganda, it is often responsible for the most horrendous and dangerous distortions of truth, which however are commonly accepted as truth per se. Past experience--which in fact would dictate a reasonable course of action--can frequently not be utilized, as it is prevented by this filtering mechanism from entering consciousness. Consequently, identical or similar mistakes have been re-enacted throughout history under the guise of "truth."

In reality, they are caused by the very inability of the social apparatus to face truth, as all access roads are blocked by subconscious resistance. Neither can objective thought prevail in a society where organized repression is the order of the day. Truth may therefore be found primarily in the realm of the unconscious: "The unconscious is the whole man--minus that part of him which corresponds to his society."[17] Therefore, hope for the liberation of humanistic consciousness can neither lie in Soviet communism nor in Western monopolistic capitalism, as both systems are repressive in their approach to truth. Their very existence requires a propaganda machinery designed for erecting huge stumbling blocks on the road to awareness. Radical humanism, as it is practiced by "small groups of humanist socialists" all over the globe, must be activated on a broad front and organized into an international movement if humanity, after millennia of bloody trial and error, is finally to be liberated from the chains of illusion.

In conclusion, Fromm offers a socialist-humanistic "credo" which distills the essence of his theoretical work as well as the various co-efficients of a new humanistic order as he envisions it. A New Man must be created who will be the center of a unified world order based on reason and peace. He concludes with the fervent plea for reversal of the "old," detrimental course humanity has steered throughout history. His final sentence betrays at least some ambivalence with regard to the actual chances that such a reversal will take place: "I believe in the perfectibility of man, but I doubt whether he will achieve his goal, unless he awakens soon."[18] At the very end of the book, Erich Fromm returns, despite all doubts, to the foundation on which all his thinking rests: to the principle of human perfectability. This humanistic credo is an admirable and deeply moving statement. Chances, however, that it will one day replace the obligatory pledges of allegiance to one nation or another in school classrooms and elsewhere are slim indeed. Humanity appears not yet ready to accept the notion of humanitarian internationalism.

The Revolution of Hope: Toward a Humanized Technology was, as mentioned earlier, meant to appear before the 1968 presidential elections, as Fromm hoped it would provide additional momentum to the popular movement centered around Robert Kennedy and, after his assassination, Eugene McCarthy. Hubert H. Humphrey, to whom the Democratic nomination finally fell, had neither the charisma nor the political profile of Kennedy and McCarthy. But it has to be kept in mind that during the later 1960s in the United States, there was indeed a relatively broad popular basis which supported discontinuation of the Vietnam War and, moreover, sought societal change in the interest of racial and economic equality. All this fizzled out within a few years and did not--as opposed to some Central European countries where the "student revolution" in particular brought about greater societal re-orientations--leave a lasting imprint on the country's social structure. But it is precisely this feeling of fermentation and optimistic anticipation shared not only by intellectual liberals but also by thousands of U.S. citizens in 1968 which prompted Fromm to write this book. Astonishingly enough, he does not mention any of the actual political events of this epoch, which began with the Berkeley student revolt in 1964, nor does he directly address the enormous pacifistic mass movement which originated on American campuses and swept like a firestorm on through Europe within a few years. Fromm is consistent in his approach. He refuses to pin his own hopes for societal evolution on any particular class or stratum of the population. In fact, he does not *want* any individual group to assume leadership within the envisioned mass movement. In this respect, he remains a faithful disciple of Max Horkheimer, who had, already in his very first writing on Critical Theory, denied any single class the claim to a leading role in the evolutionary process he hoped for. Needless to say, both Fromm and Horkheimer stand in this respect in direct opposition to Karl Marx and the particular emphasis he placed on the proletariat as history's one and only propelling force.

Although the study is a sequel to both *The Sane Society* and *May Man Prevail?*, it is somewhat disappointing in its lack of truly original concepts. The book appears to have been whipped up in great haste, and is poorly structured. Both its title and the pervading leitmotif of *hope* are heavily indebted to Ernst Bloch, whose philosophical magnum opus *Das Prinzip Hoffnung (The Principle of Hope* [1959]) had been published in Germany a decade earlier. Bloch's influence on Fromm's thinking--although acknowledged only in passing in *The Revolution of Hope* by a single footnote--became increasingly strong during the 1960s. (One should also keep in mind that Fromm had met Bloch fifty years earlier, and already then had been deeply moved by his *Spirit of Utopia*.[19]) The principle of hope, as defined by Bloch, is founded on dialectic materialism. It is centered on the vision of a new, yet unconstructed homestead for all of humanity which will emerge from the shambles of the old order. Unfulfilled hope--or, in Bloch's terminology, the "nothing"--is the eternal striving force within the human self: the drive to fill the void with "something," and thus the ultimate principle of both creativity and revolution. For Bloch, Marx has provided a concrete framework for the realization of hope. And humanity is entitled to finally achieve its goal of a full, non-alienated life in the near future. Similar to Fromm's work, atheism and messianic faith are closely linked in Bloch's philosophy. It is not possible to further delineate in this context the complex argumentation of Bloch's book. Suffice it to say that it has to be regarded as one of the most profound achievements in twentieth-century philosophy. *The Principle of Hope* has left an indelible imprint throughout *The Revolution of Hope*.

Hope, as Fromm defines it in accordance with Bloch and, to a certain extent, along the lines of Paul Tillich, is an *active* feeling directed not toward the acquisition of things, but toward the fulfillment of a vision. Its goals--a "state of greater aliveness," the liberation from an undignified existence, salvation, or revolution--are situated in the future, yet they are attainable. Future as such can not be worshipped in the spirit of hope, as Robespierre did in the French Revolution of 1789. Only if the future holds a *valid* promise for the fulfillment of messianic hope, can it be regarded as a vessel for the spirit of humanistic evolution. Lack of hope, conversely, is the absence of love for life. Here, Fromm launches a violent attack against Herbert Marcuse, his former colleague at the Institute of Social Research, who in his studies *Eros and Civilization*[20] and *One Dimensional Man*[21] painted a dismal picture of human existence in the technological world of late capitalism. Marcuse's work is denounced as a "naive, cerebral daydream, essentially irrational, unrealistic, and lacking love of life."[22] The ability to disagree while maintaining a basis of mutual respect has been conspicuously absent from some of Fromm's writings, and not only in his controversy with Marcuse.

Hoping, says Fromm, is a "state of being." A readiness which is intense, yet not released into "activeness." He uses the term *activeness*--which he owes to Michael Maccoby--throughout the book as the opposite of *passiveness*, in order to denote an attitude rather than a state of action or inaction. Intricately linked to hope are the notion of faith, the virtue of fortitude, and, finally, humanity's capacity for messianic thinking. The present state of American society is seen as a crossroads leading either to the fulfillment of messianic hope or into the abyss of a fully dehumanized mode of living, culminating in the year 2000. In his description of this hypothetical robotized society, Fromm relies heavily on the perceptive works of Lewis Mumford, especially his *The Myth of the Machine*,[23] and *In the Name of Sanity*,[24] as well as on the incisive diagnosis presented by the French sociologist Jacques Ellul in *The Technological Society*.[25] Once more, as in *The Sane Society* and other writings, Fromm emphasizes his own faith in humanity and its innate force of reason, which can orchestrate sudden, large-scale societal change propelling it away from doom (i.e. ultimate robotization and war) and toward a truly humane environment. He takes issue with anthro-

pological and instinctivistic theories founded on the assumption
that humans are strongly influenced by their instinctual organization and thus prone to certain animalistic behavior patterns. In
particular, he refutes the theories of Konrad Lorenz (*On Aggression*)[26] and Desmond Morris (*The Naked Age*),[27] as they presumably pander to the dream of many people ". . . to combine the emotions of a primate with a computerlike brain." He argues that the
enormous increase in size and complexity of the human brain, especially the greatly enlarged neocortex (located in the neen-
cephalon) are responsible for a noticeable decrease in instinctual
motivation, in exchange for a predominance in human self-awareness. Therefore, humans can no longer expect that their decisions
be "made for them" by instinct. They have to accept responsibility
for making them on the basis of *rational insight*. The time has
come, says Fromm, to halt galloping dehumanization in its tracks.
The ultimate obligation for doing so rests with each individual.

   The prophetic tone of his writing betrays little patience with
human and societal inertia. Although he excludes force as a viable
means for change--and therefore refuses to follow up on the
promise made by the book's title, as non-violent revolution may
well be regarded a contradiction in terms--and postulates evolution
instead, Fromm is simply not realistic in his assumption that evolutionary processes can take place practically overnight. In his messianic fervor, Erich Fromm consistently displayed a blind spot for
the *real* obstacles on the way to humanity's better future. Evolution takes time and unceasing effort. The road to enlightening the
masses is long and rocky. And the outcome of *any* socio-historical
process, be it revolutionary or evolutionary in nature, is never pre-
dictable. Paradoxically, it is the grand vision of the *unachievable*
change of present conditions with makes him lose sight of the *feasible*: the small but tenacious steps that could realistically be taken.

   What, then, are the "steps to the humanization of technological
society" offered by this study? Certain conditions which resulted
from the second industrial revolution are obviously irreversible.
Fromm cites the centralization of production and distribution typical for both communist and capitalist countries. In addition to cen-

tralized enterprise, centralized planning is an indispensable pre-requisite for the functioning of the economy as a whole. And finally, "cybernation"--i.e. computerized planning and the automation of actual labor--has become the backbone of modern industry and cannot be abolished without grave detriment to the production process. Given these non-variables, three alternative approaches are conceivable. First, a continuation of the present system of producing and rapidly consuming mostly unnecessary goods. The end result of this perseverance would be "severe human pathology" and/or nuclear warfare. Second, a change of course could be brought about by means of forceful revolution. This, says Fromm, would cause the total collapse of the economic system and produce a dictatorial regime. Third, and most important, a grand-scale humanization of the *existing* system might be implemented to ensure humanity's "well-being and growth." It would involve four concrete steps, which would have to be taken simultaneously. The reader is already familiar with this concept to a great extent from *The Sane Society*, and it can be briefly summarized here for the sake of further evaluation.

1. Humanistic planning. Government controls, as well as stringencies imposed on industry by concerned consumer groups, would lead to more human-centered industrial planning: " . . . man, not technique, must become the ultimate source of values; optimal human development and not maximal production the criterion for all planning."[28] Management should be re-structured in such a way that both "optimal centralization" *and* "optimal grass-roots participation" are guaranteed. Priorities have to be changed in order to alter the greater economic structure so that it becomes supportive of, and not adverse or outright hostile to human existence.

2. Abandonment of alienated bureaucracy in favor of organized mass participation in decision-making. Fromm proposes the institution of localized *groups* for the purpose of political debate and informed discussion of current issues. Such groups would function as social nuclei. Each member could know all other members personally, hence the anonymity of the political apparatus would give way to a basic parliamentarian system as outlined in *The Sane Society*

and modeled after the commissariat government propounded in
the German revolution of 1918/19 (i.e. *Räterepublik*) or the Soviet
system (a council of workers, farmers, and soldiers). The town
meeting as a primary political cell might be used as an effective tool
to break up the increasingly opaque interrelations of the military-industrial complex with practically all branches of the legisla-
tive and executive apparatus in the United States.

3. Drastic changes in society's consumption pattern as a whole.
Humanized consumption would aim at freeing the consumer from
the absurd dictates of the current market, which is exclusively
profit-oriented. Individual and collective greed would have to be
abandoned and replaced by a new humanistic orientation toward
production and consumption. Fromm concedes that this will be
possible only through a long and drastic process or re-thinking:
"The *revolution of the consumer* against the domination by industry
has yet to come."[29] He propagates legal controls on advertising,
with the ultimate goal of banning misleading indoctrination of con-
sumers. Once more, he does not realize the mutual sustenance of
production, the advertising industry, and the media in the United
States. To unravel this network of profit-shuffling based on daily
brainwashing and the subsequent consumption of throw-away
"goods" would be a truly Herculean task.

4. As a final step, the "emergence of new forms of psychospiri-
tual orientation and devotion" is proposed. This brief section of
the book is derived both from *Zen Buddhism and Psychoanalysis*
and, particularly, the final pages of *The Sane Society*. As it offers
no further insights, it need not be discussed in detail.

In conclusion, Fromm suggests the immediate constitution of a
movement which he calls the "Voice of American Conscience." A
steering group of fifty persons "whose integrity and capability are
unquestioned" should serve as a national core organization, which
would be in constant touch with the larger grass-roots bodies.
These would be organized in groups of approximately 25 members
and in broader assemblies of 100 to 300 people. The latter Fromm
calls "clubs," in allusion to the original political organization of the
instrumental factions in the French Revolution of 1789. A new

consciousness would arise from the principle of direct democracy and humanistic planning/production. Thus the mode of "having" prevalent in contemporary North America would ultimately be replaced by an existence founded on the principle of "being."

Especially the conclusive pages of *The Revolution of Hope* anticipate many central ideas of *To Have or to Be?*, Fromm's final popular study, which was to be published eight years later. *To Have or to Be?* is an extremely puzzling and contradictory book. Gone from its pages are the exuberance of the author's earlier treatises on social change. He even makes the doleful suggestion that it might in fact already be too late for humanity to radically change course. On the other hand, a strong undercurrent of hope remains visible: an almost desperate hope for a potential renewal of human life, after all. At the end of the book, Erich Fromm does not acknowledge defeat. He does, however, for the first time in his exploration of the art of living, concede that chances for a humanistic revival are exceedingly slim.

The effect of this study on the reader is ambivalent. Once again, one can not help but be captivated by the urgency of Fromm's plea for reason and sanity. At the same time, one remains conscious throughout the book of the obvious futility of his vision in the face of overwhelming factual evidence of dehumanization in Western societies. Fromm must have sensed the ambiguity of his effort. His diction is cool and almost detached. Transitions are often abrupt. Although the study contains much material from his previous writings, the customary repetitive pattern of argumentation is less apparent here, due to the fact that certain concepts are presented in a strongly abbreviated, even condensed form. The book was, once more, originally published in the *World Perspectives* series and has, as a paperback reprint, reached a broad readership since it appeared.[30] Not many reviews greeted its publication in the United States; their tenor was generally noncommittal. Interestingly enough, when the book appeared in German in 1976, it caused a flood of both sharply critical and strongly supportive reviews and commentaries. This fervent and controversial response of the

West German reading public is an illuminating testimonial to the immediate relevance of Fromm's ideas in his former homeland.

The title *To Have or to Be?* is a direct allusion to two books published some years earlier which had presented related ideas from a different viewpoint: Gabriel Marcel's *Being and Having*,[31] and the Swiss psychologist Balthasar Staehelin's *Haben und Sein* (*Having and Being*).[32] Marcel is primarily interested in the theological and philosophical ramifications of his topic. Staehelin, on the other had, is more psychologically oriented and emphasizes the importance of materialist thinking for modern science. Characteristically, Fromm tries to surpass both his antecedents by means of his proven synthetic approach. Once more, the book is divided into three parts. The first attempts a predominantly philosophical definition of the two modes in question, the "having" and the "being" forms of human existence. In part two, Fromm then delineates the socio-psychological factors responsible for each orientation. The final part is devoted to the conditions necessary for change from the "old" having-orientation to the "new" mode of being.

A brief introduction precedes the text. It focuses on the question why the second industrial revolution failed in its great promise to secure happiness for humanity. The reason, says Fromm, is two-fold. First, radical hedonism, i.e. the immediate satisfaction of any desire or material wish a person may feel, does not lead to a fulfilled human existence. And second: egotism, selfishness, and greed--the very foundations of the capitalist system--produce neither individual harmony nor peace between nations. In fact: *"Greed and peace preclude each other."*[33] Both premises are certainly acceptable as such. Fromm postulates that, in order to achieve mental health for the individual members of Western societies *and* to procure lasting peace, a "radical change of the human heart" must be instigated. Together with the economist E.F. Schumacher, the author of *Small is Beautiful*,[34] he stands convinced that there must be a fourth alternative to the presently prevailing three economic systems: " . . . to the models of corporate capitalism, social democratic or Soviet socialism, or technocratic 'fascism with a smiling face'." (It certainly is interesting to note that Fromm rather indiscriminately lumps together social democracy and Soviet socialism. The two actually have little in common--at least at this time in history. Fromm's misleading classification of European social democratic movements, to which many of his own ideas are indebted, is one more example of subconscious repression at work.)

The proposed fourth alternative rests on the essential difference between *having* and *being*. These concepts represent two fundamentally different modes of existence, whose predominance in the individual and the social character orientation is responsible for diametrically opposed life experiences. Various examples from poetry and literature, as well as from everyday language are provided to demonstrate the fact that humans have gradually acquired the tendency to define themselves on the basis of what they possess or what they consume. Alienated persons are predominantly receptive in their character orientation which, in turn, mirrors the social character of capitalist society as a whole. Learning is perceived as the accumulation of data and information, not as dynamic growth and exchange of ideas. Many areas of activity and social interaction can be approached from these two radically divergent standpoints: the "having" person will invariably rely on material possessions, status, accumulated knowledge etc., where the "being" personality reacts spontaneously to the given challenge or encounter. Particularly dangerous is the former when endowed with power, as he/she wields authority without commanding it. A political leader "... can be stupid, vicious, evil, i.e. utterly incompetent to *be* an authority, yet he *has* authority." The receptive or having character (cf. the characterological traits discussed in *Man for Himself* and *The Heart of Man*) is also essentially unable to love, as productive loving has nothing in common with possession of the beloved one. The chapter on love presents an extremely condensed version of some central ideas in *The Art of Loving*.

In part two of the book, Fromm recapitulates many concepts from his earlier writings. In addition to Master Eckhart--who gave a succinct definition of both modes--he quotes R.H. Tawney, Max Stirner's perceptive work *The Ego and His Own: The Case of the Individual Against Authority*,[35] and, last but not least, Karl Marx in his description of the "acquisitive society." The bourgeois obsession with property has gradually led to a total degeneration of all interpersonal relations. Persons are regarded as things and manipulated accordingly. Capitalist society has raised the individual's ego-consciousness to perverse heights: one's own ego is the most valuable property, to be defined in terms of physical qualities, skills, social status, wealth etc. Acquisition, then, is the ultimate goal of most actions. As opposed to nineteenth-century capitalism, commodities lose their intrinsic value once they have been acquired. They are readily discarded and replaced by newer and better "models." The process of consuming and throwing away constantly feeds the ego of the receptive personality, but it does little or nothing to enrich one's life. To the contrary: the more one becomes obsessed with having and consuming (the latter frequently involving wheeling and bartering to get the best "deal," which in turn provides a temporary ego boost), the less maturation and growth of internal strength is possible. Or, in other words, behind every ego inflated by goods and possessions, there is but a shriveled relic of a human personality.

Many among the younger generation--especially during the 1960s--rejected mindless consumerism and the having mode of existence. They set out to liberate themselves from their parents' misery, but failed, as Fromm correctly diagnoses, to simultaneously establish a new and radically different value system. Mere protest and negation surely are insufficient tools for the creation of "new" humanity. Valid and lasting counter-concepts have to be wrought in order to sustain a revitalization movement. As these were lacking, many young people failed in their quest. True, their rebellion brought them freedom "from" the acquisitive society, but it did not lead to a form of freedom "to" achieve a mature state of existence. Ultimately, many resigned themselves and rejoined the old lifestyle they had briefly left behind: "Not all who had started with great hopes ended up with disappointment, however, but it is unfortunately impossible to know what their number is."[36] Nevertheless, there is still hope that the flames of quiet rebellion might be rekindled: rebellion against consumerism and the having mode, and toward society's metamorphosis from sick to sane.

Regarding the mode of being, Fromm presents two fundamental requirements: *activity* and *altruism*. Both these character traits and their spiritual models--the philosophies of Aristotle, Master Eckhart, Spinoza, and Marx--have been discussed extensively in his prior writings, beginning with *Escape from Freedom* through the major studies on characterology and *The Sane Society*. A new and important aspect, however, is introduced with the differentiation between *solidarity* and *antagonism* as two socially conditioned, diametrically opposed forms of coexistence. Human relations in an acquisitive society are mostly characterized by greed, ruthless competition, and antagonism. Fear of losing one's possessions or, even more widespread, of losing the competitive battle for more commodities and increased status, is a crippling force. Both individuals and groups are deformed in their character structure by this all-pervading fear. Antagonism, instead of solidarity, governs most social interaction. Greed, the other side of the same coin, can never really be satisfied, as its "consummation does not fill the inner emptiness, boredom, loneliness, and depression it is meant to overcome."[37] Many of these observations can already be found in the works of the nineteenth-century socialist Moses Hess, in Schopenhauer's aphorisms, and in later writing by both the French philosopher Georges Bataille and the existentialist Martin Heidegger. The originality of Fromm's approach--this applies equally to the comparison with Gabriel Marcel's thoughts on "being" as an ontological category--lies, once more, in the cogent causalities he is able to establish between individual and social character orientation. From there, it is only logical that he extends his theory to the greater community of nations and their modus vivendi. On this global scale, the interplay of greed and fear as the determining factors in relations between various nations presents a permanent threat to peace. Fromm rightly concludes that durable peace can only be attained by replacing the having orientation by the being orientation. Solidarity between nations must be established, antagonism eradicated.

The final section of the book ("the new man and the new society") deals with the practical aspects of exchanging the detrimental having mode for the human-oriented being mode. It is not possible, argues Fromm, to accomplish wholesale change exclusively through drastic reorganization of the economic structure. He also rules out the idea that a change of individual character orientation alone could spawn the emergence of a new society. Even if such an isolated evolution of individual consciousness were possible, it would be ineffectual in terms of the greater societal organization, and would remain restricted to the private sphere. He observes that in recent years the marketing character orientation, alongside with "cybernetic religion," has gained enormous ground in Western societies. As opposed to the receptive type (who may still display traces of rudimentary individuality), the marketing character no longer possesses even a discernible ego. Perfect adaptability to the dictates of the personality market is his primary trait. Marketing persons do not experience feelings; they neither love nor hate. They are the pure incarnation of Marx's definition of the fully alienated being. (More exhaustive discussion of this character type is provided in chapters seven and eight of this study in conjunction with the respective analyses of *The Heart of Man* and *The Sane Society*.) In this context, Fromm cites two field studies completed by Michael Maccoby and Ignacio Millan. Both investigate the predominant emotional and temperamental disposition of corporate executives, and are indeed supremely illuminating with regard to the new breed of the total marketeer. In combination with cybernetic religion, i.e. the galloping advance of their unlimited faith in the predictability and manipulability of *all* forms of human existence through data processing, this character orientation presents a formidable obstacle to any humanistic revival. In Fromm's opinion, only radical humanism and simultaneous reshaping of both the social character *and* the individual's outlook on life can bring about the changes necessary for the survival of the human race.

Fromm postulates that the present situation where "a healthy economy is possible only at the price of unhealthy human beings" must be put to an end. Given the present character orientation of both capitalist and communist societies, Fromm is realistic enough to concede that the having orientation is an unavoidable part of human nature--at least in its present stage of evolution. He insists, however, that it can no longer be allowed to run amok: it must be controlled and contained by reason. In other words, *the having mode must be dominated by a new resurgence of the being mode.* In addition to E.F. Schumacher, he quotes works by the American ecologists Paul R. Ehrlich and Anne H. Ehrlich (*Population, Resources, Environment: Essays in Human Ecology*[38]) and the German Social Democrat Erhard Eppler,[39] all of which are focussed on the rampant depletion of Earth's natural resources and the willful self-destruction of human existence. Insanity, as contagious as it may be, must be halted now. A new "science of man" must be created with the goal of implementing control over both rampant technology and institutionalized humanity.

As a first step, Fromm proposes a restructuring of industrial production toward "sane" consumption. Government bodies along the lines of the existing FDA would have to be instituted for the purpose of determining norms for healthy consumption. This massive regulation could only be enforced if stockholders'/management's control over production were drastically curtailed, both by decree and by renewed consumer awareness (=boycotting useless and/or damaging commodities). All this can materialize only under the condition that ". . . the giant corporations' big hold on the government (which becomes stronger daily) and on the population (via thought control through brainwashing) is broken."[40] Anyone with even a rudimentary knowledge of the given political and economic power structure in the United States will immediately realize that this is an utterly utopian proposal. Fromm obviously does not. He continues his plan for revitalization of the being mode with a brief reiteration of the political and cultural changes he suggested in *The Sane Society* and *The Revolution of Hope*, namely the institution of a national council of responsible citizens; a grass-roots movement for the direct implementation of participatory democracy; decentralization on a smaller scale and the involvement of labor in pro-

duction planning; and the granting of an annual minimum income
to every member of society.

From there, he presents a set of essential conditions to be met by
the emerging new society, which can be briefly summarized. All
"brainwashing methods" in both industrial and political advertising
have to be banned. The rich nations must cease to exploit less developed countries. Women must be liberated from subjugation by
a patriarchal system. Accurate information must be disseminated
by effective means. Scientific research may no longer be employed
either for profit or for defense. And finally: nuclear disarmament
must be enacted immediately. Without being caustic, the astute
reader will recognize that the *voluntary* implementation of these
conditions by the present political and economic apparatus in the
United States would be tantamount to the system committing suicide. Political and economic power structures--which terms are
practically synonymous with regard to both Western capitalism and
Eastern communism--simply to not self-destruct, no matter how
many rational arguments support the dismantling of their monolithic domination over all aspects of life. The existing vicious circle
of indoctrination for the sake of consumption and consumption for
the sake of satisfying the artificial needs created by indoctrination
can not be broken up as easily as Fromm proposes. Large-scale societal changes *within* the given system are extremely time-
consuming and tedious. In some Western European countries,
such attempts as reshaping public consciousness of ecological and
defense problems have led to concrete political change within the
past decade. In West Germany, for example, the party of the
"Greens" has recently rallied considerable public support. The ultimate outcome of these as yet subtle and tentative changes in the
societal climate, however, can not be predicted.

In conclusion, Erich Fromm voices his own skepticism regarding
the fulfillment of messianic hope. Given the overwhelming power
of corporate industry and given both the powerlessness and the
horrifying apathy of the masses, there might be a two percent
chance at best for reversing the having modes. If this proposition
were a business deal, he concedes, no reasonable person would in-

vest any money in it. With this statement, Fromm returns to the gist of his seminal article "The Feeling of Powerlessness" of 1937,[41] in which he had so accurately described the prevalent social character of the German bourgeoisie before and after the ascent to power of the National Socialist party. Now, forty years later, he is faced with essentially the same conclusion: that most of those exploited by a seemingly almighty system are essentially unable--and unwilling--to act and to think independently. But unconditional surrender to doom is not compatible with Fromm's character. The book's final pages, once again, summon the vision of a new society, populated by free and productive beings. Fromm calls this noble mirage a dialectic synthesis of the medieval City of God and the modern Earthly City--*The City of Being.*

Even among his ardent followers, the publication of *To Have or to Be?* caused some consternation. Fromm's acute social diagnosis can not be easily reconciled with the solutions he propagates. Metaphorically speaking, almost every line of the book bends under the strain of the clearly impossible resolution of the dilemma. The author must have realized that he extended his own vision of a better future to the breaking point--and even beyond. Rolf Denker, one of his more sympathetic reviewers, expresses serious doubt about the possibility of actualizing his proposals.[42] Many other critics accused his suggested practical solutions of being naive and unrealistic. This is certainly true. Equally problematic, however, is the book's basic premise, as it links a *socio-psychological theory* (that of the different character orientations) with an *ethical doctrine.* The latter may be compressed into the formula that having is "evil," being is "good." Methodologically, Fromm's approach is most questionable. Social psychology and ethics have always been closely related in his writings. Their guileless amalgamation as practiced here, however, must necessarily result in oversimplification. The ethical differentiation between having and being, at least in this rather simplistic presentation, obfuscates Fromm's social pathology. Instead of strengthening his plea for humanistic revival, the unilateral praise awarded the being orientation and the equally categorical condemnation of the having principle have

failed to convince many of his readers. He constantly overstresses
his point through an inappropriate--and, in anthropological terms,
untenable--denunciation of *all* having as the root of every evil. He
fails to differentiate (as he did in his earlier writings, especially
Marx's Concept of Man and *The Sane Society*) between the natural
and even beneficial drive of humans to acquire a certain amount of
possessions required for a comfortable standard of living, and the
amassment of capital leading to exploitation and alienation.
Therefore, the very *totality* of his approach leads into pitfalls. In
the final analysis, the radical alternative between having and being
must appear contrived and unconvincing. Even Rainer Funk, one
of his closest associates, carefully describes the book as ". . . an *attempt* to synthesize sociopsychological insights and humanist religion and ethics."[43] Gonsalv K. Mainberger, much less considerate
in his critical assessment, calls the volume a "journalistic collage"
and a juggling act in which Fromm uses prophecy to pass over the
obvious gaps in his own analytical method.[44] His whole outlook on
history, Mainberger claims, is lopsided: history can not be taken
back on the strength of the two simple terms *having* and *being*.

More benevolent critics of the book rightly admire the immedi-
acy of its appeal to a large readership and its potential to instill a
new form a self-awareness in those individuals whose own discon-
tent with society and their own existence it will reinforce. Nevertheless, there seems to be at least some consensus regarding the
naiveté of its conception as a whole, particularly in light of recent
findings on human aggressions by other researchers such as
Alexander Mitscherlich. Admirable as Fromm's uncompromising
proposal for grand societal re-orientation may be, it has to be recognized as a route which not many will choose. An interesting
sidelight: one year after the publication of *To Have or to Be?*, the
Swiss writer Otto F. Walter published is novel *Die Verwilderung*
(*Gone Wild* [1977]).[45] Written under the direct influence of
Fromm's book, the novel describes the fate of two young people
who leave affluent society (i.e. the having mode) behind to create a
mini-community founded on the principles of altruistic cooperation
and the sharing of possessions (i.e. the being mode). Walter's fic-

tionalization of Fromm's ideas is quite convincing. Whether it can actually serve as a model for the emergence of new social cells imbued with the spirit of productive humanism remains yet to be seen.

In the wake of the strong and controversial reception of his last popular book, Erich Fromm was interviewed by the Austrian social scientist Adelbert Reif for the magazine *Pardon* in 1977.[46] Some of his answers shed additional light on the intent of his study. When questioned on the abolition of private property as a possible step toward realizing the being mode, Fromm stated that this measure would be totally ineffective. Not the actual distribution of possessions is the issue, he argues, but a general change in consciousness toward having and being. If having were to lose its overwhelming importance in people's minds, the question of who has a little more or less would become irrelevant. The present state of indoctrination prevents this very change, as it furthers stupidity, i.e. the absence of reason. Fromm correctly differentiates between intelligence/cunning (*Verstand*) and reason (*Vernunft*). Stupidity is not the consequence of mental retardation; it is the coefficient of a lack of freedom. Reif inquires whether it is at all possible to activate critical reason and independence in a world dominated by propaganda. Fromm, in return, expresses his hope that progress will not fail, despite mass indoctrination: "mutations" in human consciousness have always taken place throughout history, and are still conceivable. Those responsible for mutations are humans who lived in their own times and were still able to envision a totally different configuration for the future. What he describes here might be called the *revolutionary* character orientation, which has in the past propelled the evolution of history.

As the central cause for the present predominance of the having mode, Fromm pinpoints the absence of faith in millions of humans. Faith has been replaced by the obsession with things. But a radical and swift aboutface is more than a moral and ethical issue: it bears directly on the very preservation of the human species. Therefore, reason and the will for self-preservation should be enough to make humanity ready for change. Ultimately, unlived life is the primary

cause of destructiveness. Humanity will eventually self-destruct if
no drastic change of course can be implemented. With his
concluding remarks, Fromm reiterates one of the most important
theses from *The Anatomy of Human Destructiveness*, published
three years prior to *To Have or to Be?*.

His last popular work, despite its weaknesses and the obvious
oversimplifications it employs in formulating its premises, must be
regarded as a poignant exhortation addressed primarily to those
who are still able and willing to re-assess the direction of their own
lives. Admittedly, this is an autumnal book. It lacks the freshness
and the cohesion of many of its predecessors. Although not sum-
marily persuasive, it contains a wealth of individual insights into the
human psyche and the exterior forces at work on us. Above all, it is
the final major utterance of a great humanist, much more personal
in its contents than the somewhat detached style betrays. As such--
and *not* as a stringent scientific statement on human nature--it still
deserves a wide readership, at least among those who have not fully
abandoned the utopian ideas of solidarity and peace.

10

Looking Into the Abyss. The Theory of Human Aggression (1973-1975)

During the final years of his life, Erich Fromm was a very ill man. In 1974, the year after *The Anatomy of Human Destructiveness* was published, he and his wife decided not to return to Mexico, but instead to remain permanently in Muralto (canton Ticino), where he was named an honorary citizen. He traveled regularly to the Salzburg symposia on humanism and kept in close contact both with the media (through interviews) and with humanistically oriented individuals and societies, particularly with the "Praxis" group, a consortium of philosophers and other public figures devoted to socialist humanism. He also served as co-editor of their periodical, *Praxis*. In 1970, he had edited a collection of essays under the title *The Crisis of Psychoanalysis*,[1] which contained some rather awkward translations of articles from the 1930s and an important newer contribution on the present state of psychoanalysis. This essay, also entitled "The Crisis of Psychoanalysis," is definitely worthwhile reading from today's viewpoint. Here Fromm once more challenges current analytical trends as dangerous and often deformative, since they tend to enforce an individual's adaptation to the norms and behavioral patterns of a sick society. In other words: if a person is regarded as mentally ill according to commonly accepted standards of interaction, it might well be that the social character on the whole is insane--and not the nonconformist per se. Between the lines of this perceptive contribution, Fromm's own frustration with his fellow-analysts is discernible, especially with those who had ostracized him and accused him of Freudian "revisionism."

Erich Fromm remained a devoted Buddhist for the rest of his life. Every morning, he practiced meditation and engaged in concentration exercises. (His mentor was the above-mentioned monk Nyanaponika Mahatera, author of *The Heart of Buddhist Meditation*.[2]) Moreover, he conducted self-analysis of his dreams and subconscious activities on a daily basis. It is safe to say that he adhered strictly to the principles put forth in his own 1960 publication *Zen Buddhism and Psychoanalysis*. Indisputably, Fromm retained tremendous intellectual self-discipline and concentration, even when he was physically frail and impaired by various illnesses.

On the occasion of his seventy-fifth birthday, Boris Luban-Plozza and Rainer Funk organized a symposium on the past, present, and future of psychoanalysis. This took place in Locarno under the auspices of the Gottlieb Duttweiler Institute (Zurich). Fromm delivered the central lecture, distilled in fact from his approximately four decades of practical experience as a therapist. The contents of this quintessential lecture are known through the brief resume published by Luban-Plozza. Among other questions of concern in contemporary psychotherapy, Fromm enumerated the following conflict areas as primary threats to human sanity: a) consciousness of *freedom* and freedom as an unconscious phenomenon versus organized manipulation of consciousness and the dictatorship of administration; b) consciousness of a good *conscience* as opposed to unconscious feelings of guilt; c) consciousness of *honesty* versus unconscious fraud toward one's own self and toward others; d) consciousness of *individualism* versus an unconscious existence composed of clichés; e) consciousness of *identity* versus the unconscious concern about how one is perceived by others; g) consciousness of *faith* in opposition to an unconscious absence of faith; h) consciousness of *loving* versus unconscious indifference, hatred, and aggression; i) consciousness of *activity* in opposition to passiveness of the soul; j) consciousness of a *realistic relationship* to one's surroundings versus an unconscious irrationalism.[3]

All these individual stress areas can easily be related to Fromm's written work on individual and social characterology. Once more, his goal is to demonstrate the friction between pre-fabricated consciousness (i.e. the result of indoctrination) and the reality of human needs, which are all too often repressed into the unconscious. And again, the deep antagonism between human nature--as he perceives it--and contemporary civilizational and social institutions comes into sharp focus. Similar in essence to *To Have or to Be?*, this survey is determined by Fromm's bleak view of humanity's current development. He undoubtedly saw the human race--already caught in the two-fold deadly threat of ecological and/or nuclear catastrophe--as suffering from an inexorable, steady reduction in mental and emotional capacities. But he also believed that this spiraling descent toward the ultimate stage of total robotism might possibly be halted by faith and reason--if it is not already too late.

Completing *To Have or to Be?* taxed Fromm's strength unduly. His heart condition was aggravated by repeated attacks in 1977 and 1978. In 1979, when the city of Dortmund awarded him the Nelly-Sachs-Prize for outstanding contributions to cultural life, poor health prevented Fromm from attending the ceremony. His acceptance speech was read in his absence. Entitled "The Vision of our Time," it contains a touching and fervent plaidoyer for the creation of a new man in a new society. The final--and most important--sentence reads: "The vision which should guide us is a new human being, a free human being living in a sensible and humane reality, a human being able to love without subjugation or domination."[4]

Six days prior to his eightieth birthday, Erich Fromm died of heart failure in Muralto. The city of his birth and of the formative childhood and adolescent years, Frankfurt, had intended to honor him on the occasion of his birthday with the Goethe Medal: the highest distinction Frankfurt has to give. This medal had previously been awarded to both Max Horkheimer and Theodor W. Adorno. For Fromm, this distinction arrived too late. His widow accepted it posthumously in March, 1981.

A major factor in Fromm's growing reputation during the 1970s on the European continent was the publication of his most imposing work, *The Anatomy of Human Destructiveness*.[5] This study was conceived as the first part of a trilogy on psychoanalytical theory; the remaining two volumes were never completed. As opposed to most of his other writings, Fromm's magnum opus never achieved great resonance with the lay public. Its style and terminology are not addressed primarily to a general readership, but rather to the professional psychologist and therapist. Nevertheless, large portions of the book are by far less forbidding than they appear at first glance. The educated non-specialist reader will find Fromm's prose here far less dry than comparable texts by Freud and Sullivan. One intention of the following analysis is to introduce this remarkable book to a larger readership. No serious student of Fromm's thought should shun the comparatively small effort of following him into the abyss of human destruction. Fromm may not be Virgil, and his reader not Dante, but his exploration of the underworld of human nature is surely no less fascinating than their journey through the mythological inferno.

Erich Fromm worked for more than six years on *The Anatomy of Human Destructiveness*. Over five hundred pages long, this imposing volume is clearly intended to provide the scientific foundations many of his critics had previously found lacking or insufficient in his characterology. Its author takes considerable pains to refute past accusations raised against his work, especially regarding its "popular" style and general lack of solid academic documentation. In his preface, Fromm promises his reader "a global view" of the phenomenon of human destructiveness, which he indeed delivers. To accomplish this, he had to immerse himself in various areas of knowledge which he had not touched on before or, at best, treated only in passing. Not only does he now delve into the fields of instinctivism and behaviorism, he also offers some insights into the medical and particularly the neurophysiological aspects of the topic. For a scholar who had no medical training, a scientifically valid discussion of these fields required considerable effort. Regarding the work as a whole, one can not help being profoundly impressed by its encyclopedic scope. To be sure: the study does display certain weaknesses, one of them being an occasional lack of depth. But, one might argue, the tendency toward shallowness is characteristic of all of Fromm's work after the 1930s. And on the other hand, it is safe to assume that he withheld some ideas for later in-depth exploration, since the book was meant to be only *one* segment of a tripartite effort. Nevertheless, it can very well stand on its own merits. The following analysis will again concentrate both on its insights and on its more controversial facets.

Part One presents Fromm's lucid discussion of the prevalent theories on human aggression. Both the neoinstinctivists--namely Freud and Lorenz--and the neobehaviorists offer only limited and partially false evidence to explain this phenomenon. Konrad Lorenz, author of the extremely popular works *Evolution and Modification of Behavior*[6] and *On Aggression*,[7] relegates *all* human aggression to the phylogenetically programmed sphere, i.e. to the instinctual apparatus of the species *homo sapiens*. With this theory, Lorenz generally follows Freudian tradition: Freud had earlier divided human instinctual equipment into two categories, the sexual or life instinct (*Eros*) and the death instinct, later to be called *Thanatos* by some of his pupils. This "destructive" instinct, according to Freud, can be partially controlled. But the human organism still represents a dichotomy of two conflicting forces. Aggression may therefore assume a dominant role at any time and become the controlling factor in human behavior. Fromm's critique of Freud's rather elementary theory rightly stresses its failure to rest on *empirical* evidence. He points out that Freud's pioneering effort concentrated primarily on *typological* aspects of human psychic orientation. *Societal* factors played, at best, a subordinate role in his approach.

In Freud's wake, Lorenz then presented his "hydraulic" model of animal and human aggression. Energy, says Lorenz, tends to build up to a specific pressure point within the living organism (as in an hydraulic system), until an explosion of pent-up aggression occurs. From there, he purveys the assumption that aggression is a vital instinctual function, insofar as it secures the survival of the individual and the given species. In Fromm's terms: "The logic of Lorenz's assumption is that man *is* aggressive because he *was* aggressive and he *was* aggressive because he *is* aggressive."[8] The circular argumentation of the instinctivists provokes Fromm's contempt. He objects even more strongly to the fact that Lorenz' theses are based on his observation of *animal* behavior and resulting analogies between geese, fish, etc. and human beings. It may be added to Fromm's pointed criticism at this point that the wide following Lorenz has found in recent years is indeed astonishing. Lorenz consistently displays strong Darwinist traits, and in 1940 he even wrote an essay which could be interpreted as a de facto condonement of Nazi racist policy. For many modern critics, his findings are not only inconclusive but extremely contrived. Fromm rightly criticizes the element of brutality underlying some of his more recent writings, in which military enthusiasm and militant patriotism are hailed as creative forces within the historical process. It is hardly necessary to pursue Fromm's attack on instinctivism any further here. Instinctivism, especially in its modern manifestations, is a poor excuse for scientific thought. More often than not, it is an even poorer justification for the lowest varieties of human behavior.

As opposed to the instinctivist camp, the environmentalist (not to be confused with the newer meaning, i.e. those dedicated to the preservation of the ecological "environment") and the behaviorist schools of thought raised the claim that human action/interaction is exclusively the product of the given societal environment. John Broadus Watson, author of the innovative work *Behavior: An Introduction to Comparative Psychology*,[9] may be called the modern founding father of this method which, in turn, is rooted in nineteenth-century positivism. Burrhus F. Skinner is the best-known representative of the neobehaviorist school in the United States today. His major work *Science and Human Behavior*[10] and some of his subsequent publications, notably *Walden Two*, are still required reading for many college undergraduates. In sharp contrast to the neoinstinctivists, behaviorists are primarily interested in the process and results of human interaction and societal conditioning.

Fromm gives Skinner credit for documenting that human behavior--regardless of its "innate tendencies" or any given instinctual orientation--can be molded to a great degree by exterior stimuli, i.e. "positive" and "negative" reinforcement etc. He does take issue, however, with Skinner's apparent indifference toward the *deeper* motivation of human actions. Further, he challenges Skinner on the grounds of his questionable value system, which allows for the possible exploitation and subjugation of one group by another for supposedly noble purposes. He arrives at the conclusion that ". . . neobehaviorism is based on the quintessence of bourgeois experience: the primacy of egotism and self-interest over all human passions."[11]

Skinner's popularity in North America, says Fromm, is due to his skillful blending of scientific thought with the ideology and socio-economic reality of monopolistic capitalism. His approach to human behavior is nothing more than "the psychology of opportunism dressed up as a new scientific humanism."   Apart from Noam Chomsky, who built a very persuasive case against Skinnerism, Fromm is one of the few American scholars who have been able to pinpoint the dangers inherent in this highly popular theory. His criticism is concise and thought-provoking. It might well be augmented by the observation that behaviorism--at least in the hands of Skinner and related thinkers--lends itself by nature to the infusion of ethical relativism. If one specific ideology or behavioral pattern (in Skinner's case, the value system of American democracy) can be conditioned by means of "positive" reinforcement, so can any other scale of declared "values."   Interestingly enough, most of the psychologists and sociologists who remained in National Socialist Germany employed methods derived from primitive behaviorism--exactly because this scientific methodology was acceptable to the regime. It was in fact ideally suited to the breeding and training of a supposed "master race" as envisioned by Nazi leaders. Behaviorist-oriented research was also state supported in the USSR during the Stalin era. There, some shocking but illuminating experiments were done with childrearing in a behavioristically controlled environment, away from the family unit. They resulted in the upbringing of emotional and intellectual cripples. Huxley and many other authors have used utopian literature to examine the concept of applied behaviorism. Suffice it to say that when science adopts an interchangeable conscience and abandons its firm roots in the humanistic tradition, it is *always* in danger of becoming an accomplice to the given political power structure.

Part two of the study deals with data and evidence meant to invalidate the instinctivist theory. Fromm attacks his adversary from four different directions. A brief section on *neurophysiology* presents his thesis that the human brain itself produces only one specific kind of aggression: in acts of self-defense or self-preservation. Neuroscientists will find no particularly original insights in this chapter. Similarly uninspiring is Fromm's essay on *animal behavior*. Animals frequently react to crowding and/or captivity, as well as to unidentifiable threats, with aggression. Humans, on the other hand, are often conditioned by propaganda and societal pressures to commit atrocities upon their fellow beings. This is commonly accomplished by reducing the victim to a faceless, nameless entity such as "the enemy." Fromm cites examples from the Vietnam war--cold-blooded massacres of "gooks"--and Hitler's denunciation of those he intended to destroy as "subhumans." Fromm's comparison of animals to humans merely underlines the obvious. Aggression in animals results from the demands of instinct. But humans, who are endowed with powers of reason, are motivated by individual and/or social character orientation. It is, and here Fromm coins a proverbial phrase, "man's humanity that makes him so inhuman."[12]

Arguing from the viewpoint of *paleontology*, Fromm claims that Australopithecus--one of *homo sapiens'* ancestors--cannot have been a predator. Consequently, the existence of "predatory" genes in humans can safely by excluded. Finally, recent findings in *anthropology* seem to refute the theory that more primitive societies are significantly more aggressive than those in a higher stage of evolution.

On the whole, Fromm's argumentation regarding these disciplines remains superficial. Although the data provided in this part of the book are often skimpy, Fromm nevertheless manages to provide serious food for thought. He does not demonstrate beyond doubt his theory that destructiveness is neither innate nor common to all representatives of the human species. To prove this point would probably be an impossible task. His conclusion that destructiveness as such is *not* part of human nature should not be regarded as irrevocable fact, but as a working hypothesis. It stands at the pivotal point of his study and serves as the theoretical foundation for the third part, devoted to the actual exploration of several varieties of aggression and destructiveness and their respective causes.

Prior to a discussion of this central part of the book, one important omission in its critical apparatus should be mentioned. Between instinctivism and behaviorism, the two schools he rightly criticizes, Fromm fails to give any credit whatsoever to Wilhelm Reich's characterological work which, in fact, foreshadows much of his own. Both Reich's *The Mass Psychology of Fascism*[13] and his *Charakteranalyse. Technik und Grundlagen (Character Analysis: Technique and Foundations)*[14] were first published in 1933 and had considerable impact on Fromm's own development. The two studies were reviewed by Karl Landauer in the *Zeitschrift für Sozialforschung* right next to one of Fromm's own reviews.[15] Reich's thesis is based on the sexual deformation of the individual in a hierarchic society. Active heterosexual drives, he claims, are subjugated through societal repression and subsequently transformed into a masochistic (or homosexual) dependence on the Führer, the state or on authoritarian religion. Reich postulates that sexual liberation is the key to political freedom. Though he goes far beyond Reich's somewhat narrow equation, Fromm's own exploration of the narcissistic and sado-masochistic foundations of human destructiveness is clearly indebted to Reich's work. Neither in *The Heart of Man* nor in *The Anatomy of Human Destructiveness*, however, is Reich's name even mentioned.

The latter study uses the same basic differentiation between "benign" and "malignant" aggression as the former. This model has been discussed above and need not be reiterated here. Two new

aspects, however, are now added: revolution and war. Revolutionary aggression is correctly subsumed under the benign variants, as it
is the utmost expression of the human drive for freedom and justice. It has been observed in previous chapters of this book that
Fromm's attitude toward revolution is extremely ambivalent. His
apparent deep-seated fear of revolution is explained in his discussion of revolutionary aggression. Defensive aggression against an
unjust political system, he says, may easily metamorphose into rampant destructiveness and the wish to reverse the previous balance
of power and oppression. In other words, the formerly oppressed
often strive to become the new oppressors. Because he sees revolution somewhat simplistically as a propelling force of self-repeti-
tive historical oppression, Fromm is reluctant to seriously consider
it as a means for legitimate social change.

Similarly noteworthy are his remarks on war. Together with
Quincy Wright (*A Study of War*[16]), he propagates the theory that
the more alienated a society is, the more warlike it becomes. Especially belligerent are those societies with a rigid class structure
and/or a strong division of labor (vide Fromm's presentation on the
alienation of work in *The Sane Society*). War is therefore seen as
an "instrumental" form of aggression which is *not* triggered by an
innate destructive instinct in humans. Its causes lie in the societal
structure/social character as such, as well as in the given ambitions
of the ruling elite. Up to this point, one can agree with Fromm.
The ensuing amplification of his theory, however, is somewhat
bizarre and pseudo-romantic. War, he claims, is "exciting," as it
breaks up boredom and routine and even obliterates class differences to a certain extent. Participation in warfare should be recognized as an "indirect rebellion against the injustice, inequality and
boredom governing social life in peacetime. . ." These are strange
words indeed from an avowed pacifist. This is, again, one of the
many inconsistencies integral to Fromm's thinking, which cannot
be extirpated by even the most sympathetic interpretation.

The following exploration of the two essential powers in human
nature--the "life-furthering syndrome" (=biophilia) and the "life-
thwarting syndrome" (=necrophilia)--as well as their dialectic

interaction is already known to the reader from *The Heart of Man*. Both character orientations can be strengthened or weakened by the existing external, i.e. social conditions. Rationality as a predominant factor in the social character tends to enhance biophilous tendencies, whereas an irrational social structure reinforces the necrophilous trait. Destructiveness per se is *not the cause of necrophilia, but its product*. This, the book's central statement, goes back directly to Fromm's first book, *Escape from Freedom*, in which he stated that "[d]estructiveness is the outcome of unlived life."[17] Now, more than three decades later, he sets out to investigate what actually constitutes *unlived life*.

Most frequently, he says, the destructive character is rooted in sadism. Nonsexual sadism seems to be both more dangerous and more widespread than sexual activity intended to hurt and subjugate the partner. As a clinical case of nonsexual sadism, Fromm presents an analysis of Joseph Stalin's character. The important conclusion of this analysis is that Stalin both vicariously enjoyed the torture he had inflicted on people by his henchmen and also, on a personal level, liked to engage in cat-and-mouse games with his victims. Whenever he feigned benevolent concern for his associates, their arrest and/or execution was often imminent. Fromm correctly diagnoses that a basic feeling of weakness or insignificance can motivate such behavior. Sadism "is the transformation of impotence into the experience of omnipotence; it is the religion of psychical cripples."[18] And powerlessness, i.e. the inability to relate in a creative and productive manner to one's surroundings, is the unavoidable coefficient of unlived life. *Quod erat demonstrandum*. This reasoning, circuitous as it may be, is in fact the grand total of Fromm's characterological work. The accurate description of sadism in his late magnum opus can be traced back in one huge arc to his early studies on social character, and thus impressively documents the unbroken continuity of his oeuvre.

Regardless of the unquestionable validity of his theory of sadistic character orientation as such, some qualifications must be made with respect to his analytical methodology. In the case of Stalin, a strong paranoid personality streak can be deduced from the given documentation and from other historical accounts. What appears to be pleasure gained through the deception, humiliation and ultimate destruction of others, may in some instances have been the desperate cunning of a paranoiac who saw himself surrounded by devious enemies. This aspect--as it relates to the apparent *clinical* pathology of the Soviet leader--is not mentioned in Fromm's analysis which therefore remains, despite its considerable refinement, inconclusive. In general, his method of analyzing historical characters *solely* on the basis of second-hand and often circumstantial evidence is viewed skeptically by many specialists. No lesser authority than Erich Fromm himself has stressed repeatedly the importance of dynamic, eye-to-eye exchange between analyst and analysand. As this element is lacking (all of his cited examples of classic malignant aggression are dead and can be analyzed only, faute de mieux, through eyewitness reports), his treatise on Stalin provides an interesting case history, but not the foundation for a full-fledged characterological theory.

The same qualification applies to the far more extensive sections on Heinrich Himmler and Adolf Hitler. Regarding the prevalent character traits of Himmler, the leader of the Third Reich's Storm Troopers, Fromm is certainly correct in his assumption that the man had strong sado-masochistic tendencies. Sado-masochistic orientation (termed here the "bureaucratic character") frequently results from a social structure oriented rigidly toward obedience, hierarchy, and law and order. Freud had called his particular conception of the bureaucratic character the "anal" personality. Fromm classifies Himmler as a clinical case of "anal-hoarding sadism." An essential part of this personality type is its readiness to submit to the powers that be. Fromm fittingly names this "subalternity." Himmler, the man directly or indirectly responsible for the terror regime in Germany and occupied Europe as well as for the most sophisticated genocidal machinery in world history, was a timid child and a typical "mother's boy." Later in life, he was beset by various fears and psychosomatic illnesses. Unlived life, in his case, amounted to an acute fear of living. A man of almost obsessive orderliness and pedantry, he desperately clung to authorities and to various father figures. Despite his utterly submissive attachment to Hitler, it is not astonishing--but rather in character--that he abandoned him when everything was lost and then deluded himself with the assumption that he could play a leading role in a post-war German government. Himmler was an "absolute opportunist." The frightening fact is that this character orientation in its peculiar mixture of weakness and total ruthlessness is extremely widespread. Fromm convincingly states: "There are thousands of Himmlers living among us."[19] A mere glance at past and present history offers immediate proof for the omnipresence of the bureaucratic character, the obedient and completely incompassionate functionary.

Nonsexual sadism and sado-masochism are defined here as preliminary stages in the development of unequivocally malignant aggression--in Fromm's terms, *necrophilia*. Once more, this character orientation is distinct from the sexual deviation as described by Richard von Krafft-Ebing[20] and modern researchers such as Hartmut von Hentig.[21] Necrophilia in the traditional sense of the word refers to sexual relations of a living person with a corpse. In Fromm's characterology, the term is first defined in *The Heart of Man*. It refers to a person who is obsessively oriented toward things and anorganic matter and, concomitantly, unable to relate to life constructively. Fromm claims that Lenin was the first to use the term in this specific meaning (he cites the Russian word *trupolozhestvo* as the equivalent). Character-rooted necrophilia has also been described by Miguel de Unamuno in the above-related episode from the Spanish Civil War.[22]

In the neurophysiological sphere, Fromm notes a gradual decrease of the instinctual apparatus throughout the evolution of the species *homo sapiens*. Through the tremendous growth of the brain per se and especially of the neocortex, both self-awareness and the various character-rooted passions have taken over the reins in determining human behavior. Social conditions have become the predominant, if not exclusive, factor in the character shaping process. A human being still possesses complete potential for development and growth. But in order to realize this potential,

the *external* conditions must be conducive to biophilous orientation. Conversely, the combined presence of narcissism, unrelated-
ness, and destructiveness in a social environment detrimental to
growth tends to produce necrophilia or, in other words, the "malignant form of the anal character." Once more, Fromm stresses the
dialectic opposition of forces which accounts for human nature:

> Destructiveness is not parallel to, but the alternative of biophilia. Love of life
> or love of the dead is the fundamental alternative that confronts every human
> being. Necrophilia grows as the development of biophilia is stunted. Man is
> biologically endowed with the capacity for biophilia, but psychologically he
> has the potential for necrophilia as an alternative solution.[23]

From there, the study engages in a lengthy analysis of Adolf
Hitler's character structure. As opposed to Winston Churchill,
who displayed his necrophilous "trend" by killing flies and lining up
their corpses on the tablecloth, Hitler is seen as the perfect example of unilateral necrophilia. His childhood and formative young
adolescent years reinforced narcissistic character traits. Later, he
vacillated between passivity--the inability to achieve and to pro-
duce--and delusions of grandeur. His character groundwork contained all elements conducive to the growth of malignant destructiveness: incestuous fixations, coldness, total lack of interest in
others, irrationality, and the inability to assess his own condition
realistically. As he did in *The Heart of Man*, Fromm again proposes
a definition of the physiognomic indicators of a necrophilous personality. It has been pointed out before that this part of his theory
is probably the least convincing.[24] In an effort to invalidate conflicting interpretations of Hitler's personality, strong emphasis is
placed on the Führer's disposition as an actor and a consummate
liar. These and other related aspects of his personality--such as his
tendency to rationalize and to establish reaction patterns which
were repeated throughout his life--are by no means valid symptoms
to back up a conclusive diagnosis of necrophilia. Fromm's overly
lengthy and verbose analysis tends to get entangled in a multitude
of less relevant aspects. He must have been aware of some imprecision in his approach at this point, as he suddenly proceeds to

build a very detailed case regarding Hitler's relationships to women. Fromm argues that both Geli Raubal, his half-niece and first lover, and Eva Braun, his mistress for many years and his wife for one day, were totally subjugated by him. The former committed suicide out of severe depression. The latter killed herself in an act of loyalty when everything was lost. On the basis of the given documentation, it is obvious that both relationships were strongly sado-masochistic in their role division. It is not difficult to conclude that Hitler was unable to experience mature love or, even, to relate to other human beings in a productive and dignified way. The only area of genuine interest in his life was architecture: "perhaps the one bridge that linked him with life." It is ironic that the most ruthless destroyer of human life in history conceived of himself as a builder: not only the architect of a new social order, but also a planner of cities and buildings. Albert Speer, author of the bestseller *Inside the Third Reich*,[25] himself an architect and one of Hitler's closer associates (to whom Fromm incidentally is indebted for various information), was regarded by the would-be architect Hitler as a colleague and therefore treated with special consideration. Even when the armament minister Speer countermanded some of the Führer's deranged final decrees, he did not lose his life for insubordination, as did many others.

To sum up: Fromm's analysis of Adolf Hitler, despite its occasional tendency to lose track of its major thrust, is an impressive document. It fulfills its goal in proving that certain characterological conditions *may* coincide with external factors to eventually form a syndrome of malignant aggression. Its overall assessment of Hitler's personality, however, is problematic. For Hitler, in Fromm's portrayal, ultimately assumes larger-than-life proportions, and becomes almost a timeless monument of absolute evil. Unwittingly, this contributes to a widespread distorted perception of the Nazi Führer, an almost mythical aggrandizement of his presumably demonic powers. Speer himself, in addition to the predominantly sober evaluations of William L. Shirer,[26] H.R. Trevor-Roper,[27] Alan Bullock[28] and, more recently, Robert Payne[29] have made considerable efforts to dispel this false and ultimately dangerous myth. Without doubt, Hitler had a tremendous gift as an orator and demagogue. On the other hand, he was the typical half-educated, resentful petit-bourgeois who, at the given time in history, could organize a mass movement highly attractive to many frustrated and often equally ignorant individuals. As stated above with regard to Himmler, Führer-figures of Hitler's general dimensions are not unique individuals, but in fact easily interchangeable and replaceable. World history gives ample demonstration of malignant destructiveness in various individual leaders throughout the centuries. In the final analysis, it is not the evil *individual* who shapes history and wreaks havoc at will, but rather the given *circumstances* which empower him to do so.

Hitler, therefore, should not be perceived as an incarnation of absolute evil, exactly because the moral category obfuscates both his specific character structure *and* the socio-historical conditions which made his ascent to power and his subsequent atrocities possible. Illuminating as Fromm's analysis of malignant destructiveness may be, it fails to take into account the greater societal and economic conditions during the 1930s in Germany. It was only within this particular framework that the Austrian vagrant and thwarted artist--the necrophilous proponent of unlived life--could become the leader of a large nation and instill in a substantial segment of the population his own drive for destruction. As an interesting sidelight, it may be mentioned in this context that Hitler's vocabulary (an aspect treated only in passing by Fromm) was exceptionally revealing for his necrophilous orientation. Both his book *Mein Kampf*[30] and especially his later speeches and conversations abound with the most brutal language. Among his favorite terms were the verbs to annihilate, to eradicate, to wipe out, and many synonyms in their German equivalent. A psycho-linguistic approach to destructive character orientation might be a very fruitful area for further research.

The Anatomy of Human Destructiveness ends with an epilogue on "the ambiguity of hope." Fromm emphasizes that, all historical evidence notwithstanding, this is neither the time for optimism nor for pessimism. Optimism, he says, "is an alienated form of faith, pessimism an alienated form of despair." Neither attitude has ever been instrumental in changing the course of history. Humanity has to learn to distrust those politicians and demagogues who advocate destruction, as much as those whose hearts have hardened and proclaim that all is well. The only answer to the given situation is a large-scale revitalization of humanistic thought: "Critical and radical thought will only bear fruit when it is blended with the most precious quality man is endowed with--the love of life."[31]

Many of the book's reviewers were impressed by its breadth and its wealth of individual insights. Almost all agreed that Fromm's theory of human destructiveness contains a plethora of documentation on the pathology of aggression--but no viable solutions for therapy. Interestingly enough, one aspect is not mentioned at all in the critical reaction to Fromm's largest work: *his own fascination with the phenomenon of evil.* And indeed, a survey of his whole oeuvre shows this fascination to be a strong, almost everpresent undercurrent. Various analyses of Stalin and Hitler in Fromm's other books attest to this, as well as the disproportionately weighty Hitler case history which fills roughly one sixth of the text proper in *The Anatomy of Human Destructiveness.* This obsessive concern with evil may in part be explained by the strong moral and ethical background of Fromm's youth and his roots in Judaism, which he never totally severed--even when he became an atheist. From all the biographical evidence available, it can be assumed beyond doubt that he himself possessed a biophilous character orientation. Why, then, was he so excessively fascinated with the incarnations of evil? His own dynamic characterology may help to explain this tendency: one element (the syndrome of growth) always stands in dialectic opposition to another (the syndrome of decay). And even if Fromm himself did not experience malignant aggression, the latent potential of this syndrome apparently served as an irresistible stimulus for its constant and ever deeper exploration in his writings.

The slim volume *Aggression und Charakter*[32] (*Aggression and Character* [1975]) should be read as a companion to *The Anatomy of Human Destructiveness.* It contains a dialogue between Erich Fromm and Adelbert Reif, which attempts to clarify some of the

questions left pending by the larger study. Here, Fromm expounds
on the problem of *boredom*, which he considers a central factor in
the development of human destructiveness. Modern industrialized
societies--despite their efforts to exploit the market for leisure activities through constantly changing crazes and fads--fail to provide
a framework for devoted and selfless fulfillment for the individual.
Work itself is often a source of boredom because it is nonproductive in a human sense; the same applies to an uncreative leisure
life. Prefabricated entertainment is the equivalent of alienated labor. Once more, *unlived life* is the soil from which senseless aggression springs.

If anyone doubts the correctness of this diagnosis, a brief look at
newscasts and dailies should provide ample evidence of vandalism,
brutality, drug abuse (especially but not exclusively among the
younger generations)--in brief, of manifold human (self-)destruc-
tiveness perpetrated by a bored and directionless population.
Under the flag of fun and excitement, hatred for life and total
indifference toward one's self run their course, symptoms of the
emotional empoverishment of Western humanity. Fromm's cultural
pessimism is exceptionally pronounced in this small but revealing
booklet. Nevertheless, he declares that change may still be possible. Some hope can always be pinned on natural "mutations" of
the social character, and on the exceptional personalities which
have emerged throughout history as engineers of revolutionary
movements.

With this tenacious assertion that there *is* still hope for humanity, Erich Fromm's oeuvre, paradoxically, comes to an inconclusive
conclusion. One would have wished for the completion of his
three-volume set on psychoanalytic theory. Equally important
would have been an exhaustive analysis of the *revolutionary character*: an elusive concept hinted at in certain passages of his characterological studies, but never fully developed.

In theoretical terms, Fromm's lasting accomplishment undoubtedly lies in his studies on individual and social character orientations. No other researcher has even approximated his insights into
the intrinsic connections between the formation of single person-

alities and the greater whole of their social environment. Through his popular writings, Fromm has influenced millions of readers in their striving toward self-awareness. He has encouraged them to abandon their illusions and, for better or for worse, to accept themselves and assume the arduous task of responding more humanely to their fellow beings. In the final analysis, his greatness as a humanist and as a thinker does not lie in the scholarly solidity of his research. The rarified air of pure science and the esoteric realm of complex philosophical constructs were never his natural habitat. His greatness rests ultimately in his unflagging faith in humanity. His credo can be summed up in the simple sentence that the world, as it is, *can* be changed and *must* be changed.

Notes

1. In the Name of Life: A Controversial Legacy

1. Bernhard Landis and Edward S. Tauber, eds., *In The Name of Life. Essays in Honor of Erich Fromm* (New York: Holt, Reinhart & Winston, 1971).

2. Cf. Don Hausdorff, *Erich Fromm*. Twayne's United States Authors Series, vol. 203 (New York: Twayne, 1972), p. 3.

3. In *Die Zeit*, 21 March 1980. The translation is mine. In this particular case, it does not attempt to smooth out the roughness of Fromm's spoken German in his later years: the content of this revealing passage remains clear enough.

4. For an introduction to the history of the Frankfurt School see Zoltán Tar, *The Frankfurt School: The Critical Theories of Max Horkheimer and Theodor W. Adorno* (New York: Wiley, 1977); Zoltán Tar: "Introduction," in Judith Marcus and Zoltán Tar, eds., *Foundations of the Frankfurt School of Social Research* (New Brunswick: Transaction, 1984), pp. 1-26; Martin Jay, *The Dialectical Imagination. A History of the Frankfurt School and the Institute of Social Research 1923-1950* (Boston: Little, Brown & Co., 1973).

2. The Beginnings: Frankfurt, Heidelberg, and Berlin

1. Strangely, Fromm's middle name is frequently given as "Pinchas." The same mistake is made by Rainer Funk, author of the biography *Erich Fromm*, rowohlts monographien, vol. 322 (Reinbek: Rowohlt, 1983), p. 14. Through the courtesy of Dr. Andernacht, City archives, Frankfurt/Main, whom I wish to thank here, I was able to ascertain Fromm's actual names.

2. In *Die Zeit*, 21 March 1980; my translation (cf. chapter 1, note 3).

3. Cf. E. F., *Escape from Freedom* (New York: Farrar & Reinhart, 1941), esp. chapters II and III.

4. Cf. E. F., *You Shall be as Gods. A Radical Interpretation of the Old Testament and its Tradition* (New York: Holt, Reinhart & Winston, 1966), esp. chapters 1-3.

5. See Funk (note 1), p. 44.

6. Gerschom Scholem, *Walter Benjamin - die Geschichte einer Freundschaft* (Frankfurt: Suhrkamp, 1975), p. 285.

7. For this and the following biographical episodes see his "intellectual autobiography" in *Beyond the Chains of Illusion. My Encounter with Marx and Freud*, The Credo Series (New York: Pocket Books, 1962).

8. *Beyond the Chains of Illusion*, p. 9.

9. Cf. Scholem, *Walter Benjamin* (note 6), p. 149. The German original reads: "Mach mich wie den Erich Fromm, / Daß ich in den Himmel komm."

10. *Das jüdische Gesetz. Ein Beitrag zur Soziologie des Diasporajudentums.* Even in Rainer Funk's comprehensive study *Erich Fromm: The Courage to be Human* (New York: Continuum, 1982), p. 374, the date is given erroneously as 1922.

11. *Das jüdische Gesetz*, p. 11. The translation is mine.

12. "Der Sabbath," *Imago. Zeitschrift für Anwendung der Psychoanalyse auf die Natur- und Geisteswissenschaften* 13 (1927): 223-234.

13. "Psychoanalyse und Soziologie," *Zeitschrift für psychoanalytische Pädagogik* 3 (1928/29): 269f.

3. Erich Fromm at the Institute of Social Research. The Foundations of his Thought

1. Cf. Funk (chapter 2, note 1), p. 59.

2. Cf. below pp. 27 - 29.

3. The *Zeitschrift für Sozialforschung* was made more accessible in 1980 as a reprint by the Deutscher Taschenbuch Verlag in Munich. For a delineation

of Horkheimer's theories cf. especially the studies by Jay and Tar (chapter 1, note 4).

4. "Geschichte und Psychologie," *Zeitschrift für Sozialforschung* 1 (1932): 125-144, here p. 135; my translation.

5. "Über Methode und Aufgabe einer analytischen Sozialpsychologie," *Zeitschrift für Sozialforschung* 1 (1932): 28-54.

6. Die Entwicklung des Christusdogmas. Eine psychoanalytische Studie zur sozialpsychologischen Funktion der Religion," *Imago. Zeitschrift für Anwendung der Psychoanalyse auf die Natur- und Geisteswissenschaften* 16 (1930): 305-373.

7. Cf. Borkenau's review in *Zeitschrift für Sozialforschung* 1 (1932): 174f.

8. "Über Methode und Aufgabe . . ." (note 5), p. 34; my translation.

9. Ibid., p. 45; my translation.

10. Ibid., p. 46; my translation.

11. This argument is already proposed in Fromm's brief article "Politik und Psychoanalyse," *Psychoanalytische Bewegung* 3 (1931): 440-447; cf. p. 441.

12. "Die psychoanalytische Charakterologie und ihre Bedeutung für die Sozialpsychologie," *Zeitschrift für Sozialforschung* 1 (1932): 253-277; here p. 269.

13. In: *Zeitschrift für Sozialforschung* 3 (1934): 196-227.

14. "Robert Briffaults Werk über das Mutterrecht," *Zeitschrift für Sozialforschung* 2 (1933): 382-387.

15. In: *Zeitschrift für Sozialforschung* 4 (1935): 365-397.

16. "Die gesellschaftliche Bedingtheit . . ." (note 15), p. 397. The quotation is taken from the article's English summary. Although the stylistic infelicities are obvious, Fromm's message is perfectly clear.

17. "Sozialpsychologischer Teil," in: Max Horkheimer, ed., *Studien über Autorität und Familie*, Forschungsberichte aus dem Institut für Sozialforschung, 1. Abteilung: Theoretische Entwürfe über Autorität und Familie (Paris: Félix Alcan, 1936), pp. 77-135.

18. *Zeitschrift für Sozialforschung* 6 (1937): 95-118.

19. "Zum Gefühl der Ohnmacht" (cf. note 18), p. 95; my translation.

20. Ibid., p. 114; my translation.

21. Wolfgang Bonss, ed. and translator, *Arbeiter und Angestellte am Vorabend des Dritten Reiches. Eine sozialpsychologische Untersuchung* (Stuttgart: Deutsche Verlags-Anstalt, 1980).

22. (Cambridge, Mass.: Harvard University Press, 1984).

23. Cf. note 17.

24. Theodor W. Adorno with Else Frenkel-Brunswik, Daniel J. Lewinson, and R. Nevitt Sanford, *The Authoritarian Personality* (New York: Harper & Bros., 1950). A brief, but convincing assessment of Fromm's related work is provided by Franco Ferrarotti, "The Struggle of Reason against Total Bureaucratization," in: Marcus/Tar (chapter 1, note 4), pp. 235-252, esp. pp. 241ff.

25. Erich Fromm and Michael Maccoby, *Social Character in a Mexican Village. A Sociopsychoanalytic Study* (Englewood Cliffs, N.J.: Prentice-Hall, 1970).

26. Jay (cf. chapter 1, note 4), p. 117.

27. Ibid., p. 39.

28. See the excellent studies by Tar and Jay (chapter 1, note 4).

29. For some conflicting versions of this dispute cf. Jay (chapter 1, note 4), p. 101, and Funk (chapter 2, note 1), p. 68f.

30. Some details on Fromm's separation from the Institute have recently been published by Bonss (chapter 3, note 22), p. 29.

4. The Synthesis: Escape from Freedom (1941)

1. Jay (chapter 1, note 4), p. 114.

2. For a more detailed account of their friendship cf. Jack L. Rubins, *Karen Horney - Gentle Rebel of Psychoanalysis* (New York: The Dial Press, 1978), passim.

3. Abram Kardiner, *The Individual and His Society. The Psychoanalysis of Primitive Social Organization* (New York: Columbia University Press, 1939).

4. Some background is given by Rubins (note 2), chapter 18.

5. *Beyond the Chains of Illusion* (cf. chapter 2, note 7), p. 10.

6. Franz Borkenau, *Der Übergang vom feudalen zum bürgerlichen Weltbild* (Paris: Félix Alcan, 1934).

7. *Escape from Freedom* (chapter 2, note 3), p. vii.

8. These essays are discussed in some detail in chapter 3.

9. *Escape from Freedom* (chapter 2, note 3), p. 283.

10. Wilhelm Reich, *Massenpsychologie des Faschismus. Zur Sexualökonomie der politischen Reaktion und zur proletarischen Sexualpolitik* (Copenhagen: Verlag für Sexualpolitik, 1933), p. 39; my translation. Incidentally, the book was reviewed by Karl Landauer in *Zeitschrift für Sozialforschung* 3 (1934): 106f.; the English translation appeared in 1946.

11. *Escape from Freedom* (chapter 2, note 3), p. 284.

12. Ibid., p. 290.

13. Ibid., p. 289.

14. For a good analysis of the dynamic concept of social character see Uschi Essbach-Kreuzer, "Die Theorie des Sozialcharakters in den Arbeiten von Erich Fromm," *Zeitschrift für psychosomatische Medizin* 18 (1972): 171-191.

15. *Escape from Freedom* (chapter 2, note 3), p. 22.

16. Ibid., p. 42.

17. Ibid., p. 54.

18. Cf. in particular Richard Henry Tawney, *Religion and the Rise of Capitalism* (New York: Harcourt, Brace & Co., 1926).

19. *Escape from Freedom* (chapter 2, note 3), p. 62.

20. Max Weber, *The Protestant Ethic and the Spirit of Capitalism* (New York: Charles Scribner's Sons, 1930).

21. "Selfishness and Self-Love," *Psychiatry* 2 (1939): 507-523.

22. Harry Stack Sullivan, *Conceptions of Modern Psychiatry*, William Alanson White Memorial Lectures, vol. 1 (Washington: William Alanson White Institute, 1948).

23. *Escape from Freedom* (chapter 2, note 3), p. 101.

24. Ibid., p. 109f.

25. Ibid., p. 128.

26. Ibid., p. 140.

27. Cf. Karen Horney, *The Neurotic Personality of Our Time* (New York: W. W. Norton, 1937); also by this author: *New Ways in Psychoanalysis* (New York: W. W. Norton, 1939).

28. K. H., *Our Inner Conflicts. A Constructive Theory of Neurosis* (New York: W. W. Norton, 1945).

29. *Escape from Freedom* (chapter 2, note 3), p. 221.

30. Cf. Harold D. Lasswell, *Politics. Who Gets What, When, How* (New York: McGraw-Hill, 1936). Lasswell's book was reviewed favorably by Fromm in *Zeitschrift für Sozialforschung* 6 (1937): 220f.

31. *Escape from Freedom* (chapter 2, note 3), p. 243.

32. Ibid., p. 248.

33. Ibid., p. 251.

34. Erich Fromm, *Aggression und Charakter. Ein Gespräch mit Adelbert Reif* (Zurich: Die Arche, 1975), p. 20; my translation.

35. *Escape from Freedom* (chapter 2, note 3), p. 273.

36. Ernest G. Schachtel, review of *Escape from Freedom* in *Zeitschrift für Sozialforschung* 9 (1941): 491-495, here p. 495.

37. J. Stanley Glen, *Erich Fromm: A Protestant Critique* (Philadelphia: Westminster Press, 1965), p. 21.

38. John H. Schaar, *Escape from Authority. The Perspectives of Erich Fromm* (New York: Basic Books, 1961), p. 295.

39. Cf. Thomas Harvey Gill in *Psychiatry* 5 (1942): 109-111; M. F. Ashley Montagu, ibid., pp. 122-129; Patrick Mullahey, ibid., pp. 118-122. See also the reviews in the same issue by Anton T. Boisen (pp. 113-117); Lewis B. Hill (pp. 117f.); Ernest E. Hadley (pp. 131-134), and Louis Wirth (pp. 129-131).

5. Psychoanalysis, Ethics, and Religion: Toward a Humanist Credo (1944-1950)

1. Cf. Rainer Funk (chapter 2, note 1), p. 110.

2. *Psychoanalysis and Religion* (New Haven: Yale University Press, 1950).

3. C. G. Jung, *Psychology and Religion* (New Haven: Yale University Press, 1938).

4. Cf. E. F., *Man for Himself. An Inquiry into the Psychology of Ethics* (New York: Rinehart & Co., 1947). The text is quoted after the paperback edition (New York: Fawcett Premier, 1965).

5. Cf. Funk (chapter 2, note 10), p. 7.

6. *Man for Himself* (note 4), p. 22.

7. Ibid., p. 39, note 17.

8. Ibid., p. 71.

9. Ibid., p. 81.

10. "Individual and Social Origins of Neurosis," *American Sociological Review* 9 (1944): 380-384.

11. For the following discussion, see Fromm's charts: *Man for Himself* (note 4), p. 120f.

12. Cf. Herbert Marcuse, *One Dimensional Man. The Ideology of Industrial Society* (Boston: Beacon Press, 1964).

13. *Man for Himself* (note 4), p. 104.

14. Cf. Hausdorff (chapter 1, note 2), esp. pp. 50f.

15. Max Wertheimer, *Productive Thinking* (New York: Harper & Bros., 1945).

16. Karl Mannheim, *Ideology and Utopia* (New York: Harcourt, Brace & Co., 1936).

17. Cf. Mauro Torres, *El Irracionalismo en Erich Fromm. La posición científica del psicoanálisis*, Monografías Psicoanaliticas, vol. 6 (Mexico City: Editorial Pax-Medico, 1960), p. 120f.; my translation.

18. *Man for Himself* (note 4), p. 145.

19. Ibid., p. 192.

20. Cf. chapter 3, pp. 31ff. above.

21. Cf. chapter 2, note 10.

22. Cf. chapter 3, note 6.

23. "Faith as a Character Trait," *Psychiatry* 5 (1942): 307-319; cf. also *Man for Himself* (note 4), pp. 197-210.

24. London: Rider, 1950.

25. London: Rider, 1950.

26. London: Rider, 1955.

27. *Psychoanalysis and Religion* (chapter 4, note 2), p. 62.

28. Ibid., p. 95.

29. See above, chapter 5, p. 68f.

30. Hausdorff (chapter 1, note 2), p. 63.

31. Torres (note 17), p. 122; my translation.

6. Forgotten Languages: Fromm's Dream Theory. Studies on Zen, Freud and Marx

1. Cf. Hausdorff (chapter 1, note 2), p. 78.

2. Ibid.

3. *The Forgotten Language. An Introduction to the Understanding of Dreams, Fairy Tales and Myths* (New York: Rinehart & Co., 1951), p. 16; emphasis mine.

4. Ibid., p. 25.

5. Ibid., p. 36.

6. Richard I. Evans, *Dialogue with Erich Fromm*, Dialogues with Notable Contributors to Personality Theory, vol. 2 (New York: Harper & Row, 1966), p. 36.

7. Ibid., p. 74.

8. Cf. "The Oedipus Complex and the Oedipus Myth," in: Ruth Nanda Anshen, ed., *The Family: Its Functions and Destiny* (New York: Harper & Bros., 1949), pp. 334-358; also under the title "Oedipus Myth," *Scientific American* 180 (1949): 22-27; cf. *The Forgotten Language* (note 3), pp. 196-230.

9. See Hausdorff (chapter 1, note 2), p. 76.

10. D. T. Suzuki, Erich Fromm, and Richard De Martino, *Zen Buddhism and Psychoanalysis* (New York: Harper & Row, 1950), p. 112.

11. Evans (note 6), p. 33.

12. See Carl A. Rogers, *Casebook of Non-Directive Counseling* (Boston: Houghton Mifflin, 1947).

13. See *Zen Buddhism and Psychoanalysis* (note 10), p. 112.

14. Cf. Evans (note 6), p. 43.

15. See especially Herbert Marcuse, "The Social Implications of Freudian 'Revisionism'," *Dissent* 2 (Summer, 1955): 221-240, and Marcuse, "A Reply to Erich Fromm," *Dissent* 3 (Winter, 1956): 79-81. Fromm's arguments can be found in "The Human Implications of Instinctivistic Radicalism. A Reply to Herbert Marcuse," *Dissent* 2 (Summer, 1955): 342-349, and "A Counter-Rebuttal to Herbert Marcuse," *Dissent* 3 (Winter, 1956): 81-83.

16. Evans (note 6), p. 58f. and passim.

17. Ibid., p. 59.

18. Torres (chapter 5, note 18), p. 81; my translation.

19. New York: Basic Books, 1955.

20. The review appeared in: *Saturday Review* 41 (14 June 1958): 11-13, 55f. *The Dogma of Christ and Other Essays on Religion, Psychology, and Culture* (New York: Holt, Rinehart & Winston, 1963), pp. 135-148.

21. Hausdorff (chapter 1, note 2), p. 122.

22. *Sigmund Freud's Mission. An Analysis of His Personality and Influence* (New York: Harper & Row, 1959), p. 23, note 9.

23. Ibid., p. 31.

24. Ibid., p. 100.

25. Cf. Hausdorff (chapter 1, note 2), p. 121.

26. Hilde L. Mosse, "Bypaths on the Road to Vienna," *Psychiatry* 22 (1959): 39f.

27. Ibid.

28. *The Crisis of Psychoanalysis: Essays on Freud, Marx, and Social Psychology* (New York: Holt, Rinehart & Winston, 1970), pp. 42-61.

29. See above, chapter 3, pp. 30ff.

30. *Greatness and Limitations of Freud's Thought* (New York: Harper & Row, 1980), p. 132f.

31. *Zen Buddhism and Psychoanalysis* (note 11), p. 95.

32. Ibid., p. 109.

33. Esp. pp. 95f. and 101.

34. Ibid., p. 94.

35. Hausdorff (chapter 1, note 2), p. 109.

36. Ibid.

37. Torres (chapter 5, note 18), p. 52.

38. *Zen Buddhism and Psychoanalysis* (note 11), p. 98.

39. Ibid., p. 107.

40. *Marx's Concept of Man. With a Translation from Marx's Economic and Philosophical Manuscripts by T. B. Bottomore* (New York: Frederick Ungar, 1961), p. 6.

41. Ibid., p. 33, note 23.

42. Ibid., p. 23.

43. Ibid., p. 29.

44. Ibid., p. 34.

45. Ibid., p. 59; Fromm quotes Tillich's important work *Protestantische Vision* (Stuttgart: Ringverlag, 1952).

46. In: *Social Science Information* 7 (3/1968): 7-17; cf. also: *The Crisis of Psychoanalysis* (note 28); pp. 62-76.

47. *Marx's Concept of Man* (note 40), p. 79.

7.   The Heart of Man. Deeper Probings in Characterology and Religion (1964-1970)

1. *War Within Man: A Psychological Inquiry into the Roots of Destructiveness. A Study and Commentary.* Comments by J. Frank and others (Philadelphia: American Friends' Service Committee, 1963).

2. *The Heart of Man: Its Genius for Good and Evil*, Religious Perspectives, vol. 12 (New York: Harper & Row, 1964); the book is quoted here after the Perennial Library edition, New York, 1971; cf. pp. 3f., note 1. Fromm denounces Sartre's "psychological thinking" as "superficial and without sound clinical [sic] basis." This reproach toward Sartre is not only absurd (Sartre never intended to contribute to "clinical" psychology), it must also be seen as an instructive example of Fromm's often unqualified and irrelevant polemics.

3. Guyton B. Hammond, *Man in Estrangement. A Comparison of the Thought of Paul Tillich and Erich Fromm* (Nashville, Tenn.: Vanderbilt University Press, 1965), p. 43.

4. *The Heart of Man* (note 2), p. 15.

5. Cf. chapter 10 of this study, esp. pp. 216ff.

6. Cf. esp. "Eichmann in Jerusalem" (an exchange of letters between Hannah Arendt and Gershom Scholem), *Encounter* (January, 1964): 51-56.

7. Cf. chapter 6 of this study, esp. pp. 86ff.

8. *The Heart of Man* (note 2), p. 49.

9. Fromm specifically refers to Sigmund Freud, *New Introductory Lectures on Psycho-Analysis* (New York: W. W. Norton, 1933).

10. *The Heart of Man* (note 2), p. 54.

11. Karl Jaspers, *Allgemeine Psychopathologie* (Berlin: Springer Verlag, 6th edition, 1953).

12. Nikolaus Petrilowitsch: *Abnorme Persönlichkeiten* (Basel: S. Karger, 3rd edition, 1966).

13. *The Heart of Man* (note 2), p. 56.

14. Ibid., pp. 65f.

15. Ibid., p. 106.

16. Cf. Schaar (chapter 4, note 38), p. 93.

17. *The Heart of Man* (note 2), p. 113.

18. Cf. ibid., p. 144, Fromm's own graph, which is confusing and does little to clarify the actual configuration of the various spheres.

19. Ibid., p. 147.

20. Cf. Hammond (note 3), p. 40.

21. *The Heart of Man* (note 2), p. 149.

22. Hammond (note 3), p. 63.

23. *The Heart of Man* (note 2), p. 192.

24. Hausdorff (chapter 1, note 2), p. 143.

25. *You Shall be as Gods* (chapter 2, note 4), p. 7.

26. Cf. Hausdorff (chapter 1, note 2), p. 145.

27. *You Shall be as Gods* (chapter 2, note 4), p. 31.

28. Ibid., p. 34.

29. Cf. chapter 2, note 12.

30. Theodor W. Adorno, *Negative Dialektik* (Frankfurt: Suhrkamp, 1966); see also the English translation *Negative Dialectics* (New York: Seabury, 1973). For a critical appraisal refer to Wolf Heydebrand and Beverly Burris, "The Limits of Praxis in Critical Theory," in Marcus/Tar (chapter 1, note 4), pp. 401-417.

8.   Toward a Sane Society. Fromm as a Political Thinker (1955-1968)

1. See Evans (chapter 6, note 6), p. 57.

2. *Beyond the Chains of Illusion* (chapter 2, note 7), pp. 10-12.

3. Cf. chapter 3, note 11; here p. 441.

4. *Journal of Home Economics* 34 (April, 1942): 220-223.

5. *The Heart of Man* (chapter 7, note 2), p. 18.

6. "Should We Hate Hitler?" (note 4), p. 222.

7. *Look*, 5 May 1964, pp. 50f.

8. Ibid., p. 51.

9. Cf. Funk (chapter 2, note 10), p. 119.

10. *The Sane Society* (New York: Rinehart & Winston, 1955); the book is quoted here after the paperback edition (New York: Fawcett, 1962). The above quoted passage is on p. 30.

11. Ibid., p. 84.

12. Ibid.

13. Ibid., p. 123.

14. Ibid., p. 143.

15. Ibid., p. 180.

16. New York: Harcourt, Brace & Co., 1920.

17. New York: The Macmillan Co., 1933.

18. Frank Tannenbaum, *A Philosophy of Labor* (New York: Alfred A. Knopf, 1952).

19. New York: The Macmillan Co., 1949.

20. Cf. chapter 3 of this study on Critical Theory, esp. pp. 25ff.

21. George Douglas Howard Cole and W. Mellor, *The Meaning of Industrial Freedom* (London: G. Allen & Unwin, 1918).

22. *The Sane Society* (note 10), p. 248.

23. In: Robert Theobald, ed., *The Guaranteed Income, Next Step in Economic Evolution?* (New York: Doubleday & Co., 1966), pp. 174-184. The text was reprinted in Erich Fromm, *On Disobedience and Other Essays* (New York: Seabury Press, 1981), pp. 91-101.

24. Cf. chapter 7 of this study, esp. pp. 131ff.

25. Cf. note 23; pp. 58-74.

26. *A Nation of Sheep* (New York: W. W. Norton, 1961).

27. "The Case for Unilateral Disarmament," *Daedalus* (Fall, 1960): 1015-1028; republished in *On Disobedience* (note 23), pp. 102-119. Cf. also Charles E. Osgood, "Suggestions for Winning the Real War with Communism," *Conflict Resolution* 3 (4 December 1959): 131 ff., and "A Case for Gradual Unilateral Disarmament," *Bulletin of Atomic Scientists* 16, No. 4, pp. 127ff.

28. George F. Kennan, *The Atom and the West* (New York: Harper & Bros., 1957), esp. pp. 54f.

29. Princeton: Princeton University Press, 1960.

30. In: *Commentary. A Jewish Review* 33 (1962): 11-23.

31. *May Man Prevail? An Inquiry into the Facts and Fictions of Foreign Policy* (Garden City, N.Y.: Doubleday & Co., 1961), p. 132.

32. Ibid., p. 211.

33. Cf. above note 29.

34. Henry A. Kissinger, *The Necessity for Choice* (New York: Harper & Bros., 1961).

35. *May Man Prevail?* (note 31), p. 197.

36. Erich Fromm and Hans Herzfeld in collaboration with Kurt R. Grossmann, *Der Friede. Idee und Verwirklichung. The Search for Peace. Festgabe für Adolf Leschnitzer* (Heidelberg: Lambert Schneider, 1961); here p. 25.

37. "Remarks on the Policy of Détente," in *Détente. Hearings before the Committee on Foreign Relations, United States Senate, 93rd Congress, Second Session, On United States Relations with Communist Countries* (Washington: U.S. Government Printing Office, 1975).

38. Cf. chapter 1, note 1.

39. Cf. Hausdorff (chapter 1, note 2), p. 168, note 8.

40. George Gilder, *Wealth and Poverty* (New York: Bantam Books, 1981), p. 3.

9. The Art of Living. Fromm's Popular Writings Reconsidered (1956-1976)

1. For a few examples cf. Funk (chapter 2, note 1), pp. 125ff.

2. *The Art of Loving*, World Perspectives, vol. 9 (New York: Harper & Row, 1956). The book will be quoted here after the paperback edition (New York: Perennial Library, 1974).

3. See chapters 4 and 5 of this study, esp. pp. 55ff. and 73ff.

4. *The Art of Loving* (note 2), p. 3.

5. Ibid., p. 6.

6. Cf. chapter 8 of this study, esp. p. 150f.

7. *The Art of Loving* (note 2), p. 26.

8. Ibid., p. 35.

9. Ibid., p. 47.

10. Ibid., p. 28.

11. Cf. Hausdorff (chapter 1, note 2), p. 99.

12. *The Art of Loving* (note 2), p. 53.

13. Ibid., p. 110.

14. *Beyond the Chains of Illusion* (chapter 2, note 7), p. 9.

15. Ibid., p. 10; my emphasis.

16. Ibid., p. 20.

17. Ibid., p. 139.

18. Ibid., p. 198.

19. Cf. chapter 2 of this study, esp. p. 10.

20. Boston: Beacon Press, 1955.

21. Cf. chapter 5, note 12.

22. *The Revolution of Hope. Toward a Humanized Technology*, World Perspectives, vol. 38 (New York: Harper & Row, 1968), p. 9.

23. New York: Harcourt, Brace & World, 1966.

24. New York: Harcourt, Brace & Co., 1954.

25. New York: Alfred A. Knopf, 1964.

26. New York: Harcourt, Brace & Jovanovich, 1966.

27. New York: McGraw-Hill, 1967.

28. *The Revolution of Hope* (note 22), p. 96.

29. Ibid., p. 124.

30. *To Have or to Be?*, World Perspectives, vol. 30 (New York: Harper & Row, 1976); the book will be quoted here after the paperback edition (New York: Bantam Books, 1981).

31. *Being and Having. An Existentialist Diary* (New York: Harper & Row, 1965).

32. Zurich: Editio Academica, 1969.

33. *To Have or to Be?* (note 30), p. xxviii.

34. *Small is Beautiful. Economics as if People Mattered* (New York: Harper & Row, 1973).

35. New York: Dover, 1973.

36. *To Have or to Be?* (note 30), p. 63.

37. Ibid., p. 99.

38. San Francisco: W. H. Freeman, 1970.

39. *Ende oder Wende* (Stuttgart: Kohlhammer, 1975).

40. *To Have or to Be?* (note 30), p. 166.

41. Cf. chapter 3 of this study, esp. pp. 31ff.

42. "Ein Weg, den man nicht gehen wird," *Frankfurter Allgemeine Zeitung* 23 February 1977.

43. Cf. Funk (chapter 2, note 10), p. 8; my emphasis.

44. "Mahnmal in verwüsteter Landschaft. Erich Fromm, Psychoanalytiker und Visionär," *Neue Zürcher Zeitung No. 106, 7/8 May 1977.*

45. Reinbek: Rowohlt, 1977.

46. "Die große Jagd auf das Falsche," *Pardon* 6 (June, 1977): 68-70.

10. Looking into the Abyss. The Theory of Human Aggression (1973-1975)

1. Cf. chapter 6, note 28.

2. New York: Samuel Weiser, 1970.

3. In: *Deutsches Ärzteblatt* No. 41, 9 October 1980.

4. "Die Vision unserer Zeit," in: *Erich Fromm. Kulturpreis der Stadt Dortmund. Nelly-Sachs-Preis 1979,* Mitteilungen aus dem Literaturarchiv bei der Stadt- und Landesbibliothek Dortmund, vol. 7 (Dortmund: Stadt- und Landesbibliothek, 1979), pp. 29f.; my translation.

5. *The Anatomy of Human Destructiveness* (New York: Holt, Rinehart & Winston, 1973).

6. Chicago: University of Chicago Press, 1965.

7. New York: Harcourt, Brace & Jovanovich, 1966.

8. *The Anatomy of Human Destructiveness* (note 5), p. 19.

9. New York: H. Holt, 1914.

10. New York: Macmillan, 1953.

11. *The Anatomy of Human Destructiveness* (note 5), p. 41.

12. Ibid., p. 125.

13. Cf. chapter 4, note 10.

14. Vienna: Selbstverlag, 1933.

15. Cf. *Zeitschrift für Sozialforschung* 3 (1934): 106f.

16. Chicago: Chicago University Press, 2nd edition, 1965.

17. *Escape from Freedom* (chapter 2, note 3), p. 184.

18. *The Anatomy of Human Destructiveness* (note 5), p. 290.

19. Ibid., p. 323.

20. *Psychopathia Sexualis* (Stuttgart: J. B. Metzler, 1886).

21. *Der nekrotope Mensch* (Stuttgart: F. Enke, 1964).

22. Cf. p. 120 of this study.

23. *The Anatomy of Human Destructiveness* (note 5), p. 366.

24. Cf. p. 120f. above.

25. New York: Macmillan, 1970.

26. *The Rise and Fall of the Third Reich* (New York: Simon & Schuster, 1960).

27. *The Last Days of Hitler* (New York: Macmillan, 1947).

28. *Hitler: A Study in Tyranny* (New York: Harper & Row, 1962).

29. *The Life and Death of Adolf Hitler* (New York: Popular Library, 1973).

30. Translated by R. Manheim (Boston: Houghton Mifflin, 1943).

31. *The Anatomy of Human Destructiveness* (note 5), p. 438.

32. Cf. chapter 4, note 34.

Bibliography

I Works by Erich Fromm (in chronological order)

Das jüdische Gesetz. Ein Beitrag zur Soziologie des Diasporajudentums. Doctoral dissertation, University of Heidelberg, 1925. Typescript.

"Der Sabbath." *Imago. Zeitschrift für Anwendung der Psychoanalyse auf die Natur- und Geisteswissenschaften* 13 (1927): 223-234.

"Psychoanalyse und Soziologie." *Zeitschrift für psychoanalytische Pädagogik* 3 (1928/29): 269f.

"Die Entwicklung des Christusdogmas. Eine psychoanalytische Studie zur sozialpsychologischen Funktion der Religion." *Imago. Zeitschrift für Anwendung der Psychoanalyse auf die Natur- und Geisteswissenschaften* 16 (1930): 305-373.

"Politik und Psychoanalyse." *Psychoanalytische Bewegung* 3 (1931): 440-447.

"Die psychoanalytische Charakterologie und ihre Bedeutung für die Sozialpsychologie." *Zeitschrift für Sozialforschung* 1 (1932): 253-277.

"Über Methode und Aufgabe einer analytischen Sozialpsychologie." *Zeitschrift für Sozialforschung* 1 (1932): 28-54.

"Robert Briffaults Werk über das Mutterrecht." *Zeitschrift für Sozialforschung* 2 (1933): 382-387.

"Die sozialpsychologische Bedeutung der Mutterrechtstheorie." *Zeitschrift für Sozialforschung* 3 (1934): 196-227.

"Die gesellschaftliche Bedingtheit der psychoanalytischen Theorie." *Zeitschrift für Sozialforschung* 4 (1935): 365-397.

Arbeiter und Angestellte am Vorabend des Dritten Reiches. Eine sozialpsychologische Untersuchung, ed. and transl. by Wolfgang Bonss. Stuttgart: Deutsche Verlags-Anstalt, 1980 (cf. also the English edition: *The Working Class in Weimar Germany. A Psychological and Sociological Study.* Cambridge, Mass.: Harvard University Press, 1984).

"Sozialpsychologischer Teil." In: Max Horkheimer, ed. *Studien über Autorität und Familie.* Forschungsberichte aus dem Institut für Sozialforschung, 1. Abteilung: Theoretische Entwürfe über Autorität und Familie. Paris: Félix Alcan, 1936, pp. 77-135.

"Zum Gefühl der Ohnmacht." *Zeitschrift für Sozialforschung* 6 (1937): 95-118.

"Selfishness and Self-Love." *Psychiatry* 2 (1939): 507-523.

Escape from Freedom. New York: Farrar & Rinehart, 1941.

"Faith as a Character Trait." *Psychiatry* 5 (1942): 307-319.

"Should we Hate Hitler?" *Journal of Home Economics* 34 (April, 1942): 220-223.

"Individual and Social Origins of Neurosis." *American Sociological Review* 9 (1944): 380-384.

Man for Himself. An Inquiry into the Psychology of Ethics. New York: Rinehart & Co., 1947; quoted here from the paperback edition: New York: Fawcett Premier, 1965.

"The Oedipus Complex and the Oedipus Myth." In: Ruth Nanda Anshen, ed. *The Family: Its Functions and Destiny.* New York: Harper & Bros., 1949. (Identical to "Oedipus Myth." *Scientific American* 18 [1949]: 22-27; also in: *The Forgotten Language*, pp. 196-230.)

Psychoanalysis and Religion. New Haven: Yale University Press, 1950.

————, Suzuki, D.T. and De Martino, Richard. *Zen Buddhism and Psychoanalysis.* New York: Harper & Row, 1950.

The Forgotten Language. An Introduction to the Understanding of Dreams, Fairy Tales and Myths. New York: Rinehart & Co., 1951.

"The Human Implications of Instinctivistic Radicalism. A Reply to Herbert Marcuse." *Dissent* 2 (Summer, 1955): 342-349.

The Sane Society. New York: Rinehart & Winston, 1955; quoted here from the paperback edition: New York: Fawcett, 1962.

"A Counter-Rebuttal to Herbert Marcuse." *Dissent* 3 (Winter, 1956): 81-83.

The Art of Loving. World Perspectives, vol. 9. New York: Harper & Row, 1956; quoted here from the paperback edition: New York: Perennial Library, 1974.

Sigmund Freud's Mission. An Analysis of His Personality and Influence. New York: Harper & Row, 1959.

"The Case for Unilateral Disarmament." *Daedalus* (Fall, 1960): 1015-1028. Also in: *On Disobedience and Other Essays*, pp. 102-119.

———— and Herzfeld, Hans, in collaboration with Kurt R. Grossmann, eds. *Der Friede. Idee und Verwirklichung. The Search for Peace*. Festgabe für Adolf Leschnitzer. Heidelberg: Lambert Schneider, 1961.

Marx's Concept of Man. With a Translation from Marx's Economic and Philosophical Manuscripts by T. B. Bottomore. New York: Frederick Ungar, 1961.

May Man Prevail? An Inquiry into the Facts and Fictions of Foreign Policy. Garden City, N.Y.: Doubleday & Co., 1961.

Beyond the Chains of Illusion. My Encounter with Marx and Freud. The Credo Series. New York: Pocket Books, 1962.

———— and Maccoby, Michael. "A Debate on the Question of Civil Defense." *Commentary. A Jewish Review* 33 (1962): 11-23.

The Dogma of Christ and Other Essays on Religion, Psychology, and Culture. New York: Holt, Rinehart & Winston, 1963.

"War Within Man: A Psychological Inquiry into the Roots of Destructiveness." In: *War Within Man: A Psychological Inquiry into the Roots of Destructiveness. A Study and Commentary*. Comments by J. Frank and others. Philadelphia: American Friends' Service Committee, 1963.

"The Psychological Aspects of the Guaranteed Income." In: Theobald, Robert, ed. *The Guaranteed Income, Next Step in Economic Evolution?* New York: Doubleday & Co., 1966, pp. 174-184; see also: *On Disobedience and Other Essays*, pp. 91-101.

You Shall be as Gods. A Radical Interpretation of the Old Testament and its Tradition. New York: Holt, Rinehart & Winston, 1966.

"Marx's Contribution to the Knowledge of Man." *Social Science Information* 7 (3/1968): 7-17; see also *The Crisis of Psychoanalysis*, pp. 62-76.

The Revolution of Hope. Toward a Humanized Technology. World Perspectives, vol. 38. New York: Harper & Row, 1968.

The Crisis of Psychoanalysis. Essays on Freud, Marx, and Social Psychology. New York: Holt, Rinehart & Winston, 1970.

———— and Maccoby, Michael. *Social Character in a Mexican Village. A Sociopsychoanalytic Study.* Englewood Cliffs, N.J.: Prentice-Hall, 1970.

The Heart of Man: Its Genius for Good and Evil. Religious Perspectives, vol. 12. New York: Harper & Row, 1964; quoted here from the paperback edition: New York: Perennial Library, 1971.

The Anatomy of Human Destructiveness. New York: Holt, Rinehart & Winston, 1973.

Aggression und Charakter. Ein Gespräch mit Adelbert Reif. Zurich: Die Arche, 1975.

"Remarks on the Policy of Détente." In: *Détente. Hearings before the Committee on Foreign Relations, United States Senate, 93rd Congress, Second Session, On United States Relations with Communist Countries.* Washington: U.S. Government Printing Office, 1975.

To Have or to Be? World Perspectives, vol. 30. New York: Harper & Row, 1976; quoted here from the paperback edition: New York: Bantam Books, 1981.

"Die Vision unserer Zeit." In: *Erich Fromm. Kulturpreis der Stadt Dortmund. Nelly-Sachs-Preis 1979.* Mitteilungen aus dem Landesarchiv der Stadt- und Landesbibliothek Dortmund, vol. 7. Dortmund: Stadt- und Landesbibliothek, 1979.

Greatness and Limitations of Freud's Thought. New York: Harper & Row, 1980.

On Disobedience and Other Essays. New York: Seabury Press, 1981.

For the Love of Life. Hans Jürgen Schultz, ed. New York: The Free Press, 1986 [contains the following essays: "Affluence and Ennui in Our Society," "On the Origins of Aggression," "Dreams are the Universal Language of Man," "Psychology for Nonpsychologists," "In the Name of Life: A Portrait Through Dialogue," "Hitler - Who was He and What Constituted Resistance Against Him?," "The Relevance of the Prophets for Us Today," "Who is Man?"].

II Related Works

Adorno, Theodor W.; Frenkel-Brunswik, Else; Lewinson, Daniel J.; and Sanford, R. Nevitt. *The Authoritarian Personality.* New York: Harper & Bros., 1950.

Adorno, Theodor W. *Negative Dialektik.* Frankfurt: Suhrkamp, 1966. (In English translation: *Negative Dialectics.* New York: Seabury, 1973.)

Borkenau, Franz. *Der Übergang vom feudalen zum bürgerlichen Weltbild.* Paris: Félix Alcan, 1934.

Bullock, Alan. *Hitler: A Study in Tyranny*. New York: Harper & Row, 1962.

Cole, George Douglas Howard and Mellor, W. *The Meaning of Industrial Freedom*. London: G. Allen & Unwin, 1918.

Ehrlich, Paul R. and Ehrlich, Anne H. *Population, Resources, Environment: Essays in Human Ecology*. San Francisco: W.H. Freeman, 1970.

Ellul, Jacques. *The Technological Society*. New York: Alfred A. Knopf, 1964.

Eppler, Erhard. *Ende oder Wende*. Stuttgart: Kohlhammer, 1975.

Ferrarotti, Franco. "The Struggle of Reason against Total Bureaucratization." In: Marcus/Tar. *Foundations of the Frankfurt School of Social Research*, pp. 235-252.

Freud, Sigmund. *New Introductory Lectures on Psycho-Analysis*. New York: W. W. Norton, 1933.

Gilder, George. *Wealth and Poverty*. New York: Bantam Books, 1981.

Hentig, Hartmut von. *Der nekrotope Mensch*. Stuttgart: F. Enke, 1964.

Horkheimer, Max. "Geschichte und Psychologie." *Zeitschrift für Sozialforschung* 1 (1932): 125-144.

Horney, Karen. *The Neurotic Personality of Our Time*. New York: W. W. Norton, 1937.

_____. *New Ways in Psychoanalysis*. New York: W. W. Norton, 1939.

_____. *Our Inner Conflicts. A Constructive Theory of Neurosis.* New York: W. W. Norton, 1945.

Jaspers, Karl. *Allgemeine Psychopathologie.* Berlin: Springer Verlag, 6th edition 1953.

Jay, Martin. *The Dialectical Imagination. A History of the Frankfurt School and the Institute of Social Research 1923-1950.* Boston: Little, Brown & Co., 1973.

Jones, Ernest. *The Life and Work of Sigmund Freud.* 3 vols. New York: Basic Books, 1955.

Jung, C.G. *Psychology and Religion.* New Haven: Yale University Press, 1938.

Kahn, Herman. *On Thermonuclear War.* Princeton: Princeton University Press, 1960.

Kardiner, Abram. *The Individual and His Society. The Psychoanalysis of Primitive Social Organization.* New York: Columbia University Press, 1939.

Kennan, George F. *The Atom and the West.* New York: Harper & Bros., 1957.

Kissinger, Henry A. *The Necessity for Choice.* New York: Harper & Bros., 1961.

Krafft-Ebing, Richard von. *Psychopathia sexualis.* Stuttgart: J. B. Metzler, 1886.

Lasswell, Harold D. *Politics. Who Gets What, When, How.* New York: McGraw-Hill, 1936.

Lederer, William J. *A Nation of Sheep.* New York: W. W. Norton, 1961.

Lorenz, Konrad. *On Aggression.* New York: Harcourt, Brace & Jovanovich, 1966.

_____. *Evolution and Modification of Behavior.* Chicago: University of Chicago Press, 1965.

Mannheim, Karl. *Ideology and Utopia.* New York: Harcourt, Brace & Co., 1936.

Marcel, Gabriel. *Being and Having.* An Existentialist Diary. New York: Harper & Row, 1965.

Marcus, Judith and Tar, Zoltan, eds. *Foundations of the Frankfurt School of Social Research.* New Brunswick: Transaction, 1984.

Marcuse, Herbert. *Eros and Civilization.* Boston: Beacon Press, 1955.

_____. *One Dimensional Man. The Ideology of Industrial Society.* Boston: Beacon Press, 1964.

_____. "A Reply to Erich Fromm." *Dissent* 3 (Winter, 1956): 79-81.

_____. "The Social Implications of Freudian 'Revisionism'." *Dissent* 2 (Summer, 1955): 221-240.

Mayo, Elton. *The Human Problems of an Industrial Civilization.* New York: The Macmillan Co., 1933.

Morris, Desmord. *The Naked Ape.* New York: McGraw-Hill, 1967.

Mumford, Lewis. *In the Name of Sanity.* New York: Harcourt, Brace & Co., 1954.

_____. *The Myth of the Machine.* New York: Harcourt, Brace & World, 1966.

Osgood, Charles E. "A Case for Gradual Unilateral Disarmament." *Bulletin of Atomic Scientists* 16, No. 4, pp. 127ff.

_____. "Suggestions for Winning the Real War with Communism." *Conflict Resolution* 3 (4 December 1959): 131ff.

Payne, Robert. *The Life and Death of Adolf Hitler.* New York: Popular Library, 1973.

Petrilowitsch, Nikolaus. *Abnorme Persönlichkeiten.* Basel: S. Karger, third edition 1966.

Reich, Wilhelm. *Charakteranalyse. Technik und Grundlagen.* Vienna: Selbstverlag, 1933.

_____. *Massenpsychologie des Faschismus. Zur Sexualökonomie der politischen Reaktion und zur proletarischen Sexualpolitik.* Copenhagen: Verlag für Sexualpolitik, 1933.

Rogers, Carl A. *Casebook of Non-Directive Counseling.* Boston: Houghton Mifflin, 1947.

Rubins, Jack L. *Karen Horney - Gentle Rebel of Psychoanalysis.* New York: The Dial Press, 1978.

Scholem, Gerschom. *Walter Benjamin - die Geschichte einer Freundschaft.* Frankfurt: Suhrkamp, 1975.

Schumacher, E. F. *Small is Beautiful. Economics as if People Mattered.* New York: Harper & Row, 1973.

Schweitzer, Albert. *Philosophy of Civilization.* New York: The Macmillan Co., 1949.

Shirer, William L. *The Rise and Fall of the Third Reich.* New York: Simon & Schuster, 1960.

Skinner, Burrhus F. *Science and Human Behavior.* New York: Macmillan, 1953.

Speer, Albert. *Inside the Third Reich.* New York: Macmillan, 1970.

Staehelin, Balthasar. *Haben und Sein.* Zurich: Editio Academica, 1969.

Stirner, Max. *The Ego and His Own: The Case of the Individual Against Authority.* New York: Dover, 1973.

Sullivan, Harry Stack. *Conceptions of Modern Psychiatry.* William Alanson White Memorial Lectures, vol. 1. Washington: William Alanson White Institute, 1948.

Suzuki, Daisetz Taitaro. *Living by Zen.* London: Rider, 1950.

_____. *Manual of Zen Buddhism.* London: Rider, 1950.

_____. *Studies in Zen.* London: Rider, 1955.

Tannenbaum, Frank. *A Philosophy of Labor.* New York: Alfred A. Knopf, 1952.

Tar, Zoltán. *The Frankfurt School. The Critical Theories of Max Horkheimer and Theodor W. Adorno.* New York: Wiley, 1977.

Tawney, Richard Henry. *Religion and the Rise of Capitalism.* New York: Harcourt, Brace & Co., 1926.

_____. *The Acquisitive Society.* New York: Harcourt, Brace & Co., 1920.

Tillich, Paul. *Protestantische Vision*. Stuttgart: Ringverlag, 1952.

Trevor-Roper, H. R. *The Last Days of Hitler*. New York: Macmillan, 1947.

Walter, Otto F. *Die Verwilderung*. Reinbek: Rowohlt, 1977.

Watson, John Broadus. *Behavior: An Introduction to Comparative Psychology*. New York: H. Holt, 1914.

Weber, Max. *The Protestant Ethic and the Spirit of Capitalism*. New York: Charles Scribner's Sons, 1930.

Wertheimer, Max. *Productive Thinking*. New York: Harper & Bros., 1945.

Wright, Quincy. *A Study of War*. Chicago: Chicago University Press, second edition 1965.

III Selected Critical Writings on Fromm

1 **Bibliographies**. The two major printed sources are contained in Funk, Rainer (III,2). *The Courage to be Human*, pp. 374-407, and Funk, Rainer (III,2). *Mut zum Menschen*, pp. 361-412.

For ongoing information see the *Newsletter* of the "International Erich Fromm Society." Write to: Internationale Erich-Fromm-Gesellschaft, Rappenberghalde 17, D-7400 Tübingen 1, Federal Republic of Germany.

2 Monographs and Anthologies

Evans, Richard I. *Dialogue with Erich Fromm*. Dialogues with Notable Contributors to Personality Theory, vol. 2. New York: Harper & Row, 1966.

Funk, Rainer. *Erich Fromm: The Courage to be Human*. New York: Continuum, 1982. In German original: *Mut zum Menschen. Erich Fromms Denken und Werk, seine humanistische Religion und Ethik*. Stuttgart: Deutsche Verlags-Anstalt, 1978.

_____. *Erich Fromm*. rowohlts monographien 322. Reinbek: Rowohlt, 1983.

Glen, J. Stanley: *Erich Fromm: A Protestant Critique*. Philadelphia: Westminster Press, 1965.

Hammond, Guyton B. *Man in Estrangement. A Comparison of the Thought of Paul Tillich and Erich Fromm*. Nashville, Tenn.: Vanderbilt University Press, 1965.

Hausdorff, Don. *Erich Fromm*. Twayne's United States Authors Series, vol. 203. New York: Twayne, 1972.

Knapp, Gerhard P. *Erich Fromm*. Köpfe des 20. Jahrhunderts, vol. 97. Berlin: Colloquium, 1982.

Landis, Bernhard and Tauber, Edward S. *In the Name of Life. Essays in Honor of Erich Fromm*. New York: Holt, Rinehart & Winston, 1971.

Reif, Adelbert, ed. *Erich Fromm. Materialien zu seinem Werk*. Vienna: Europaverlag, 1978.

Tauscher, Petra. *Nekrophilie und Faschismus. Erich Fromms Beitrag zur soziobiographischen Deutung Adolf Hitlers und weitere sozialpsychologische Interpretationen*. Frankfurt: Haag + Herchen, 1985.

Torres, Mauro. *El Irracionalismo en Erich Fromm. La posición científica del psicoanálisis*. Monografías Psicoanaliticas, vol. 6. Mexico City: Editorial Pax-Mexico, 1960.

Schaar, John H. *Escape from Authority. The Perspectives of Erich Fromm*. New York: Basic Books, 1961.

Werder, Lutz von, ed. *Der unbekannte Fromm. Biographische Studien*. Frankfurt: Haag + Herchen, 1987.

3 Selected Articles and Essays

Anshen, Ruth Nanda. "Authority and Power: Erich Fromm and Herbert Marcuse." *Journal of Social Philosophy* 5 (Sept., 1974): 1-8.

Appel, Werner. "Erich Fromms Dialog mit dem Buddhismus." In: L. v. Werner. *Der unbekannte Fromm*, pp. 71-91.

Balmer, Hans Peter. "Befreiung von der Destruktivität? Erich Fromm in der Debatte und die menschliche Aggression." In: A. Reif. *Erich Fromm*, pp. 109-124.

Banks, Robert. "A Neo-Freudian Critique of Religion: Erich Fromm on Judeo-Christian Tradition." *Religion* 5 (1975): 117-135.

Caparrós Benedicto, Antonio. "El caractér social según Erich Fromm." *Convivium* 42 (1974): 3-27.

Eßbach-Kreuzer, Uschi. "Die Theorie des Sozialcharakters in den Arbeiten von Erich Fromm." In: A. Reif. *Erich Fromm*, pp. 299-326 (also in: *Zeitschrift für psychosomatische Medizin* 18 [1972]: 171-191).

Forsyth, James J. and Beniskos, J.M. "Biblical Faith and Erich Fromm's Theory of Personality." *Revue de l'Université d'Ottawa* 40 (1970): 69-91.

Friedenburg, Edgar Z. "Neo-Freudianism and Erich Fromm." *Commentary. A Jewish Review* 34 (1962): 305-313.

Green, Arnold W. "Sociological Analysis of Horney and Fromm." *American Journal of Sociology* 51 (1945/46): 533-540.

Heigl, Franz. "Die humanistische Psychoanalyse Erich Fromms." *Zeitschrift für psychosomatische Medizin* 7 (1961): 77-84; 153-161; 235-249.

Heller, Agnes. "Aufklärung und Radikalismus. Kritik der psychologischen Anthropologie Erich Fromms." In: A. Reif, *Erich Fromm*, pp. 162-213.

Heydebrand, Wolf and Burris, Beverly. "The Limits of Praxis in Critical Theory." In: Marcus/Tar, *Foundations of the Frankfurt School of Social Research*, pp. 401-417.

Jungk, Robert. "Ein Gespräch mit Erich Fromm." *Bild der Wissenschaft* 11 (October, 1974): 59-62.

Landis, Bernhard. "Erich Fromms Theorie der Biophilie-Nekrophilie. Ihre Auswirkungen auf die psychoanalytische Praxis." In: A. Reif, *Erich Fromm*, pp. 88-108.

Luban-Plozza, Boris and Biancoli, Romano. "Erich Fromms therapeutische Annäherung an die Kunst der Psychotherapie." In: L. v. Werder, *Der unbekannte Fromm*, pp. 101-146.

Mosse, Hilde L. "Bypaths on the Road to Vienna." *Psychiatry* 22 (1959): 39f.

Reif, Adelbert. "Vom Haben zum Sein. Aufzeichnungen nach einem Gespräch mit Erich Fromm." In: A. Reif, *Erich Fromm*, pp. 219-247.

Rickert, John. "Erich Fromms Institut in Mexiko." In: L. v. Werder, *Der unbekannte Fromm*, pp. 46-54.

Schneider-Flume, Gunda. "Leben dürfen oder leben müssen. Die
    Bedeutung der humanistischen Psychoanalyse Erich Fromms
    für die theologische Anthropologie." In: A. Reif, *Erich
    Fromm*, pp. 135-161.

Werder, Lutz von. "Erich Fromms produktiver Charakter." In: L.
    v. Werder, *Der unbekannte Fromm*, pp. 4-31.

Wiegand, Ronald. "Psychoanalyse und Gesellschaft bei Erich
    Fromm." *Psychologische Menschenkenntnis* 6 (1970):
    257-273.

_____. "Zum Problem des Sozialcharakters." In: A. Reif, *Erich
    Fromm*, pp. 280-298.

Index

270   Index

John Frederick Loase

SIGFLUENCE
Enduring Positive Influence

American University Studies: Series VIII (Psychology). Vol. 10
ISBN 0-8204-0534-5   269 pages   hardcover US $ 46.50*

*Recommended price – alterations reserved

We lack a word in the English language to define significant, long-term, positive inter-
personal influence – defined by this researcher as sigfluence. Sigfluence represents a
fundamental will of person – paralleling Viktor Frankl's will-to-meaning.
The work first scrutinizes the autobiographies of sixteen famous contemporaries for
their accounts of the people and forces that shaped their lives (and ours).
The next four chapters analyze sigfluence from the academic perspectives of statistics,
psychology, linguistics, sociology, and education. The last two chapters feature
societal and personal applications of the new construct.
The work ranges over a variety of academic disciplines, cites several hundred references, and recommends several future joint disciplinary research avenues in order to
improve upon our primitive understanding of this elusive phenomenon.

«Loase has written a provocative book on a topic of critical value to the human condition, and we are all in his debt.» (Eigil Pedersen, McGill University)
«This publication is recommended for clergy and professional counselors, particularly
those dealing in family, crises intervention and supportive counseling.» (Dr. Alan G.
Robertson, City University of New York)
«I feel this book will make a real impact in its field and Professor Loase is to be com-
mended for his very fine work.» (G. Richard Dimler, Editor, Thought)

PETER LANG PUBLISHING, INC.
62 West 45th Street
USA – New York, NY 10036

Robin Robertson

C. G. JUNG AND THE ARCHETYPES
OF THE COLLECTIVE UNCONSCIOUS

American University Studies: Series VIII (Psychology). Vol. 7
ISBN 0-8204-0395-4   272 pages   hardcover US $ 30.50*

*Recommended price – alterations reserved

The author presents a stimulating panorama of Jung's psychology, and shows how accurately it corresponds to the strange world described by twentieth-century scientists in fields other than psychology. He traces the development of the concept of the archetypes of the collective unconscious from the dawn of the scientific method in the Renaissance to twentieth-century mathematician Kurt Gödel's proof of the limits of science. Robertson's presentation of Jung's psychology is the most complete to date, treating it as a connected whole, from the early experimental studies to the final work using alchemy as a model of psychological dynamics.

PETER LANG PUBLISHING, INC.
62 West 45th Street
USA – New York, NY 10036